A

MANUAL COMMENTARY

ON THE

GENERAL CANON LAW AND THE CONSTITUTION

OF THE

Protestant Episcopal Church

IN THE

UNITED STATES.

BY

FRANCIS VINTON, S. T. D., D. C. L.

"CHARLES AND ELIZABETH LUDLOW PROFESSOR OF ECCLESIASTICAL POLITY AND LAW"
IN THE GENERAL THEOLOGICAL SEMINARY, AND ASSISTANT MINISTER OF
TRINITY CHURCH, NEW YORK.

NEW YORK:
E. P. DUTTON AND COMPANY,
713 BROADWAY.
1870.

Windham Press is committed to bringing the lost cultural heritage of ages past into the 21st century through high-quality reproductions of original, classic printed works at affordable prices.

This book has been carefully crafted to utilize the original images of antique books rather than error-prone OCR text. This also preserves the work of the original typesetters of these classics, unknown craftsmen who laid out the text, often by hand, of each and every page you will read. Their subtle art involving judgment and interaction with the text is in many ways superior and more human than the mechanical methods utilized today, and gave each book a unique, hand-crafted feel in its text that connected the reader organically to the art of bindery and book-making.

We think these benefits are worth the occasional imperfection resulting from the age of these books at the time of scanning, and their vintage feel provides a connection to the past that goes beyond the mere words of the text.

As bibliophiles, we are always seeking perfection in our work, so please notify us of any errors in this book by emailing us at corrections@windhampress.com. Our team is motivated to correct errors quickly so future customers are better served. Our mission is to raise the bar of quality for reprinted works by a focus on detail and quality over mass production. To peruse our catalog of carefully curated classic works, please visit our online store at www.windhampress.com.

PART I.

THE COMMON LAW OF THE PROTESTANT EPISCOPAL CHURCH IN THE UNITED STATES, WITH APPENDIX, EXPLAINING

1. THE SPIRITUAL COURTS AND PROCEEDINGS OF THE CHURCH OF ENGLAND.

2. THE MANNER OF ELECTING AND CONSECRATING ARCHBISHOPS AND BISHOPS IN THE CHURCH OF ENGLAND.

PART II.

1. PRELIMINARY HISTORY OF THE CONSTITUTION OF THE PROTESTANT EPISCOPAL CHURCH IN THE UNITED STATES.

2. THE LEGISLATIVE POWERS AND AUTHORITY OF THE GENERAL CONVENTION.

3. THE CONSTITUTION OF THE CHURCH.

TO THE READER.

THE Statutes of the General Theological Seminary assign to the Chair of "Ecclesiastical Polity and Law" these three topics: "The Principles of Ecclesiastical Polity, with a particular Explanation of that of the Protestant Episcopal Church;" "General Canon Law;" "Constitution and Canons of the Church in the United States."

The Professor has been constrained to compose a Text-book from the ample materials scattered through our Libraries and furnished by the erudition of Canonists of our own Church, and of England, and of the Continent.

This Manual Commentary on the General Canon Law and the Constitution of the Protestant Episcopal Church is the first-fruits of my Professorship, which I now humbly offer to CHRIST and the CHURCH.

I have concentrated the subject into the form of Questions and Answers, rather through habit than by premeditated design; following herein the familiar system of Catechising, as the best of all methods of instruction. And as a Catechism is the Ultimate Analysis of any subject, so Questions and Answers presuppose and demand the utmost brevity, correctness, and utility, at the cost of the profoundest meditation and the best knowledge of the author.

This plan, though spontaneous and original, I find sanctioned by such teachers as Grey, in his "Ecclesiastical

Law," and Bates, in his " College Lectures on Ecclesiastical History." I have found this method very convenient in lecturing; for I could take the QUESTION as a Text, making my comments, while driving at the ANSWER, wherein is contained the gist and end of my discourse. The Students, meanwhile, jotted down the Lecture in their note-books.

This MANUAL, together with the student's notes, makes a tolerable mental furniture for his future ministry in this department of Theological Learning.

I am hopeful that this publication may serve the same purpose in aid of other teachers, and to the edification of other pupils. And these are not merely the Professors and Students of our Theological Schools, but likewise the Deputies to the General Convention; the Delegates to Diocesan Conventions; the Clergy and Wardens and Vestrymen of our Parishes; the members of Ecclesiastical Courts; the Judges, the Lawyers, and the Lay Assessors, who are likely to be employed as Advocates and Counselors at ecclesiastical Tribunals. The intelligent laymen, too, who desire to understand the Polity and Law of their Church; the gentlemen of the learned callings, and professions of secular interest, and those who belong to various religious bodies, may discover and reap some advantage from this Manual Commentary. All these "sorts and conditions of men" might find this Handbook a convenience, and these Commentaries a prompter to thoughtful study. For the Index contains a catalogue of " Questions " which may arise, ranged under their several proper Heads of Subjects; while the copious References to Authorities in the " Answers " will repay a diligent research into the mine of wealth which they open and expose to view. The student will discern therein some of the ore that is embedded in the Church of past ages, whence the Jurisprudence of the modern world derives the grandest and loveliest gems of Justice and of Equity.

In conclusion, I venture to sketch the Plan of Lectures in my mind, suited, as it appears to me, to a liberal and edifying Course of Study in Ecclesiastical Polity and Law.

1st. *The History of Roman Law*, from the Twelve Tables to the Institutes, the Pandects, the Code, and the Novels of the Emperor Justinian (A. D. 528–534). This Body of the Civil Law, which has so largely ruled the Civilized Nations, was reverently published by the Emperor, "IN NOMINE DOMINI NOSTRI JESU CHRISTI."

Hence, 2d. *The influence of Christianity on the Roman Law* suggests the theme for a following Lecture.

CHRISTIANITY, since the conversion of Constantine, had had the providential opportunity of two Centuries to infuse its blessed Charities into the Soul of the Law of the Roman Empire, and to bring it to that perfection which won a willing submission to its rule from the Nations and the Church of Europe.

Hence, 3d. The *agency of the Civil Law in shaping the Canon Law*, becomes the next theme in course.

4th. A collateral topic is the crystallizing of the *new Canon Laws and Constitution of the Church of Rome into the mould of the old Roman Empire*, through the False Decretals of Isidore, and their adoption by Popes, from Adrian to Nicholas (A. D. 785 to 836); and thenceforward to the present time. This side-issue forms a topic, for the elucidation of which, the imminent threatening aspect of the Roman Communion challenges the scholar, who is both Catholic and Protestant, to burnish his weapons.

5th. The introduction and authority of the *Catholic and of the New Canon Law in the Church and Kingdom of Great Britain*, should be the next theme.

Finally, 6th. *The passage of the Ecclesiastical Law of the Church of England into the Colonies and States of America.*

This final theme is the foremost Head of this Manual Commentary, which may be entitled "The COMMON LAW of the Protestant Episcopal Church." All the themes that precede it are links in the chain that leads to the Twelve Tables; and beyond them, to the Court of the Gentile Nations, to the Jews, to Moses, to Divine Revelation, to the Bosom of God, — wherein is the **Seat of Law**, " whose Voice is the Harmony of the World."

The writer may not live to compose a Series of Lectures on all these themes appertaining to his Professorship. Yet they are the measure of its importance, and of its grandeur.

He has, therefore, not refrained from suggesting them to the consideration of his successors, while he humbly contributes what he could do, amidst the urgencies of parochial duties, for the instruction and benefit of his pupils in Ecclesiastical Polity and Law.

F. V.

NEW YORK, *Eastertide*, A. D. 1870.

ABBREVIATIONS OF SOME OF THE AUTHORITIES.

Alumni Association Publications	Pub. Alum. Assoc.
Bingham's Ecclesiastical Antiquities	Bingham, Ecc. Antiq.
Bishop Gibson's Codex Juris Ecclesiastici Anglicani	Gibson's Codex.
Bishop White's Memoirs of the Episcopal Church	Mem. of Ch.
Bishop White's Article on Primitive Facts	Bp. White, Prim. Facts.
Bishop White's Comparative Views on the Arminian and Calvinistic Controversy	Bp. White, Ar. & Calv. Cont.
Bishop White on the Ordination Office	Bp. White, Ord. Off.
Dawson's Origo Legum	Dawson's Or. Leg.
Digest of Canons	Dig.
Hawks, F. L., D. D., LL. D., Contributions to Ecclesiastical History	Hawks' Contrib.
Hawks' Commentary on the Constitution and Canons	Hawks' Cons. & Can.
Hoffman, Murray, V. Chancellor, on the Law of the Church	Hoff. L. C.
Hoffman, Murray, Ecclesiastical Law of New York	Hoff. Ec. L. of N. Y.
Journal of the General Convention	Jour. Gen. Conv.
Kenneth's Ecclesiastical Synods	Kenneth's Ec. Syn.
Lyndwood's Provincial Constitutions	Lyndwood's Prov. Con.
Wilkins's Concilia Magnæ Britannicæ et Hibernicæ	Wilkins's Concil.
Wilson's Memoir of the Life of Bishop White	Wilson's Mem. Bp. White.

Manual Commentary

ON THE

ECCLESIASTICAL POLITY AND LAW

OF THE

PROTESTANT EPISCOPAL CHURCH

IN THE

UNITED STATES OF AMERICA.

Question. WHAT are the Grand Divisions of the Law of the Church in the United States?

Answer. (1) The General Canon Law, and the Ecclesiastical Law of England, applicable to the Church in the United States, and not abrogated by Constitution nor Canons, being THE COMMON LAW OF THIS CHURCH.

(2) The Constitution and Canons of the General Convention.

(3) The Constitution and Canons of the several Dioceses.

(4) The Rubrics of the Church and (in some particulars) the Articles.

(5) The Secular Laws of the State, affecting Churches in regard to Corporate and personal rights, and the acquisition and preservation of property.

PART I.

THE COMMON LAW OF THE PROTESTANT EPISCOPAL CHURCH IN THE UNITED STATES.

EXTENT OF AUTHORITY OF ENGLISH CANON LAW.

Q. What is the relation of the Church of England and the Protestant Episcopal Church in the United States?

A. They are identical; as sisters in the Family of the Catholic Church.

Q. What is the Extent of Authority of the Ecclesiastical Law of England in the United States?

A. (1) Our ancestors from England brought "as much of English Law and Liberty with them as the nature of things will bear," both in Church and State. Kent's Commentaries, vol. i. p. 472. Chalmers' Opinion of Eminent Lawyers, vol. i. p. 194. As to Ecclesiastical Law, Gaskins *v.* Gaskins, 3 Iredell's Law Rep. 155, N. Car.

(2) The Canon Law is a part of the Common Law of the State (*e. g.* as to Testaments), except where our Statutes have altered it. Bogardus *v.* Smith, 4 Paige Rep. 178.

Limitations. *Q.* What are the Restraints on the Canon Law of England in this country?

A. In all things where the Church is considered as an Establishment, as (1) The Royal Supremacy. 26 Henry VIII. c. i. (2) Statutes of Uniformity. 13 Car. II. c. 4; 6 Anne, c. 5.

IDENTITY OF THE CHURCH OF ENGLAND IN THE COLONIES.

Q. What Acts of Legislation demonstrate the Identity of the Church of England and the Protestant Episcopal Church?

A. The Acts of the Colonial Governments. Hoff. L. C. pp. 16 et seq.
  (1) COLONY OF NEW YORK.
    Charter of the Duke of York (1664 to 1683) excluded all but Protestant ministers. People were assessed for support of the ministry in A. D. 1672, 1675, 1693, 1695, 1705, and until 1784. <small>Acts of the Colonies.</small>
  (2) SOUTH CAROLINA.
    Charter to Earl of Clarendon and others gave them right of Patronage and Advowson according to Ecclesiastical Law of the Church of England, with exemption from Conformity to Liturgy and Articles. Act of Legislature gave liberty of Conscience, A. D. 1696, 1697. Act of Legislature established Church of England in A. D. 1698 and in A. D. 1706. Continued to the Revolution, A. D. 1783.
  (3) VIRGINIA.
    Colonial Legislature. Church of England established in A. D. 1619, 1621, 1622. Clergy endowed with Glebe of 100 acres and revenue £200. Canons of Church of England made obligatory, A. D. 1624. Subscription to Constitution and Laws of Church of England required, A. D. 1642, and Letters of Ordination by a Bishop of Church of England, A. D. 1662. Vestrymen must make Oath of Allegiance and Supremacy, and subscribe Declaration of Conformity to Doctrine and Discipline, A. D. 1662. The English Act of Toleration applied to Virginia, A. D. 1745, under which Presbyterianism arose and flourished. All Qualifications and Restrictions removed by repeal, A. D. 1776.

(4) MARYLAND.

Colonial Legislature. Church recognized as an Establishment, A. D. 1692, and endowed. Tax laid for support of Episcopal Clergy, A. D. 1692. All rights, privileges, etc., of Church of England then or *thereafter* established by Laws of England were established, A. D. 1696. This Act failed of Royal assent, but was renewed and perfected, A. D. 1702. English Act of Toleration was extended to Quakers and Protestant Dissenters, A. D. 1702. A rigid intolerance, in this Law, towards Papists was passed unanimously, A. D. 1702. The Legislature, in a violent reaction, persisted in assaults upon the Church and the rights and property of the Clergy, "even to outrage," till A. D. 1776. The Church was disestablished by law in November, A. D. 1776. Henceforward there were no taxes for support of Clergy; yet the Legislature secured to the Church, Glebes and other property.

Q. By whom was the Church of England established in this country?

A. By the Colonial Assemblies.

Q. Did the Government of England prescribe the Establishment?

A. No.

Q. Did Parliament?

A. No.

Q. Did the King?

A. Yes. By Instructions and Proclamations.

Q. What authority had the King in the premises?

A. None.

Q. What power in England could establish the Church?

A. The King and Parliament and Convocation.

Q. What was the Supreme Authority in the Saxon Church?

A. The Monarch, Priests, and Nobles framed Laws for both Church and State in the Witenagemote. See Dawson's Origo Legum, Book vi. chaps. 3, 4; Churton's Early British Church; Sharon Turner's Anglo Saxons; Palgrave's Anglo Saxons.

Q. How did the Royal Governors in the Colonies justify their acts—for example, not to prefer any to Ecclesiastical Benefices, except persons lawfully ordained?

A. By the Instructions and Proclamations of the King?

Q. What effect on Colonial Society did the Governors' recognition of the King's sole prerogative produce?

A. Agitation, dissatisfaction.

Q. What apology for the Royal Governors may be offered?

A. Some believed in the legality of the Royal Proclamations and Instructions. Some believed that there was no salvation out of the Church of England. Some acted in the spirit of Intolerance.

Q. What was the spirit of the age?

A. That of Intolerance.

Q. Mention an Act of Intolerance of the Virginia Legislature in A. D. 1642? Hoff. L. C. p. 24.

A. The Delegates from the Ministers of Boston were silenced under pain of banishment.

Q. Mention contemporaneous Legislation in Massachusetts?

A. The exiled Quaker was doomed to death if he returned.

Q. Did the Church of England in the Colonies owe its existence and support to the Government of England?

A. Not at all; it was neglected and unnoticed.

Q. What notable example of earnest and successful rebuke of the indifference of Parliament occurred about this time?

A. That of George Berkeley, Dean of Derry, afterwards Bishop of Cloyne. The Parliament, during Walpole's administration, A. D. 1723 to 1742, appropriated £20,000 to found a College in America (Bermuda), A. D. 1727. Hawkins' Historical Notices, pp. 168–174.

Q. Was the money paid?

A. No! Walpole sequestered the money, and plundered the fund, to swell the nuptial pomp of the Royal Princess. Ibid.

Q. What else characterized the age?

A. Philosophic infidelity.

Q. To whom, under God, is the Church indebted, in this country, for existence, for support, and for the spread of sound doctrines and the Catholic faith?

A. To "the Society for the Propagation of the Gospel in Foreign Parts," with the exception of Virginia and Maryland, where the Church was endowed. Ibid. Preface, p. 6.

Q. What, briefly, will you say of this venerable Society?

A. It was incorporated by King William III. June 16, A. D. 1701, specially by exertions of Dr. Bray, Commissary for Maryland, with devout men of England. Its object was "Receiving and managing contributions for religious instruction of emigrants, maintenance of clergymen in the plantations, colonies, etc., and for 'the general Propagation of the Gospel.'" Hoff. L. C. p. 25. The Archbishop of Canterbury, President. Since the Foundation of the Society, all the Bishops, Directors. Ibid. pp. 10–17.

Q. Who was the "Ordinary" or Bishop of the Church in the Colonies?

A. Bishop of London.

Q. Whence did he derive his authority?

A. From the King's Commission, A. D. 1723.

Q. How did the Bishop of London exercise a personal oversight?

A. By Commissaries for various Colonies.

Q. Name the Commissaries of the Bishop of London in the Colonies?

A. Rev. Mr. Johnson for South Carolina, A. D. 1707; Rev. Messrs. Henderson and Wilkinson, Maryland, Eastern and Western Shores, A. D. 1716; Rev. Dr. Bray, North Carolina, A. D. 1703; Rev. Dr. Blair, Virginia, A. D. 1689; Rev. Mr. Vesey, New York, A. D. 1713. Hoff. L. C. p. 26, note.

Q. Did the Colonial Church apply for Commissaries?

A. Yes; Maryland in A. D. 1687.

Q. What attempt by a Colonial Legislature was made against the rights of the Clergy and the prerogative of the Bishop of London?

A. By the Assembly of South Carolina in A. D. 1704, depriving a Clergyman, Rev. Edward Marston, of his Ecclesiastical Function and Office; also, in A. D. 1704, by establishing a Lay Tribunal for the trial of Clergymen.

Q. Was this Act of the Legislature resisted?

A. Yes; by Churchmen, by Dissenters, by the House of Lords, and by the V. S. P. Gospel.

Q. How was the outrage remedied?

A. The Queen (Anne) declared the Laws null and void, and the Colonial Assembly repealed them in A. D. 1706.

Q. What other instances of attempts to bring Clergymen of the Church under Lay jurisdiction?

A. In Maryland, by one of the Parishes, on appeal to the Governor in A. D. 1704. Again: In Maryland, by Beardsley introducing a Bill to establish a Court of Laymen for the trial of Clergymen.

Q. What course was pursued in conformity with Ecclesiastical Law?

A. The Governor sent three Clergymen into the Parish as a Commission of Inquiry, to obtain facts "*to lay before the Bishop,*" and thus conformed to the Law and usage of the Church of England.

Q. What Ecclesiastical Law of England ruled the case?

A. By Canons 109, 110, 111, 112, 113, the Church-warden, the Church-warden with the Minister, or the minister alone, present to the Bishop charges against both Ministers and Laymen.

Q. What Acts further confirmed the exclusive jurisdiction of the Bishop of London?

A. The attempt to procure an Act from the Assembly of Maryland, recognizing the authority of the Bishop of London, sought for by the Governor: but opposed by the Bishop and by the Commissary, the Rev. Mr. Henderson, as *unnecessary*, because the Bishop possessed the authority already, by Divine right, and by the Law of England. Hoff. L. C. 28, 29; Hawks' Contributions, vol. ii. p. 139.

Q. What was the effect, finally, of these struggles?

A. The general acquiescence in the Ecclesiastical Law of England in the premises, and the facilitating of the *exercise* of the exclusive jurisdiction of the Bishop of London.

Q. What do these Acts of the Colonies demonstrate in a general way?

A. The *Identity of the Colonial Church* and *the Church of England.*

Q. What custom of the Clergy, in Connecticut *specially*, exhibits the Identity of the Church of England and the Church in the Colonies?

A. (1) The Custom of the Clergy in Connecticut to meet in *Convention*, and to transact such business as lay in their power.

(2) The style of their address, "We, the Clergy of the Church of England, in voluntary Convention, assembled, May 28, A. D. 1776, Wallingford."

(3) In the recognition of the Bishop of London as their Diocesan, to ordain to Holy Orders Abraham Beach, J. Nichols, and others; and in acquainting the Bishop of London with the conduct and condition of the Churches: this recognition running through several years, A. D. 1774–1781.

Q. In what particulars do these historical facts indicate the Identity of the Church of England and the Episcopal Church in the Colonies?

A. Their essential Identity, in the pervading spirit of the Ecclesiastical Law, and in the Faith, the Doctrine, and the Discipline of the Church of England, avowed and practiced in the Church of the Colonies.

Q. Was the Ecclesiastical Law of England in any way modified?

A. Yes; by the Colonial usages and jurisprudence, as the offspring of their necessities and position among Dissenters.

Q. How did this Common Law of the Protestant Episcopal Church in the United States develop itself?

A. By peculiar Usages and Statutes in the Colonies, and by the Independence of the United States.

Q. Was there any violent disruption at the Revolution, between the Church of England and the Episcopal Church in the United States?

A. No; "The daughter glided from the mother's side, by the allotment of Divine Providence, but maintained her spiritual union of Faith, of Worship, and of Discipline."

IDENTITY OF THE CHURCH OF ENGLAND IN THE UNITED STATES.

Q. What were some of the Acts of the Church in the several STATES evincing its Identity with the Church of England? *Acts of the States.*

VIRGINIA.

A. (1) The Convention of Virginia, on July 5, A. D. 1776, altered the Book of Common Prayer to accommodate it to the change of political relations with England. Hoff. L. C. pp. 31, 32.

(2) The Act of the Assembly of Virginia in A. D. 1784 required Vestrymen to subscribe a Declaration of Conformity to the Doctrine, Discipline, and Worship of *the Protestant Episcopal Church.*

(3) The Assembly of A. D. 1785 ordered that the Liturgy of the Church of England should be used with such alterations *only* as the American Revolution had rendered necessary.

(4) The Convention of Virginia, A. D. 1790, Resolved, that the Glebes and other property held by the Church of England, in Virginia, at the commencement of the Revolution, were exclusively owned by the Protestant Episcopal Church in Virginia. This heritage of succession was confirmed to the Protestant Episcopal Church, in A. D. 1799, by the opinions of Bushrod Washington, Edmund Randolph, and others. Hoff. L. C. pp. 31, 32. Hawks' Contrib. vol. i. p. 209.

MARYLAND.

(1) The civil authority of Maryland, in A. D. 1775, prescribed the form of prayer for the new Government, and required an oath of the clergy to support it.

(2) The Church of Maryland, in A. D. 1783, declared her "*right to preserve and complete herself as an entire Church, agreeably to her ancient usages and professions;*" and that she "possessed the Spiritual powers essential to the being of a Church, independent of foreign jurisdiction, so far as consistent with the civil rights of society." Hoff. L. C. p. 32. Hawks' Contrib. vol. ii. p. 330.

(3) That the Glebe and other property of the Church of England had passed to the Protestant Episcopal Church in Maryland.

(4) That it would be the duty of the Church, when duly organized in a Synod of the different orders of her *ministers and people*, to revise the Liturgy, etc., in order to adapt it *to the local circumstances of America, without any other departure from the Church of England than may be found expedient in the change of a daughter to a sister Church.* Hoff. L. C. p. 32.

(4) The Vestry Act of the State of Maryland was adopted by the Church as part of its organization, and

contains the clause expressly recognizing the Church of England as having been *the same* as the Protestant Episcopal Church of Maryland. See Compilation of Constitution, Balt. 1849, p. 275. Hawks' Contrib. vol. iv. p. 330.

SOUTH CAROLINA.

The Constitution of South Carolina, May 31, A. D. 1786, declared that the Doctrines of the Gospel be maintained in conformity, as near as may be, to the Liturgy of the Church of England. Dalcho's History, p. 474.

PENNSYLVANIA.

In the fundamental Articles adopted by Pennsylvania, May, A. D. 1784, one of them was that, "the Liturgy of the Church of England should be the Liturgy of the Protestant Episcopal Church as far as shall be consistent with the American Revolution and the Constitution of the several States.' Mem. of Ch. p. 73.

MASSACHUSETTS.

Massachusetts declared certain articles in language almost identical with that of Pennsylvania. Ibid. p. 69.

NEW JERSEY.

New Jersey set forth rules and regulations, May, A. D. 1786. The 9th Rule required from every clergyman that he engage to conform to the discipline, doctrines, and worship of the Church, as contained in the Book of Common Prayer of the Church of England, " except the political alterations in the mode of worship made therein by the Convention held in Philadelphia, from the 27th September to the 7th October, A. D. 1785." Hoff. L. C. pp. 33, 34.

This Convention, after debate (A. D. 1786), memorialized the General Convention to "remove every cause that may have excited any jealousy or fear that the Episcopal Church in the United States of America has any intention or desire, essentially to depart, either in doctrine or discipline, from the Church of England; but, on the contrary, to convince the world that it is their wish and intention to maintain the doctrines of the Gospel as now held by the Church of England, and to adhere to the Liturgy of the said Church, as far as shall be consistent with the American Revolution and the Constitutions of the several States." Proceedings of the Convention of N. J., Trenton, A. D. 1787.

In the same memorial is this passage: "We are very apprehensive, that, until alterations can be made *consistent with the customs of the Primitive Church, and with the rules of the Church of England*, from which it is our boast to have descended, a ratification of them would create great uneasiness." Mem. of Ch. p 299.

NEW YORK.

In New York the Convention, in A. D. 1790, "Resolved, That the *Articles of the Church of England*, as they now stand, except such part thereof as affect the political government of this country, be held in full force and virtue until a further provision is made by the General Convention." Journals, A. D. 1790, p. 39. In A. D. 1801 the Church in New York instructed the Deputies to advocate the Resolution of A. D. 1790, in the General Convention. Journal N. Y. Convention, A. D. 1801. Hoff. L. C. p. 34.

CONNECTICUT.

A letter of Doctor (afterwards Bishop) Jarvis, dated May, A. D. 1786, expresses the views of the clergy of Connecticut, that, "In the planting and growth of the Church in America, the Church of England was perpetuated and enlarged. That our Church was, in her original, a part, and is, in her formation, the image of the Church of England, and that it was expedient to declare so authoritatively." Hoff. L. C. p. 35.

<small>Acts of the Protestant Episcopal Church in General Convention.</small> *Q.* What were the Acts of the Protestant Episcopal Church in General Convention?

A. (1) The Bishops, the Clergy, and the Laity in General Convention, A. D. 1789 (16th October), set forth "*the Book of Common Prayer, Admin-*

istration of the Sacraments, and other Rites and Ceremonies," declaring it to be the Liturgy of this Church, to be in use on and after the 1st day of October, A. D. 1790.

(2) In A. D. 1801 the General Convention established the *Articles of Religion,* "agreeing, as far as possible, with those of the Church of England."

(3) In A. D. 1814 the House of Bishops and the House of Clerical and Lay Deputies united in this Declaration: "It having been credibly stated to the House of Bishops that on a question in reference to property devised before the Revolution to congregations belonging to the Church of England, and to uses connected with that name, some doubts have been entertained in regard to the *Identity of the Body* to which the two names have been applied; the House thinks it expedient to make these declarations, and to request the concurrence of the House of Clerical and Lay Deputies therein, namely: *That the Protestant Episcopal Church in the United States of America is the same body heretofore known in these States by the name of the Church of England, — the change of name, although not of religious principle in doctrine, or in worship, or in discipline,* being induced by a characteristic of the Church of England, supposing the independence of the Christian Churches under the different sovereignties, to which respectively their allegiance, in civil concerns, belongs." Hoff. L. C. pp. 35, 36. Jour. Gen. Conv. A. D. 1814.

Q. What are the Acts of the Protestant Episcopal Church in General Convention, with the acquiescence of the whole Church? <small>Acquiescence of the whole Church.</small>

A. The Preface to the Book of Common Prayer expresses the voice of the Supreme Legislature and of the Church at large, from A. D. 1789 to this day, in this passage: "It seems unnecessary to enumerate all the different alterations and amendments. They will appear, and it is to be hoped the reason of them also, upon a comparison of this with the Book of Common Prayer of the Church of

England. In it will also appear, that this Church *is far from intending to depart from the Church of England in any essential point of doctrine, discipline, or worship, or further than local circumstances require.*"

Q. What do these acts prove beyond contradiction?

A. The IDENTITY of the Protestant Episcopal Church in the United States and the Church of England.

Q. What is the summary of the proofs that the Protestant Episcopal Church in the United States is Identical with the Church of England: and as such, is a living and independent branch of the Church Catholic, and subject to the Catholic Law of the Church and to the Ecclesiastical Law of England, so far as those laws are applicable, and not superseded by Special Canon Law of the Protestant Episcopal Church in the United States?

A. (1) The decided voice of the Church, separately expressed by the Churches in the Colonies and in the States; and (2) uttered by the representative body of the whole Union in General Convention; and (3) by official action; and (4) especially, by the adoption of the "*Book of Common Prayer and Administration of the Sacraments, and other Rites and Ceremonies of the Church, declaring it to be the Liturgy of the Church, and requiring that it be received as such by all the members of the same;*" and (5) by the establishment of the "Articles of Religion;" *departing from the Church of England in not any essential point of doctrine, discipline, or worship, or further than local circumstances require;* and (6) by the unbroken acquiescence and consent of the whole people; and (7) by the decisions of Secular Courts of Law, vesting the rights to property held by the Church of England in the Colonies, in the Protestant Episcopal Church in the United States.

Q. In what does the IDENTITY of the Church of England with the Protestant Episcopal Church consist?

A. (1) In that the Liturgy of the Church of England was substantially retained.

(2) In that the Articles were established with some appropriate variations.

(3) In that the Faith was adhered to, whole and undefiled.

(4) In that the Sacraments were duly preserved and administered.

(5) In that the Apostolic Episcopal regimen was transmitted and received.

(6) In that the discipline of the Church of England — including Laws and Canons for rule and government — as far (and in every particular as far) as it was not necessarily, or by express enactment, changed, was continued and perpetuated. Hoff. L. C. p. 38.

Q. What opposing view of the relation of the Church of England with the Protestant Episcopal Church in the United States has been entertained and debated?

A. " That the Protestant Episcopal Church possesses no Institutions until made for her specially;" or in other words, that "we are no further bound, by either the Catholic or English Canons, when confessedly applicable, than as we distinctly and by legislation recognize them." Hoff. L. C. p. 37, note. Wilson's Mem. Bp. White, Appendix, p. 348. Pub. Alum. Assoc. p. 59.

Q. What distinguished body set forth this opponent view?

A. The House of Clerical and Lay Deputies in A. D. 1789.

Q. Where will you find a full account of those discussions?

A. In Bishop White's Memoirs of the Church, p. 175, *et seq.*

Q. What does Bishop White say of these opponent opinions expressed in the lower House in A. D. 1789?

A. He says, "If the matter had been so understood at the close of the Revolutionary War, and there had been among us such spirits as I can now designate, it would have torn us to pieces." Appendix to Wilson's Mem. Bp. White, p. 348. Hoff. L. C. p. 37.

Q. Did the opinion of the House of Clerical and Lay Deputies of A. D. 1789 prevail?

A. No. It was opposed to that of the House of Bishops in that General Convention, and to that of both Houses in the previous and subsequent Conventions: and being confined to the one house, and not, at any time, pursued afterwards, it may not be considered as having prevailed in the Church.

Q. What would such opinions, if prevailing, reduce the Church to?

A. They would have reduced the Protestant Episcopal Church in the United States to the level of one of the sects of Christianity.

Q. What just dignity do the prevailing sentiments of the Protestant Episcopal Church, in regard to her continuous relations with the Mother or Sister Church of England exhibit?

A. They illustrate her dignity as a component part of the One, Holy, Catholic, and Apostolic Church, inheriting the promises of her Lord to the organic Body and amenable to the unrevoked and applicable Laws of the whole Church.

Q. State some of the Dicta of received and learned commentators on the question.

A. (1) Bishop White. "In all other respects, except in prayers for Civil Rulers (a duty bound on us by a higher authority than that of the Church), I hold the former ecclesiastical system (of the Church of England) to be binding." Appendix to Wilson's Mem. Bp. White, p. 347. "The Episcopal Church in the United States of America is precisely in succession, the body formerly known as the Church of England in America." Bp. White, Ar. & Calv. Cont. vol. ii. p. 191.

(2) Dr. Hawks. "The opinions which were entertained in the mother country, and the decisions which had been made on matters of Ecclesiastical Law, or usage, up to the severance of these Colonies by the Revolution, were,

as far as applicable, held to be the guide of the Church of England here; and although the independence of the United States dissolved the connection, it evidently did not destroy the prevailing opinions among Churchmen as to matters and usages touching the Church. To the Common and Canon Law of England we must therefore look, if we would fully understand the origin of much of the Law of our own Church." Hawks' Cons. & Can. p. 265.

(3) Hoffman on the Law of the Church. Introduction, and throughout.

(4) Bishop Odenheimer. Quotes Bishop White from the "Church Register," January, 1826, on "Primitive Facts." "In the Church of England it is provided that nothing shall be adjudged heresy, besides what has been pronounced such by some one of the first four General Councils; and although this rests on the authority of an Act of Parliament, which is of no force in the Church of the United States, it is historic evidence of the sense of the Church of England, and of course ours, *which has inherited from her all the principles of our ecclesiastical system.* In that point of view it remains in proof of the respect for the sense of the early ages of the Church which has descended to us."

Again, in his work on "the Ordination Office," Bishop White says: "He considers all ecclesiastical institutions which existed before the American Revolution as continuing after it, until altered by competent authority." "From a consideration, therefore, of the *principle* on which our Church assumed her present independent position," Bishop Odenheimer says, "it appears to me a true view to maintain our right to the Ante-Revolution Canon Law of the English Church, in all points applicable, and where it has not been distinctly rejected or provided for by our own Canonical Legislation." See Odenheimer's Essay, Pub. Alum. Assoc. 1847, pp. 58, 59.

Q. What is the relation of the Protestant Episcopal Church to the General Canon Law?

<small>Amecability of the Protestant Episcopal Church to the General Canon Law of the Catholic Code.</small>

A. Whatever Canon Law was received by the Church of England up to the period of our separate organization belongs to us, in all points applicable, as matter of right.

In the first place, as claiming to be a branch of the Catholic Church, we possess as part of our Canon Law, the Catholic Code.

In addition, I would say, that as originally a portion of the English Church under the jurisdiction of the Bishop of London, we possess as our birthright the Catholic Code, as part of English Ecclesiastical Law. The Catholic Canon Law, in all points applicable, belongs to us, until we expressly disclaim its possession. This disclaimer has not been made and can never be made with safety to our claim to be a branch of the Church Universal. For, in the language of Bishop Beveridge (Conc. ad Synod, A. D. 1689), "Illud abrogare, aut rejicere, quod semper et ubique observatum fuit, non est Ecclesiasticum tantum ritum, sed ipsam ecclesiam mutare, et diversam efficere ab omnibus aliis Dei ecclesiis." Odenheimer's Essay, Pub. Alum. Assoc. 1847, p. 55.

Q. What do the Homilies teach on this question?

A. Constant references are made in the Homilies to "the usages of the Primitive Church," and "the sentences and judgments of the most ancient, learned, and godly Doctors of the Church." See, also, "Judgment of Sir R. Phillemore, D. C. L., in case of *Martin* v. *Mackonochie*, 1868.

Q. Will you mention a recognition of the "Ancient Canons" as being cognate with Holy Scripture and as authority in this Church.

A. At the consecration of a Bishop, the Presiding Bishop, sitting in his chair, shall say to him that is to be consecrated, "Brother, forasmuch as the Holy Scripture and the Ancient Canons command," etc.

Q. Do these Ancient Canons form part of the Catholic Code?

A. Yes.

Q. What practice of this Church in the consecration of Bishops follows the injunctions of the Catholic Code?

A. The practice of requiring three Bishops to consecrate a Bishop according to Apostolic Canons.

Q. Recite the first of the Apostolic Canons.

A. Canon I. Let a Bishop be ordained by two or three Bishops.

Q. What practice of this Church, in other ordinations, is enjoined by Canon in conformity with the Catholic Code?

A. Section VI. of Canon 4 of Title I. General Canons, declares, That " *agreeably to the practice of the Primitive Church,* the stated times of ordination shall be on the Sundays following the Ember weeks," etc.

Q. Where is this practice of Ember weeks enjoined in the Primitive Church?

A. Gelasius' Decrees (2), 5th century, A. D. 492. But upon urgent occasions Bishops may be authorized to give Holy Orders, *extra tempora prescripta.* Gibson's Codex, p. 160.

Q. Does our Church, in recognizing Ancient Law and the Ecclesiastical Law of England, follow the example of the English Church in yielding obedience to the Catholic Code or Body of the Canon Law, and also to the Foreign Canon Law.

A. Yes. Bishop Gibson says, "As in all cases where no rule was provided by our Domestic Laws, the Body of the Canon Law was received by the Church for a rule; so there was no objection against receiving 'foreign or Ante-Reformation Canon Law' in any instance whatever, *unless it appeared, in that particular instance, to be foreign to our Constitution or contrary to our Laws.*" Can. XXXI. Church of England also refers to " Ancient Fathers."

Od. Essay, Pub. Alum. Assoc. p. 56. Gibson's Codex, Introd. Dis. p. 28. Grey's Ec. Law, p. 10.

Q. What is the Analogy precisely?

A. Both Churches are amenable to the Body of the Canon Law when it is not superseded by Domestic Law. As the Ante-Reformation (or Foreign) Law (imposed by Rome) is to the English Church, so is the English Canon Law to the Church in the United States. In other words, the Catholic Code is absolutely obligatory when no rule is provided: the Foreign Code of laws (*e. g.* the English Ecclesiastical Laws in the United States) is obligatory with two restraints: (1) that " they are adapted to the Constitution of this Church, and so are *proper;* (2) and not contradicted by the Laws of the land and of this Church, and so are *legal* rules." 25 Hen. VII. c. 21, 1. Gibson's Codex, Introd. Dis. pp. 27, 28.

Q. Is every member of the Church bound to obey the Canons of the Catholic Code, and of the English Church, with the restraints abovenamed?

A. Yes; on "the footing of consent, usage, and custom in this Church," or *Jus non Scriptum Ecclesiasticum.* Gibson's Codex, Introd. Dis. 28. Grey's Eccl. Law, pp. 9, 10.

Q. May any member of the Church, on his own motion, decide what is the Common Law or custom of the Church?

A. No. He must first have the express warrant of ecclesiastical authority for the introduction of ceremonies or novel practices in this Church.

Q. Quote authority for the restraint on private action.

A. Preface to Prayer Book of Church of England, on " Rites and Ceremonies." " No man ought to take in hand, nor presume to appoint or alter any publick or common order in Christ's Church, except he be lawfully called and authorized thereunto."

Q. Who or what are the authorities that may decide on the Law of the Church in England, and of the Protestant Episcopal Church in the United States?

A. (1) The Law of the Church of England is determined by the Convocation, by Parliament, by accepted commentators, as expounded in her Ecclesiastical Courts. They are the witnesses to the members of that Church of what is Catholic and Canon Law.

(2) The law of the Protestant Episcopal Church is determined by the Constitution and Canons of the General Convention; and of the several Dioceses; and of the Rubrics; and by the Articles of Religion; and by the Civil Laws of the State in the premises, as expounded by the Courts, ecclesiastical and secular, in their respective spheres.

(3) There is likewise the *Law* of " consent, usage, and custom" in this Church; which, together with the decisions of the English ecclesiastical tribunals, respecting the interpretation of Rubrics and rules common to both Churches, is the *Jus non Scriptum Ecelesiasticum*, or Common Law of this Church. Hoff. L. C. p. 44.

(4) The Laws Catholic, to which all separate or national Churches are bound to conform.

Q. What other restraint on individual and private judgment, in respect of doctrine or practice in the Church, may you name?

A. (1) The restraint on Laymen to "do nothing without the Bishop," according to St. Ignatius' maxim; nor without the advice and consent of the Priest and Pastor under whose guidance the Layman has voluntarily submitted himself.

(2) The restraint on Deacons, as being specially under the advice and control of the Bishop.

(3) The restraint on Priests as well as Deacons, in their ordination vow, to "reverently obey their Bishop and other chief ministers, who, according to the Canons of the Church, may have charge and government over them; following with their glad mind and will their godly admonitions, and submitting themselves to their godly judg-

ments." And furthermore, the vow of the Priest to "maintain and set forward as much as lieth in him, quietness, peace, and love, among all Christian people, and especially among them that are committed to his charge."

(4) The restraint on the Bishop to set forward charity and peace (the same as that of the Priest), together with his vow to "diligently exercise such discipline as by the authority of God's word and by the order of this Church is committed to him."

Q. Will you illustrate by some examples of the just restraint on private judgment and action in respect of doctrine and practice?

A. (1) Lay Baptism. No one should enforce and put in practice his private views of the invalidity of Lay Baptism;

(2) Nor of the propriety or impropriety of the use of the Surplice or Gown in preaching;

(3) Nor of the Choral Service;

(4) Nor of Processional and Recessional Hymns;

(5) Nor of wearing the Alb and Chasuble in consecrating the Holy Communion;

(6) And such like doctrines and practices. These should not be enforced nor insisted on by private will and judgment to the peril of peace and quietness; nor against the decision of the Ecclesiastical Authority;

(7) Nor should they be objected to by private will and judgment, if not forbidden by Ecclesiastical Authority.

Q. What further statement, in the Preface to the Book of Common Prayer, confirms the declaration "that this Church was far from intending to depart from the Church of England in any essential point of doctrine, discipline, or worship, or farther than local circumstances require?"

A. The statement that "in every Church, whatever cannot be clearly determined to belong to doctrine must be referred to *discipline.*" Preface to Book of Common Prayer. Oct. 16, A. D. 1789.

Q. What is the sense of the term "discipline" in Ecclesiastical writings?

A. Twofold. (1) The administering of punishment for offenses. (2) The regulation and government of the Church.

Q. In which sense is the word "discipline" here used?

A. In the sense of the order and law of the Church for its proper government.

Q. Will you give examples of this use of the word?

A. In the Preface to the English Book of Common Prayer (2d and 5th Edw. VI.) it is said, "of Ceremonies, why some be abolished and some retained," "Although the keeping or omitting of a ceremony, in itself considered, is but a small thing, yet the willful and contemptuous transgression of a common order and *discipline* is no small offense before God." Again, it speaks of "those ceremonies which do serve to a decent and godly *discipline*." So likewise, HOOKER says, "As we are to believe forever the articles of evangelical *doctrine*, so the precepts and *discipline*, we are in like sort bound forever to observe."

Q. What is the argument, hence derived, that our Church retained the same Ecclesiastical Laws after the Revolution which it possessed before the Revolution, further than local circumstances required?

A. The body of English Ecclesiastical Law was an undoubted part of the "*discipline*" of the English Church; this Church retains the "discipline" of the Church of England; and therefore the English Ecclesiastical Law is affirmed to be the law of this Church, so long as it is applicable and unrevoked. Hoff. L. C. pp. 38–41.

PERIODS OF CANON LAW.

Q. How many periods are there of the Canon Law of the Church of England?

A. Four. The British, the Anglican, the Norman, and the Reformation periods.

Q. What are their respective dates?

A. (1) The British period, from the Apostles' time to the arrival of the Monk Augustine, A. D. 596. Wilkins' Concilia Magnæ Britaniæ et Hiberniæ. Councils of Great Britain and Ireland, by Haddan and Stubbs, Oxford, 1869, contains Records from A. D. 200.

(2) The Anglican period, from A. D. 596 to A. D. 1066, the coming of William the Conqueror.

(3) The Norman period, from A. D. 1066 to the Reformation, A. D. 1534.

(4) From the Reformation to this time.

British Period. *Q.* What was the origin of the Laws of the *British* Church?

A. They are derived from primitive and Apostolic times with the Episcopal regimen and authority. Augustine found the British Church in the use of the Liturgy of Gaul derived from the East.

Q. What are the earliest records of the Church in Great Britain?

A. The earliest record of Christians in Britain, A. D. 208, Tertullian Adv. Jud. VII. Origen, A. D. 239, Homily IV. and VI. Sozomen, A. D. 300, Hist. Ec. 1, 6. Eusebius A. D. 337, 340, Vit. Constantine II. 28. Hilary, *et. al.* St. Alban, Martyr, Diocletian Persecution, A. D. 304. British Bishops at Council of Arles, A. D. 314. British Bishops, A. D. 325, assent to Council of Nice respecting Arianism and Easter. British Bishops at Council of Sardica, A. D. 350, and at the Council of Ariminium, A. D. 359. See documents in Haddan and Stubbs, Ox. 1869.

Q. How were the Ancient Laws of the British Church to be changed?

A. Ecclesiastical Laws could not be changed except by a National Synod, consisting of "Bishops and other learned men of the clergy." Hoff. L. C. p. 48. Dawson's Or. Leg. bk. vi. cap. 4.

Anglican Period. *Q.* What were the sources of Ecclesiastical Law in the *Anglican Period?*

A. (1) The Laws under the Saxon Kings; those on spiritual subjects styled " *Monumenta Ecclesiastica* " touching the Church and Clergy, and known as " Institutions."

(2) Those styled " Laws," which touched the Laity in both temporal and spiritual matters.

Q. How were these " Laws " which affected the Laity and Clergy made?

A. In the Great Saxon Council or Witenagemote of the Realm, at which there was a representation of the Laity.

Q. How were the " Institutions " or Monumenta Ecclesiastica enacted?

A. The Clergy of the Witenagemote departed into a separate Synod and made their Canons; they brought their Canons from the Synod to the Witenagemote, " to be ratified by the King with the advice of his great men, and so made the Constitutions of the Church to be laws of the Realm." " The Norman revolution made no change in this respect." Kenneth's Ec. Syn. p. 249. Hoff. L. C. p. 52.

Q. What do you learn from these Laws and Institutions respecting the British and Anglican Church?

A. That the Councils of Clergy were sufficient for the Government of the Clergy, and that where the Laity were concerned in Spiritual matters, the laws of the Church must have been passed or ratified by the Witan, in which a representation of the Laity existed. Hoff. L. C. p. 52.

Q. Give me an example of the force of this Ancient Law in modern times?

A. In a question of marriage in the case of " Queen *v.* Mills," in 1864, the decision was grounded on one of the Laws of King Edmund (A. D. 950), that the presence of the Priest at the nuptials was necessary, who should, with God's blessing, " bind the union to all prosperity." Hoff. L. C. p. 50.

Q. Were these Synods or Gemotes (as they were called) frequently held by the Bishops and Clergy?

A. Yes. Records exist, in Bede and others, of five Church Gemotes, A. D. 673 to 794.

Q. What are the sources of Common Law in England in the third, or *Norman Period,*—middle of the Eleventh Century to Reformation?

<small>Norman Period.</small>

A. " The legislation of the Church, after the Conquest to the Reformation (exclusive of the acts of Parliament) is contained in the Legatine and Provincial Constitutions." Hoff. L. C. p. 53.

Q. What are the Legatine Constitutions?

A. They are the Constitutions of Otho, the Special Legate of Pope Gregory IX. A. D. 1236, and of Othobon, Special Legate of Pope Clement A. D. 1268, in the reign of Henry III. They were made in Synods in London, wherein sat the Archbishops of both Provinces, Canterbury and York, and other dignitaries, who duly represented the whole realm, and therefore were express National Ecclesiastical Laws. Johnson's Eng. Can. vol. ii. pp. 150, 211. Grey's Ec. Law, Intro. p. 8. Gibson's Codex, Pref. 12.

Q. What are the Provincial Constitutions?

A. Such as were published from time to time by several Archbishops of Canterbury from Stephen Langton, A. D. 1206, in the time of King John, to Henry Chicheley A. D. 1414, in the time of Henry V., being 225 Constitutions of 14 Archbishops. The Province of York received these Constitutions by consent and use. Gibson's Codex, Pref. p. 10.

Q. What are the Legatine and Provincial Constitutions styled?

A. The " *Common Law of the Church of England.*" Gibson's Codex, Introd. p. 27. Grey's Ec. Law, p. 8.

Q. Where may best be learned this Common Law?

A. (1) In the Commentaries of John of Athon, on the Legatine Constitutions; and in the Commentaries of Lyndwood on the Provincial Constitutions, reigns of Henry V. and Henry VI. A. D. 1380–1446.

(2) The Courts of Civil and Canon Law in England

regard these Commentaries as "the *witnesses of the practice of the Church of England* in their respective ages; which practice having continued, in very many cases, down to the present age upon their evidence and authority, their rules are become for the most part, and in effect, the *Common Law of the Church.*" Gibson's Codex, Pref. 12. Grey's Ec. Law, Int. p. 8.

Q. What higher recognition of these laws and rules now prevails?

A. The Statute of Parliament, 21st chap. of Henry VIII., declares that the people of the realm had bound themselves to them by long use, *not as the laws of any foreign prince or prelate,* but as customs established as laws of the realm by said sufferance, consent, and custom. Hoff. L. C. p. 60.

Q. How is the English Canon Law divided?

A. Into Foreign and Domestic. Gibson's Codex, Pref. 8.

Q. What is the Foreign Canon Law?

(1) The *Apostolical Canons,* or the Code of the Primitive Church. It embraces the Canons of Bishops and Synods of the 1st and 2d centuries, being 85 in number, and collected into one body, A. D. 200. See Cotelerius Pat. Apostol. C. 16, 17. Beveridge "Synodicon et Cod. Canon Ec. Prim. vindicatus et illustratus."

(2) *Canons of the Catholic Church;* containing 207 Canons, viz: 20 Canons of Nice; 25 of Ancyra; 14 of Neo-Cæsarea; 20 of Gangra; 25 of Antioch; 59 of Laodicea; 7 of Constantinople; 8 of Ephesus; 29 of Chalcedon.

(3) *The Code of the African Church,* 138 in number.

(4) The Collection of *Johannes Scholasticus,* Patriarch of Constantinople, embracing all Canons then in force (A. D. 560), and numbering 377.

(5) *The Code of the Latin Church,* collected by Dyonisius Exiguus (A. D. 530), embracing 402 Canons; and also decrees of eight Popes, from Pope Siricius to Anas-

tasius, under whom Exiguus flourished: to which other hands have added the decrees of six Popes, from Hilary to Gregory I.

(6) The *Code of the Oriental Church*, settled in the Synod of Trullo, A. D. 683, and containing 724 Canons.

(7) The *Code of Photius*, Patriarch of Constantinople (A. D. 880). This code contained all the Laws and Canons of the Catholic Church for 800 years, which were then in use and authority, numbering 659 Canons.[1]

(8) The *Code of the new Canon Law of the Latin Church*, consisting of spurious decrees and Papal decisions and orders, invented and published, A. D. 785, by Isidore Mercator (or Peccator) under Pope Adrian, who was "the true Creator of the Modern Papacy" (See " The Papacy," by the Abbe Guettee, Paris; New York, Carleton; London, S. Low, Son & Co., 1867, p. 261, Am. Ed.). These "*False Decretals*," with other Papal decisions, were established in the Western Church, by Pope Nicholas, A. D. 836. They concentrated all authority at Rome, and are the foundation of the claims of the Papacy.

Q. How do you prove that these " Decretals " are false?

A. (1) *Cardinal Bona* frankly calls them a "pious fraud."

(2) *Baronius* would not use them in his Ecclesiastical Annals, " lest the Roman Church should seem to require suspicious documents to establish her rights." Abbe Guettee, p. 59, *et seq.*

(3) FLEURY (Eccles. Hist. xliv. liv.) says, " The subject matter reveals their spuriousness." " They speak of Archbishops, Primates, Patriarchs, as if these titles had existed from the birth of the Church. They forbid the holding any Council, even a provincial one, without permission of the Pope, etc. Finally, the principal subject of these *Decretals* is that of complaints against Bishops," etc.

---

[1] See a Minute Summary of Ecclesiastical Laws in Essay, *Pub. Alum. Assoc.* 1847, by Bishop Odenheimer.

(4) The Abbe Guettee on "The Papacy," has gathered conclusive demonstrations of the Apocryphal character of the "False Decretals." See also "Christendom's Divisions," London, 1865, 1867. Ffoulke's "Church's Creed, or the Crown's Creed," New York, Pott & Amery, 1869. "Janus," Boston, Roberts Brothers, 1870.

Q. Were these False Decretals received in England?

A. For a time, and unwillingly, but as "new Law," which crowded out the Ancient Canon Law; so that "an ingenious author, about the year 1046, in a comparison between the Churches of the East and West, says, 'In the Greek Church are many Canonists, and in the Latin Church are no Canonists, but many Decretalists.'" Dawson's Or. Leg. bk. i. ch. 15. Hoff. L. C. p. 42.

Q. How did the Reformers treat this new Law of Rome?

A. Cranmer, in the Preface to "*Reformatio Legum,*" denounces the whole of it. Hoff. L. C. p. 42. See Burnet's Hist. Refor. p. 257.

Q. What are Domestic Canons in the Church of England?

A. Those which have been made from time to time by ecclesiastical authority within the Realm, whether before or since the Reformation. Gibson's Codex, Introd. Dis. p. 29.

Q. What do you mean by Ecclesiastical Authority?

A. The Canons and Constitutions made in Provincial Synods. They were confirmed and published, before the Reformation, by the Metropolitan; after the Reformation, by Royal assent and license (ch. 25, Henry VIII.). The authority of Canons affecting the *Laity*, after the Reformation, are only those which were accepted as ancient usage, or were confirmed by Parliament. Grey's Ec. Law, Int. p. 11, note.

Q. What are the sources of English Ecclesiastical Law in the fourth, or *Reformation Period?* — Reformation Period.

A. The Ecclesiastical "Common Law," the Canons of Convocation confirmed by Royal authority, and the Statute Law of Parliament.

Q. What Canons have been authorized by Convocation?

A. Those made in Convocation of the Province of Canterbury in the first year of James I., which are therefore distinguished as the Canons of A. D. 1603, though they are taken from Canons and Constitutions made in the reign of Queen Elizabeth. They were chiefly reënacted, because the act of Elizabeth establishing them did not contain the clause continuing them after the Queen's death; these were also received and passed by the Province of York in A. D. 1605. Gibson's Codex, Pref. p. 10.

Q. What Statute Law is considered as part of the Ecclesiastical Law of England?

A. Statutes made from time to time to enforce both Common and Canon Law, for the suppression of vice and immorality, and for the protection of the Church. Gibson's Codex, Int. p. 30.

Q. Are the Rubrics in the Liturgy a part of the Statute Law?

A. Yes; as having been confirmed in Parliament by the Acts of Uniformity. 2d and 3d of Edw. VI. ch. 1. 1 Elizabeth, ch. 2. 13 and 14 Car. II. ch. 4. Gibson's Codex, Int. Dis. Pref. 10. See Judgment of Sir Robert Phillemore, Official Principal of Court of Arches, *Martin v. Mackonochie*, p. 8, 1868.

Q. Are the XXXIX. Articles of Religion a part of the Statute Law?

A. Yes; though originally made in Convocation, they are required to be subscribed and assented to by an express Act of Parliament, 13 Eliz. ch. 12. These were mostly taken from a like body of Articles compiled in the reign of Edward VI. Grey's Ec. Law, Intro. p. 13. Gibson's Codex, Intro. Dis. Pref. pp. 10, 11.

Q. What other sources of Ecclesiastical Law are to be regarded?

A. "The noble Statutes of Henry, Edward, and Elizabeth; the injunctions of the two latter in A. D. 1547 and A. D. 1559; the Synod of Archbishop Parker, A. D. 1571; the Articuli pro Clero of A. D. 1584; the Capitula of London, A. D. 1597, together with the Canons of A. D. 1603, and all previous institutions not superseded." Hoff. L. C. p. 61. Dawson's Or. Leg. bk. vi. ch. 8, p. 157.

Q. Was this body of English Canon Law the Ecclesiastical Law of the Church in the Colonies, at the date of the Royal Charters?

A. Yes; if followed by settlement and the establishment of a Church and public worship. Hoff. L. C. pp. 60, 61, note.

Q. What is the date of the first Church erected on this Continent?

A. On the 19th December, A. D. 1606, Rev. Robert Hunt, the first ordained minister of the Church of England, embarked as a Missionary for the shores of America. In the spring of A. D. 1607 the services of the Church of England were first administered on this Continent at Jamestown, Va. Hawkins' His. Notes, p. 3. Hoff. L. C. p. 61.

It is claimed that the first services of the Church of England were in Maine. See His. Soc. Rec. of Maine. The Popham Celebration in Maine annually commemorates the tradition.

Q. Were all the Ecclesiastical Laws, which we have enumerated, in full force in England at the time of the settlement of the American Colonies?

A. No. Some were modified by the Parliament, such, for instance, as related to Dissenters. Some had grown obsolete; some incapable of being enforced; others were superseded by Statute Law. Hoff. L. C. p. 61. Cardwell's Synodalia, Pref. p. 24.

The force of custom and disuse has varied or extinguished the obligation of certain Canons. Stillingfleet on Rights and Duties, pp. 261, 267. The Bishops and other high Spiritual persons, though not competent to annul a Canon formally, instructed and directed the conscience as to the observance of them. Hoff. L. C. p. 62. Card. Syn. Pref. p. 24.

Colonial modification of English Common Law.   *Q.* What exceptions and modifications in the English Canon Law did our Colonial condition superinduce?

A. The great bulk of the Canons of A. D. 1603 were not binding on the Colonial Church for various reasons.

(1) The principles of the first twelve remained, but not in the form therein declared.

(2) The 13th to the 76th inclusive, are either inapplicable (such as those relating to Colleges) or the subjects of them are provided for and regulated by Canons of our own, with a few exceptions.

(3) The Canons 77, 78, 79, are wholly inapplicable.

(4) The 127th to the 141st are local in their nature, and have no bearing here. Hoff. L. C. p. 62.

Q. Will you sum up the several ingredients of the English Ecclesiastical Law as it obtained when the Church was planted in this country?

A. First. The Body of the FOREIGN Canon Law, derived from the Papal domination, was presumptively of no force; yet those regulations which had been adopted by use, custom, and sufferance, as the "Common Law Ecclesiastical," had force in consequence; the burden of proof, however, resting on the party affirming.

The Legatine Constitutions of Otho and Othobon stand on this footing.

Second. The Provincial Constitutions have the presumption of legality and obligation: requiring the party denying, to show why they should not prevail.

Third. The decisions of Civil and Ecclesiastical tribunals; the cases and precedents in the Spiritual Courts; together with the comments and writings of eminent men, are to be named as testimonials and witnesses of the Common Law of the English Church.

Fourth. The Statutes of the Realm and the Canons of A. D. 1603. The Canons of A. D. 1603 being agreed upon in Convocation, with the Royal License under the great Seal, were binding on the Clergy; they were binding on the Laity only by long use and acquiescence, or by express recognition of the Civil tribunals. Hoff. L. C. p. 63.

Q. Did this constitute the Body of the Law of the Church in the Colonies?

A. Yes. Many modifications, however, arose from specific provisions of charters, or particular laws of Colonial assemblies, as well as from those changes in the situation and usages of the community which rendered some provisions incompatible or inapplicable. Hoff. L. C. p. 64.

Q. What change did the American REVOLUTION bring with it?

A. (1) Alterations in the Law and Discipline and Liturgy of the Church, all well defined in one system. Modification of English Canon Law by the Independence of the U. States.

(2) The Constitution of the Church at large and the organization of the several Dioceses, have established a body of regulations, partly original, partly adapted to our condition.

(3) These, together with statutes of the Civil authority, cover a very extended field of Ecclesiastical Law in the Protestant Episcopal Church.

Q. What Law prevails in cases not provided for as above? The Common Law of the Church.

A. The law of the English Church. By that law such cases are presumptively to be decided; leaving the party contradicting to show that such law is repugnant to some principle, settled custom, or institution of our own, secular or ecclesiastical. Hoff. L. C. pp. 63, 64.

Such is the COMMON LAW OF THE PROTESTANT EPISCOPAL CHURCH IN THE UNITED STATES.

APPENDIX I. — SPIRITUAL COURTS AND PROCEEDINGS IN THE CHURCH OF ENGLAND.

In the British and Anglo-Saxon periods, and until the reign of William the Conqueror, the Court for Ecclesiastical and Temporal matters was the same; namely, the *County Court*, where the Bishop and Sheriff, or their representatives, sat jointly for the administration of justice; the first, in matters Ecclesiastical, by the Laws of the Church; the second, in matters Temporal, by the Laws of the State.

William the Conqueror separated the Ecclesiastical Court from the Temporal Court, by a charter to that effect.

The Spiritual Courts are enumerated as follows: —

1. The ARCHDEACON'S COURT, with jurisdiction in his Archdeaconry. The Judge of this Court is styled " The Official of the Archdeaconry." Appeals lie to the Bishop or Diocesan. 24 Henry VIII. c. 12.

2. The CONSISTORY COURT, which is the Court of the Archbishop or the Bishop in every Diocese, held in their respective Cathedral Churches, for the trial of all Ecclesiastical causes within the Diocese. The Judge is styled " The Bishop's Chancellor." When appointed by special Commission to hear Causes in remote parts of the Diocese, the Judge is styled " Officialis Foraneus," or " Commissary." Appeals lie to " the Court of Arches " and to " the King in Chancery."

3. The COURT OF PECULIARS of the Archbishop of Canterbury and of York, and of Bishops, Archdeacons, Deans, Deans and Chapter, and Prebendaries, etc.

These are Courts to determine the privileges of these dignitaries to enjoy a peculiar jurisdiction in certain places, where their seats and possessions are, and whence their endowments are derived. The jurisdiction in the COURT OF PECULIARS is administered by Commissioners, the chief of whom is the "Dean of the Arches." The Province of Canterbury possesses more than a hundred "Peculiars" in Seven Dioceses.

4. The PREROGATIVE COURTS of the Archbishops of Canterbury and York.

In these Courts all Testaments and Wills are proved, and Administrations on the Estates of Intestates are granted. That of Canterbury is called "Doctors' Commons," in London. This Court has been modified by Act of Parliament, A. D. 1858.

5. The COURT OF ARCHES, "CURIA DE ARCUBUS," so called because it was anciently held in "Bow Church," or the Arched Church of St. Mary, in Cheapside, London, styled "*Ecclesia St. Mariæ de Arcubus.*"

The Court of Arches has jurisdiction upon appeal in *all* Ecclesiastical Causes, except what belong to the Prerogative Court.

All manner of appeals from any Bishops or their Chancellors, Commissaries, etc., are directed here; as well as all appeals from the Commissaries of the Archbishop of Canterbury.

The Judge of the Court of Arches is styled, "*The Principal Official of the Archbishop,*" — "OFFICIALIS DE ARCUBAS." This Court is held in "Bow Church," by reason of the Archbishop's having ordinary jurisdiction in that Church as the chief one of his "Thirteen Peculiars," in London, where the Dean of those Peculiars, commonly called "Dean of the Arches," held his Court. The office of the *Vicar-General* of the Archbishop, the offices of the *Official Principal,* and the office of *the Dean of the Arches,* were formerly separate, but are now united in one and the same person; while his jurisdiction is distinct as of old. As *Vicar-General* he represents the Archbishop in his absence, *except in hearing causes.* As *Dean* of the Arches, his jurisdiction is limited to the *Archbishop's Peculiars in London.* He receives appeals throughout the *Province,* not as *Dean*, but as the *Official Principal* and *Judge of the Arches* in the place of the Archbishop. Appeals lie from this Archbishop's Court to the King in Chancery.

6. The KING IN CHANCERY.

This Court was established by 25 Henry VIII. c. 19, as a Court of final appeal from the Court of Arches or the Court of the Archbishop. Upon every such appeal a Commission is directed under the Great Seal to such persons as the King shall nominate; who, on account of the Special Commission, or Delegation, are sometimes styled "*The King's Delegates.*"

The Statute which entitles the King to ultimate cognizance by Commission, does not limit him, but leaves him wholly to his own choice, with power of appointing Commissioners out of the Temporality. None but spiritual persons were Commissioned as the "King's Delegates," until A. D. 1664,—seventy years after the erection of this Court. Afterwards, but very seldom, some of the Nobility or Common Law Judges were joined in the Commission. In A. D. 1639, in the time of the Martyr King, Charles I., from whence we date the downfall of the Bishops and their jurisdiction, which ensued, we may date the present RULE of Mixture of Temporal and Spiritual Judges in that Court.

The Court now consists of the Judicial Committee of the Queen's Privy Council, of which there is no quorum in criminal cases[1] unless the Archbishop of Canterbury, the Archbishop of York, or the Bishop of London, be present and assisting. The Queen, after definitive sentence, may grant a Commission of Review;—for there are no

[1] The Archbishops and the Bishops, who are Privy Counselors, are members of the Judicial Commission only in cases of *criminal* proceedings against Clerks in Holy Orders. The prelates who did sit on this last occasion (to wit, *Liddell* v. *Westerton*, which was a case of *civil* form and procedure) sat only as *Assessors*, and not as *members*, of the Court. See judgment of Sir R. Phillimore, D. C. L., Court of Arches, in Case of *Martin* v. *Mackonochie*, A. D. 1868, p. 8.

APPENDIX TO THE COMMON LAW OF THE CHURCH. 37

words in the Statute to restrain her. The Pope, formerly, as Supreme Head, could do the like. See Gibson's Codex, pp. 1018, 1046–1083; Introductory Dis. p. 21; Wood's Inst. p. 504, &c.; Grey's Eccl. Law, pp. 362–392; 4 Ins. p. 340; Littl. p. 232.

APPENDIX II. — THE MANNER OF ELECTING AND CONSECRATING ARCHBISHOPS AND BISHOPS IN THE CHURCH OF ENGLAND.

Bishoprics in England, under the Pope's usurpation, were DONATIVES, and bestowed "*per Traditionem Annuli et Baculi.*" About the eighth year of Henry I. A. D. 1108, they begun to be elective. Being of "the King's Foundation," he is, in right thereof, "Patron" of them all.

It may be remembered that Henry I., Beauclerc, granted to the English a CHARTER, and married Maud, a Saxon: thus uniting the Norman and Saxon interests, and restoring some of the ancient privileges of the British Church, among which may be ·reckoned that of Choosing their Bishops.

The manner of Electing and Consecrating Bishops since the Reformation is as follows: —

The Dean and Chapter of the Cathedral, signifying to the King the death of the former Bishop, are to pray leave to elect another Bishop. Upon this the King grants his license to them, under the Great Seal, to proceed to an election; laying no other restraints or limitations, but only this, entreating them that the Ecclesiastic whom they would choose as their Bishop and Pastor should be a man devoted to God, loyal to the King, and manifestly a fit and trusty person in the affairs of the Kingdom. "*Rogantes — quod talem vobis Eligatis in Episcopum et Pastorem, qui Deo devotus, nobisque: et Regno nostro utilis et fidelis existat.*"

This is all the restraint they are under from the King, in his license, styled, "*Congè d'Elire.*"

But at the same time, there goes with the license a "*Letter Missive*," containing the name of the person whom they shall elect; by virtue of which they are to choose the person so named, and no other, in due form, within twelve days; and in default of that, the King may nominate, and present by his Letters-patent, to the Metropolitan, if a Bishop; or, if an Archbishop, to the Metropolitan and two other Bishops; or else to four other Bishops, who shall consecrate him.

After the person is elected, the Proctor of the Dean and Chapter exhibits to the Bishop elect the Instrument of Election, to which he gives assent, in due form, before a Notary public: thereupon the King is certified of the election made under the seal of the Dean and Chapter. Upon the certificate the person is styled, " Lord Elect of N. N.," who thereupon does "homage" to the King; and the election is certified to the Archbishop under the Great Seal. The Archbishop is required to Confirm and Consecrate him.

The method and order of *Confirmation* is a long and formal process. The Archbishop gives a Commission to his Vicar-General to "confirm the election;" who then cites all such as have any objections against the Bishop-elect to appear before him; the Proctor exhibits the Certificates of Election and of the Royal assent. After which the Vicar-General administers to the Bishop-elect the oaths of Supremacy, of Simony, and of Canonical Obedience. Whereupon the sentence is read and subscribed by the Vicar-General, and the Election is decreed to be good and *confirmed*.[1]

After Confirmation, the Archbishop and Bishops pro-

[1] In the case of Archbishop Parker " the Confirmation " was made in " Bow Church," December 9, 1559, and afterwards the Judges adjourned to " the Confirmation dinner " at the " Nag's Head Tavern," in Cheapside, close by. Hence, after forty years, the Papists started the fable of the " Nag's Head *Consecration*." See Bishop Bramhall's *Tracts*, London, 1726, p. 17, *et seq.*, and Williams Sharpe, Earbury, *Tracts*.

ceed to *Consecration*, according to the form established, to the number at least of three. Apost. Can. 1.

In the case of *Translation* of a Bishop, Confirmation, and all that precedes it, is required.

After Election and Confirmation, the Bishop is invested with a right to exercise spiritual *jurisdiction*.

So soon as he is *Consecrated*, the prior dignities and benefices of every Bishop *created* become void; or in case of *Translation*, they become void after the Bishop's *Confirmation* in his new See. Every Bishop, whether created or translated, is bound, immediately after Confirmation, to make a legal conveyance to the Archbishop of the next avoidance of one such Dignity or Benefice belonging to his See, as the Archbishop shall choose. This is called "the Archbishop's *Option*." But a writ of "*Commendam*" may intervene, which retains the Benefice in the same person wherein it was before. If the Incumbent of the Promotion chosen by the Archbishop outlives the Bishop who is to be consecrated or translated, the Option becomes void, inasmuch as the Grantor could not convey any right or title beyond the term of his continuance in that See.

After Consecration the Bishop sues for his *Temporalities*, being all things appertaining to his See, which a Bishop receives by "livery from the King,"—as manors, lands, testaments, advowsons, titles, etc.

The Bishop is next *Inthroned*, either himself or by proxy, on mandate from the Archbishop to his own Archdeacon, at which time the King makes "Restitution of the Bishop's Temporalities," and he is then completely installed as one of the "Peers of the Land," 25 Edw. III. Stat. 3, c. 6, and is a member of the "First Estate of the Realm." Gibson's Codex, pp. 12–137. Grey's Eccl. Law, p. 30, *et seq.*

Q. But what if the Dean and Chapter refuse to elect, or the Archbishop to confirm and consecrate, the nominee of the Crown?

A. "They shall incur a *Præmunire.*"

This is a Statute made in 16 Richard II., A. D. 1393, against purchasing bulls or other instruments from Rome or elsewhere in derogation of the Crown. Other transgressions were subsequently made to incur its penalty. It is called *Præmunire* from the words of the writ: *"Rex vicecomite, etc., Præmunire,* or *præmonere facias præfatum A. B. quod sit coram nobis,"* — signifying the offense, and appointing a certain day for the offender to appear and answer.

If he appear and plead, and the issue be found against him, he shall be " put out of the King's protection : " that is, be disabled from having any action or remedy by the King's laws and writs ; he shall forfeit all his goods, and be ransomed only at the King's will.

If he do not appear or cannot be found, he is proclaimed an outlaw, and all his goods and chattels are forfeited to the King. Gibson's Codex, p. 80, *et seq.*

Such is the frightful penalty of *Præmunire*, which the Dean and Chapter, if they fail to elect, and the Archbishops and Bishops, if they decline to confirm and consecrate the person nominated by the King as Bishop to a vacant Diocese, incur.

In later times, even in these days, the first Lord of the Treasury, or Prime Minister, exercises the Royal Prerogative, and names the person to be elected, who is thereupon duly chosen (or rather voted for), and consecrated to the holy office of an Apostle in the Church of God.

The liberties of the Church are thus invaded, trampled on, and set at nought by what is styled, as if in derision of the Church, " *The Union of Church and State.*"

Contrast the present subjection of the Church of England with its condition during the Anglo-Saxon and early Norman periods, as reported to us in History and by Ecclesiastical commentators !

Divers of the Kings before the Conquest, particularly

APPENDIX TO THE COMMON LAW OF THE CHURCH. 41

Edward the Elder, Edgar, Canute, and Edward the Confessor, begin their laws with special provisions for the Liberties of Church and Clergy.

The first Article of Magna Charta, or the Confirmation of Liberties, granted by Henry III., A. D. 1225, is in these words: —

"First, we have granted to God, and by this our present Charter, have confirmed for us and our heirs, forever, that the CHURCH OF ENGLAND SHALL BE FREE, and shall have all her whole Rights and Liberties inviolable."

And this Charter was confirmed, and attested, and renewed, most solemnly, by many Kings and Parliaments, by Edward I., by Edward III., and by subsequent authorities.

The first recognition of "the King as Supreme Head of the Church of England" was made by the CLERGY themselves in CONVOCATION, upon the occasion of a grant of £100,000 by them made to King Henry VIII., to purchase from him pardon for certain offenses (particularly for having submitted to the Legatine authority of Cardinal Wolsey), and to compound the forfeitures incurred by them thereby, under the Statutes of Præmunire and Provisors.

But the King refused to accept the subsidy, or grant the pardon, unless the Clergy would accompany the gift of money with the recognition of the Royal Supremacy in things Ecclesiastical and Spiritual. This novel claim was for some time under debate, and at length it was deliberately agreed upon in these words: "*Ecclesiæ et cleri Anglicani, cujus singularem Protectorem, unicum et Supremum Dominum, et quantum per Christi legem licet, etiam Supremum Caput, ipsius Majestatem recognoscimus.*" Gibson's Codex, p. 28.

The Ancient Charter of Liberties was thus virtually surrendered by the Clergy, and immediately afterwards was revoked by Parliament (26 Henry VIII. c. 1.), which established by law the Supremacy of the King and his heirs. This Statute was repealed by Queen Mary, but restored in the first year of Queen Elizabeth. The Canons of the Church (Can. 36), and the Articles of Religion (Art. 37), A. D. 1562, reaffirmed the King's Supremacy. The Canons furthermore denounce the censure of "*Excommunication ipso facto*" (Can. 2) on whomsoever impugns the doctrine, and the Parliament has decreed the penalty of "*Præmunire*" upon the refusing to take "the Oath of Supremacy." The odious "Præmunire," and the sentence of "Excommunication," applied by the joint hands of the civil and ecclesiastical authority in the sixteenth century, have riveted, even unto this day, the chains which the Church of England painfully and ignobly forged for her own slavery.

Happy are we that our fathers, in winning the political Independence of the British Colonies, have recovered, for the Protestant Episcopal Church in the United States, the rights and independence of the Apostolic British Church, and have restored to us that Catholic Liberty wherewith Christ hath made us free, — and in such measure as not to be entangled again with the yoke of bondage.

The true and Scriptural relations of the Church and State, by the Gospel, are set forth and published in *our* 37th Article of Religion, as follows: —

"The power of the Civil Magistrate extendeth to all men, as well Clergy as Laity, but hath no authority in things purely spiritual. And we hold it to be the duty of all men who are professors of the Gospel, to pay respectful OBEDIENCE TO THE CIVIL AUTHORITY, REGULARLY AND LEGITIMATELY CONSTITUTED."

PART II.

THE CONSTITUTION OF THE PROTESTANT EPISCOPAL CHURCH IN THE UNITED STATES.

I. PRELIMINARY HISTORY.

Q. WHEN did the Church in this country become Independent of the Government of the Church of England?

A. On the Fourth of July, A. D. 1776.

Q. Who was the Bishop of the Church in the Colonies?

A. The Bishop of London.

Q. What authority declares that the Jurisdiction of the Bishop of London ceased on the Fourth of July, A. D. 1776?

A. The Preface to our Book of Common Prayer, in these words: "When in the course of Divine Providence these American States became independent with respect to Civil Government, their Ecclesiastical Independence was necessarily included."

Q. What alterations in the Liturgy were made necessary by the Revolution?

A. "The attention of this Church was, *in the first place,* drawn to those alterations in the Liturgy which became necessary in the Prayers for our Civil Rulers, in consequence of the Revolution."

Q. What political condition was assumed by the Colonies after the Declaration of Independence?

A. That of Sovereign States, in the Union of Alliance, offensive and defensive; but independent of each other as of England. Articles of Confederation, A. D. 1774.

Q. What was the Ecclesiastical condition of the Church in the several States?

A. It was that of Ecclesiastical Independence, but without any Episcopal Head. See Argument in Hawks' Cons. & Can. pp. 4–8.

Q. How did the Church "in the first place" proceed to make the "necessary alterations" in the Liturgy?

A. The Church in each State assumed the authority, by virtue of its independence, to make for itself the necessary alterations.

Q. Give examples.

A. On the Sunday before the Fourth of July, A. D. 1776, the Churches of Philadelphia ceased to pray for the King. Wilson's Mem. Bp. White, p. 51. On the day after the Declaration of Independence, the Legislature of Virginia altered the Book of Common Prayer to accommodate it to the change of affairs. See Hawks' Contrib. vol. i. p. 228. "This document is found in the State Library in Albany. It contains various alterations of the Service, almost exclusively relating to Prayers for Rulers." Hoff. L. C. p. 31. By the Act of the Assembly of Virginia, of A. D. 1784, the Vestrymen were required to subscribe a Declaration of Conformity to the Doctrine, Discipline, and Worship of the Protestant Episcopal Church. Hoff. L. C. p. 31. Hawks' Contrib. p. 163.

Q. Were these examples followed?

A. Yes. The old English Prayer Books are extant, with alterations made by erasure and substitution, as used during the War of the Revolution, in the several States.

Q. How was the Independence of the Church in each State illustrated in Connecticut?

A. By the Convention of that State, so soon as peace was declared, to wit, in March, A. D. 1783, nominating the Rev. Samuel Seabury as Bishop, and sending him to Great Britain for Episcopal Consecration, with a letter, addressed to the Archbishop of York (See of Canterbury being vacant), dated April 21, A. D. 1783. Parliament declining to enact *enabling laws*, Dr. Seabury applied with his credentials to the independent Bishops of Scotland. Bishop Seabury was duly consecrated in Aberdeen, Scotland, Sunday, November 14, A. D. 1784, by Robert Kilgour, Bishop and Primus: Arthur Petrie and John Skinner, Bishops. He was welcomed and received as Bishop of Connecticut by the Diocesan Convocation, August 3, A. D. 1785, and made his Primary Charge to the Clergy the next day. His official signature was "SAMUEL, Bishop of the Episcopal Church of Connecticut." See Hawks' and Perry's Historical Notes and Documents, published by Order of General Convention, vol. i. pp. 604–624.

Q. In how many States did the Episcopal Church exist, at the date of the Declaration of Independence?

A. In all the original Thirteen States, and in the District of Maine.[1]

Q. What was the relation of the Congregations to each other during the War?

A. They were in the way of Truth, and held the Faith in unity of Spirit; but were separate and distinct, with no organization nor union, except in Connecticut.

Q. What was peculiar to Connecticut?

A. "During the Colonial period, it was the "Custom of the Clergy in Connecticut to meet in Convention and transact such business as lay in their power." They maintained their Organization during the war. "After the Consecration of Bishop Seabury, these assemblies were termed *Convocations.*" Hoff. L. C. Introd. p. 29.

Q. What was done, after the War, in other States, for the organization of the Church?

A. (1) MARYLAND.

In August, A. D. 1783, the Clergy of Maryland organized in Convention, and set forth the following Declaration: "We consider it as the undoubted right of the Protestant Episcopal Church in Maryland, to complete and preserve herself, as an entire Church, agreeably to her

[1] Maine was admitted as a State in A. D. 1810.

ancient usages and professions; and to have a full enjoyment and free exercise of those purely Spiritual Powers which are essential to the being of every Church or Congregation of the Faithful, and which, being derived from Christ and His Apostles, are to be maintained independent of every foreign or other jurisdiction: so far as may be consistent with the Civil rights of Society." Hawks' Cons. & Can. p. 5. "In June, A. D. 1784, the *Laity were introduced* into the Convention, and they ratified the previous Acts." Conventions were held every year thereafter of both Clergy and Laity. Hoff. L. C. p. 92.

(2) PENNSYLVANIA.

In May, A. D. 1784, several members of the Churches in the city of Philadelphia met together, and appointed "a Standing Committee of the Episcopal Church in this State," and authorized them "to correspond and confer with representatives from the Episcopal Church in the other States, or any of them, and assist in framing an Ecclesiastical Government."

This was the *first step* taken toward an Union of the Churches in the States generally. Mem. of Ch. p. 72. Hoff. L. C. p. 88. Hawks' Cons. & Can. p. 5.

Q. State the *fundamental principles* which the meeting in Philadelphia proposed as the basis of the Union of the Churches?

A. (1) The Episcopal Church in the United States ought to be independent of all foreign authority, Ecclesiastical or Civil.

(2) It ought to have exclusive power to regulate its own concerns.

(3) The Faith should be maintained in accordance with that professed by the Church of England, and uniformity of Worship continued, as near as may be, to the Liturgy of the English Church.

(4) That the Succession of the Ministry be the Three Orders of Bishops, Priests, and Deacons, whose rights and

powers should be ascertained, and that they be exercised according to Law.

(5) That the authority to make Canons or Laws should be none other than a Representative Body of the Clergy and Laity conjointly.

(6) That no powers be delegated to a general Ecclesiastical Government, except such as cannot conveniently be exercised by the Clergy and Laity in their respective Congregations. Mem. of Ch. p. 72. Hoff. L. C. p. 89.

Q. What seems to characterize these "fundamental principles?"

A. A desire for Episcopal Union, yet with a jealousy of Episcopal and Priestly authority, joined with the assertion of Ecclesiastical Independence, and the right of Laymen to participate in legislating for the Church.

Q. Which Articles affirm the Independence of the Church?

A. The first, and the second, and the fifth.

Q. Which express the desire and purpose of Union?

A. The third and the fourth.

Q. Which evince jealousy of Episcopal and Priestly authority?

A. The fifth, a part of the fourth, and the sixth.

Q. What sentiment in the Church does the sixth fundamental Article further evince?

A. The sentiment that the Clergy and Laity distributed in the Congregations are the constituted Body of the Church; and the suspicion and dread of the concentration of power in the proposed General Convention.

Q. Repeat the Sixth Article.

A. "That no powers be delegated to a general Ecclesiastical Government, except such as cannot conveniently be exercised by the Clergy and Laity in *their respective Congregations.*"

Q. Was there any apprehensiveness that Episcopalians of that era were disaffected towards Episcopacy?

A. Bishop White remarks (Mem. of Ch. p. 65) "that the more Northern Clergymen were under apprehensions of there being a disposition on the part of the Southern Members to make material deviations from the Ecclesiastical System of England, in the article of Church Government. Hoff. L. C. p. 89.

Q. What confirmation of this suspicion is extant?

A. The Clergy of South Carolina received the invitation to coöperate for a general Union. There was a Meeting of Vestries 8th February, A. D. 1785. Deputies were appointed by this Convention in A. D. 1785. It was resolved that the Deputies should act according to their Judgment, but with the proviso "*that no Bishop was to be settled in that State.*" Mem. of Ch. p. 91. Hoff. L. C. p. 92. Dalcho's Hist. p. 466. Hawks' Cons. & Can. p. 7.

Q. What political circumstances at that time prompted, or at least favored, the proposed introduction of this Sixth "fundamental principle" in the Constitution of the Church?

A. The time was that *transition era* of the country, when the Continental Congress was gathered under the "Articles of Confederation." The first Article was this: " Every power not *expressly* delegated to the United States in Congress assembled, shall be retained by each State." Art. I. Art. of Confed. Very many of the men, influential in the State, were traditionally or by profession, Episcopalians, who also were powerful in the organization of the Union of the Churches. And hence, it is not strange that their political predilections should be reflected on their ecclesiastical functions, and that they should attempt to organize the Church "in accommodation to the Civil System," after the model of the Republic. Mem. of Ch. p. 90.

Q. Did the Confederation of the States endure?

A. No. It was found to be inadequate as a Government for the want of *implied* powers," and in consequence, chiefly, of the "*expressly*" reserved authority of the States, whereby Congress was shackled.

Q. What was the complexion of the hindrances to Union, as revealed in the objections of the Northeastern States?

A. The reverse of Congregationalism and eminently Churchly, though impeding organization. For example, on the 8th September, A. D. 1784, the Convention of the Clergy of Massachusetts and Rhode Island was held at Boston, and addressed a letter to the Clergy of Connecticut, in which they said, " It is our unanimous opinion that *it is beginning at the wrong end*, to attempt to organize our Church before we have obtained a head. We cannot conceive it probable, or even possible, to carry the (Philadelphia) plan out into execution, before an Episcopate is obtained to direct our motions, and by a delegated authority to claim our assent. We are extremely desirous for the preservation of our communion and the continuance of uniformity of doctrine and worship, but we see not how this can be maintained without a Common Head, and are, therefore, desirous of uniting with you in such measures as shall be found expedient and proper for the common good. [Signed,] S. GRAVES, *Sec'y.*" [1]

Consult Mem. of Ch. pp. 332–338. Letter of Rt. Rev. Dr. Jarvis: Hoff. L. C. p. 91, note. Bishop White's Defense of the Lay Principle, Mem. of Ch. p. 74, *et seq.*

Q. What further objections proceeded from Connecticut?

A. The Convention of A. D. 1784 commissioned a deputy, Mr. Marshall, to attend the proposed meeting in New York, in October, to acquaint the Clergy with the reasons why the Clergy of Connecticut *cannot enter into any discussion of measures* relative to the settlement of the Church in the United States previous to the completion of the Church in this State, by having a Bishop among us. Ibid.

[1] Rector of St. John's Church, Providence, Rhode Island.

Q. What other hindrances from New Jersey?

A. In the month of May, A. D. 1784, at a meeting of the Clergymen in New Brunswick, the subject of Ecclesiastical Union was discussed. But further proceedings were postponed "in consequence of the pending application of Dr. Seabury for Consecration in England." Hoff. L. C. p. 89.

Q. Was this sixth "fundamental principle," in regard to the restricting of the powers of the General Convention to those functions which cannot be exercised by the congregations, favored by the Churches, after a second thought?

A. No It was eliminated altogether at a general meeting of *Clergymen* who, in conformity with the call of the Standing Committee of Pennsylvania, in May, were deputed by the Churches in the States, and who assembled in New York, on the following 6th of October, A. D. 1784.

Q. State the character and annals of "*this first general meeting*" of Churchmen.

A. (1) Dr. Hawks says, "It was a meeting for Conference; it was nothing more."

The Deputies recommended to the States represented, and proposed to those not represented, to organize and associate " themselves in the States to which they respectively belong, agreeably to such rules as they shall think proper," and that, then, " all should unite in a General Ecclesiastical Constitution." Hawks' Cons. & Can. p. 6.

(2) Bishop White states that "as the greater part of the Deputies were not invested with powers to bind their constituents, all that was done was to recommend a series of resolutions to the Churches of the several States, which should be considered as Fundamental Articles of Union." Mem. of Ch. p. 11. Hoff. L. C. p. 91.

Q. What were these "Fundamental Articles"?

A. First. That there shall be a General Convention of the Episcopal Church in the United States of America.

Second. That the Episcopal Church in each State send Deputies to the Convention, consisting of Clergy and Laity.

Third. That associated Congregations in two or more States send Deputies jointly.

Fourth. That the said Church shall maintain the doctrines of the Gospel as now held by the Church of England, and shall adhere to the Liturgy of the said Church, as far as shall be consistent with the American Revolution, and the Constitutions of the several States.

Fifth. That, in every State, where there shall be a Bishop duly Consecrated and settled, he shall be a Member of the Convention, *ex officio*.

Sixth. That the Clergy and Laity, assembled in Convention, shall deliberate in one body, but shall vote separately; and that the concurrence of both shall be necessary to give validity to every measure.

The 7th Article recommended the time and place of meeting (Philadelphia, September, A. D. 1785), with a request that Clerical and Lay Deputies might be sent by the Churches in the States. Hoff. L. C. p. 91.

Q. What States were represented by their Clerical Deputies at this meeting in New York, October, A. D. 1784?

A. Massachusetts, Rhode Island, New Jersey, Connecticut (by the deputy, Mr. Marshall, commissioned to object to premature union), Pennsylvania, Delaware, Maryland, New York, Virginia (by Dr. Griffith, present by permission). Hoff. L. C. p. 91. Hawks' Cons. & Can. p. 6.

Q. Why was not Virginia duly represented?

A. Because Virginia had forbidden, *by law*, her Clergy to interfere in making changes in the order, government, worship, or doctrine of the Church. Virginia asserted the entire independence of the Church within her limits of all control but her own. Hawks' Cons. & Can. p. 6.

Q. What effect followed the publication of these Fundamental Articles, in respect to the organization of the Church in the States?

A. Maryland had held a Convention of Clergy and Laity in June, A. D. 1783, after receiving the proceedings of the Clergy at the meeting of May in Philadelphia (as before stated); and resolved that Conventions should be held every year thereafter, consisting of Clergy and Laity. *This was the foremost instance in the whole Church Catholic of the introduction of the Laity, as an Order, in Church Legislation.* South Carolina organized the Church in Convention of Clergy and Laity in July, A. D. 1785. New York held its first Convention of Clergy and Laity in June, A. D. 1785; Virginia, in May, A. D. 1785; New Jersey, in July, A. D. 1785. Hoff. L. C. pp. 92, 93.

Q. What principles seem to characterize these Fundamental Articles?

A. (1) The 1st Article recognizes the Episcopal Church in the United States, as a national Branch of the Church Catholic.

(2) The 2d Article contemplates the Church in each State as a Diocese, and entitled to representation in the National Church by both Clergy and Laity.

(3) The 3d Article overleaps State lines as non-essential to Ecclesiastical jurisdiction and rights, recognizing the Churches in their Spiritual alliance alone, with an eye to convenience and ease of communication.

(4) The 4th Article piously adheres to the traditions of the Faith, Worship, and Discipline of the Primitive Church, as transmitted through the Church of England to the United States of America.

(5) The 5th Article acknowledges the Bishop as a Legislator in the Church, *ex officio;* but *not* having even *concurrent* authority in Legislation.

(6) The 6th Article regards the Laity as a *distinct Order in Church Councils, having concurrent authority* with the Clergy.

Q. Does not the analysis of these Fundamental Articles of the assembled Clergy in October, A. D. 1784, seem to depress the Episcopacy overmuch, and exalt the power of the Laity?

HISTORY OF THE CONSTITUTION. 53

A. It certainly does.

Q. State the grounds of this opinion.

A. In all the early Councils of the Church, Bishops, or their Representatives, presided. The Councils were composed of Bishops and Clergy only. See Cave on the Ancient Church, *et. al.*

(1) The first Council on Record is that of " the Apostles and Elders" (in the 15th chapter of the Acts of the Apostles); presided over by St. James, Bishop of Jerusalem.

The Church in Antioch "sent Paul and Barnabas and certain other of them to the Apostles and Elders about this question, to wit, ' Except ye be circumcised, after the manner of Moses, ye cannot be saved.' "

" The Apostles and Elders came together for to consider of this matter."

St. James pronounced the verdict of the Council. " Then pleased it the Apostles and Elders, with the whole Church, to send chosen men to Antioch, with Paul and Barnabas, namely, Judas surnamed Barsabas, and Silas, chief men among the brethren: and they wrote letters by them after this manner, The Apostles, and Elders, and Brethren send greeting unto the brethren which are of the Gentiles in Antioch, and Syria, and Cilicia." Acts xv. 22, 23.

The " brethren" who joined, in this Encyclical letter, with the " Apostles and Elders," are distinct from them. If they were laymen, " brethren," members of the Church, they were present, not having been summoned as Legislators, nor being come together as Legislators, but, at the most, as assessors without a vote, or as loyal churchmen, submissive to the authoritative voice of "the Holy Ghost," and their spiritual fathers, "the Apostles and Elders." Acts xv. 28.

These laymen possessed *influence*, and were entitled to be present in the first Council of the Church; but the record suggests for them no *power*, nor any concurrent *authority.* See Bp. White's argument *per contra*, Mem. of Ch. p. 74, *et seq.*

Every subsequent Council of the Primitive Church was constituted after this Apostolic model. Bishop White avows that he was the first one in the United States to suggest the introducing of the Laity into the Councils of the Church. See his pamphlet, A. D. 1782.

Bishop White justifies his opinion, both as to the lawfulness and expediency of the measure, and furthermore avers that " experience has confirmed his judgment." Wilson's Mem. Bp. White, p. 123. Mem. of Ch. p. 81.

In no Branch of the Church Catholic up to that time, had it ever been proposed that Laymen sit as an Order in the Legislative Ecclesiastical Councils.

(2) Even Constantine, the first Christian Emperor, and he who summoned the first Œcumenical Council, at Nice, in Bithynia, A. D. 325, presumed not to preside, nor to debate, nor to decide, " nor to prescribe his own views on points of religious faith, but to collect the suffrages of its recognized expounders, the depositories of three centuries of interpretation and tradition, the Chief Pastors of the Christian Congregations *scattered over* the face of the Empire and beyond it." Merivale. Boyle Lectures, A. D. 1864, p. 29.

For " here were assembled the most eminent among God's Ministers of all those Churches which filled all Europe, Libya, and Asia. Eusebius Pamphilias, Life of Cons. vol. iii. p. 7.

(3) The Laws of the Ancient British Church (A. D. 180–596) could not be changed, except by a National Synod, consisting of Bishops and other learned men of the Clergy. Dawson's Or. Leg. bk. vi. c. 4.

The "Institutions" under the Saxon Kings, styled " Monumenta Ecclesiastica," were laws affecting the Clergy only. The Clergy of the Witenagemote departed into a separate Synod and made their Canons; they brought their Canons from the Synod to the Witenagemote to be ratified by the King, with the advice of his great men, and so made the Constitutions of the Church to be Laws of the realm.

Ecclesiastical "Laws" affecting the Laity were made in the Great Saxon Council or Witenagemote, at which there was a representation of the Laity. See *ante*, "Common Law of the Church." Kenneth's Ec. Syn. p. 249.

Hence we learn that the Councils of the Clergy were sufficient for the government of the Clergy, and that only where the Laity were concerned in Spiritual matters the Laws of the Church must have been passed, or ratified by the Witan, in which a representation of the Laity existed. Hoff. L. C. p. 52.

(4) The Norman Conquest made no change in this respect. Ibid.

(5) The Convocations of England are composed of Bishops and Clergy, who sit in separate houses,[1] and who enact all the Spiritual laws of the Realm. But those Canons affecting the Laity are not imperative unless ratified by Parliament.

Hence, by the liberties of the Church of England, whether in the periods, British (A. D. 180–596), Anglican (A. D. 596–1066), Norman (A. D. 1066–1547), or Reformation (A. D. 1547–1870), the Clergy alone made laws for the Clergy; and the Laity had a voice in laws affecting the Laity; but no example exists in the History of Christianity where the Laity made ecclesiastical laws for the Clergy.

The conclusion, therefore, is that the "Fundamental Articles" of the Clergy assembled in New York, October, A. D. 1784, furnish us with the first instance of an organic arrangement for Laymen to sit as an *Order* in Ecclesiastical

---

[1] In the Convocation of the Province of York, the Archbishop and Bishops sit with the Clergy in one house usually, but vote separately. Yet the Constitution of the Convocation of York admits of separate houses, when demanded by the Bishops.

Councils, or of a deliberate proposal that Laymen should be admitted as a *coördinate authority* in enacting Canons affecting the Clergy.

Q. What justification may be alleged for this departure from the pattern of Primitive and Ancient Ecclesiastical Councils?

A. Expediency. The Spirit of the age repudiated ecclesiasticism among Protestants, as favoring the abuses and tyranny of the Church of Rome. The Episcopal Churches were poor, lonely, and scattered. A Bishop had never trodden the soil, nor exercised jurisdiction, except by the poor substitute of a Commissary, and the very name of Bishop was associated with Lords Spiritual. The political and sectarian antipathies to England were rampant. The Clergy felt their need of the coöperation of the episcopal Laity. The traditions of the "liberties of the British Church" made Laymen jealous of any danger of encroachment on the freedom of American Churchmen; and the apparent assimilation of the government of the Church to that of the Nation, gave a plausible argument to lessen the opposition to the organization of the Church with Laymen as a component element in its Legislature. It could not be helped, and many loved to have it so. Bishop White, in a pamphlet published in the summer of A. D. 1782, advocated it, and justified it ever afterwards. Mem. of Ch. pp. 74–92.

Q. What does Dr. Hawks say on the subject?

A. He says, "The Church in this country could never have been organized on the principle of excluding the Laity from a voice in its legislation. Judging from past experience, as a mere measure of policy, it would have been most unwise to exclude them; for they have been of great service in the deliberations of the Church. No evil worth mentioning has resulted from their admission." Hawks' Cons. & Can. p. 19.

Q. What evil in *principle* was patent?

A. The evil of admitting Laymen, *whether they were*

HISTORY OF THE CONSTITUTION.

Members of the Church or not. Men, not baptized, might be admitted to legislate for the Church of Christ. They were so admitted; exhibiting the anomaly that persons might legislate for a Society to which they did not belong; and, above all, to prescribe the Faith, Worship, and Discipline of Christ, which they practically and theoretically repudiated. This outrage on principle was mitigated by a change of the Constitution of the Protestant Episcopal Church in A. D. 1856, requiring Lay Members of the General Convention to be *Communicants* in the Church. This qualification ought, on principle, to be required of all Vestrymen in Parishes, and all Delegates to Diocesan Conventions. The example of the General Convention, it is hoped, will be potent to move the conscience of the Churches to imitate it.

Q. State what followed the adoption of the Fundamental Articles by the voluntary meeting in New York in A. D. 1784.

A. Delegates from seven States met in Philadelphia, 27th September, A. D. 1785. "On the 1st October, A. D 1785, the draft of an Ecclesiastical Constitution was submitted to the Convention, by the Rev. Dr. Smith of Maryland, the Chairman of the Committee before appointed. It was read by paragraphs, and ordered to be transcribed." Journal A. D. 1785, pp. 21, 22. Hoff. L. C. p. 23.

Q. What Churches were represented?

A. New York, New Jersey, Pennsylvania, Delaware, Maryland, Virginia, and South Carolina. All the Northeastern Churches were absent, although represented at the former Voluntary Meeting, October, A. D. 1784.

Q. What was the character and authority of this proposed Constitution of the Church?

A. Bishop White informs us that it did not form a Bond of Union among the Churches throughout the land, for it stood on *recommendation* only; and the real and only bond by which all the Episcopal Congregations in the Country were held together, until A. D. 1789, was in the common recognition of the Thirty-Nine Articles of Religion. Mem. of Ch. p. 93. Hawks' Cons. & Can. p. 7.

Q. What followed next?

A. The Second General Convention met on the 20th of June, A. D. 1786. The Constitution was taken up and debated. Several alterations were made, and on the 23d of June it was unanimously adopted. The "Fundamental Articles" were the basis of the Constitution.

Q. Did the Constitution of A. D. 1786 become the Fundamental Law of the whole Church?

A. No. The Eleventh Article was as follows: " The Constitution of the Protestant Episcopal Church in the United States of America, *when ratified by the Church in a majority of the States, assembled in General Convention, with sufficient power for the purpose of such ratification,* shall be unalterable by the Convention of any particular State which hath been represented at the time of such ratification." Jour. Gen. Conv. A. D. 1786.

Q. How was the next General Convention summoned?

A. By a Resolution of June 24, A. D. 1786, recommending "That the several State Conventions do *authorize and empower the Deputies to the next General Convention*, after we shall have obtained a Bishop or Bishops in our Church, to *confirm or ratify a General Constitution*, respecting both the doctrine and the discipline of the Protestant Episcopal Church." Jour. Gen. Conv. A. D. 1786.

Q. When did the next General Convention convene?

A. In July, A. D. 1789. Bishops Seabury, of Connecticut (A. D. 1784), White, of Pennsylvania, and Provoost, of New York (A. D. 1787), had then been consecrated. Bishop White attended and presided. Massachusetts, Connecticut, Rhode Island, and New Hampshire were not present.

Q. What was done at this Convention of A. D. 1789?

A. The Constitution having been referred to a committee of one from each State and adopted, was engrossed for signing; and on the 8th of August, it was signed by the members of the Convention.

Q. What was done to engage the Churches in the Northeastern States ?

A. The Convention was adjourned from August to 29th September, A. D. 1789. At that time the assent of the Deputies of those Churches was given, *provided*, that the Third Article should be so amended as to authorize the Bishops when sitting in a separate House, to originate any measures, and to negative the acts of the other House. The Convention agreed to them, modifying the Veto (from three fifths) so that a law might be passed if adhered to by four fifths of the House of Deputies; and changing the powers of the House of Bishops, from being a House of Revision of the acts of the lower House into a coördinate Branch of the Legislature, with the right to originate Canons. This amendment of the Third Article of the Constitution was made in the General Convention without recourse to the Diocesan Conventions for ratification. On the 2d of October, A. D. 1789, Bishop Seabury and the Deputies from Connecticut, Massachusetts, and New Hampshire, signed the Constitution, and *the Union of the Churches was consummated.* Jour. Gen. Conv. A. D. 1789, pp. 94–97.

Q. What were the several Dioceses *allowed* to retain under the Constitution of A. D. 1786 ?

A. They were allowed very clearly the following rights and privileges: —

" (1) To organize as a distinct Church within the territorial limits of each State, district, or diocese.

" (2) To elect their own Ecclesiastical Head.

" (3) To hold the sole and exclusive Jurisdiction in the Trial of offending Clergymen, within their respective limits; and to prescribe the Mode of trial.

" (4) To hold their own Ecclesiastical Legislatures, and make all such laws as they might deem necessary for their well-being, provided they did not defeat the purpose of Union, by the contravening of the Constitution and constitutional enactments of the Church General.

"(5) To have an equal Voice in the general legislation of the Church at large.

"(6) To have their respective Bishops subject to no other Prelate, and to be interfered with in the discharge of their duty by no other Bishop; but in all things belonging to their Office, to be equal to every other Bishop in the Church.

"(7) To have their several Bishops, of right entitled to a voice in the Councils of the Church, not as Representatives of Dioceses, but individually, as Christian Bishops." Hawks' Cons. & Can. p. 11.

Q. In what were the several Dioceses *prohibited;* or, as Dr. Hawks states the proposition, "What did they surrender?"

A. "As we apprehend," he says, "they surrendered the following things:—

"(1) Such an exercise of Independency as would permit them to withdraw from the Union at their own pleasure, and without the assent of the other Dioceses.

"(2) They surrendered the right of having the Bishop whom they might elect, consecrated without the consent of the Church at large.

"(3) They surrendered the right of sole and unrestricted Legislation for themselves, in the Dioceses alone; but consented that part of their laws should be made in a General Legislature of which they were members.

"(4) They surrendered the right of framing their own Liturgy, and agreed through all the Dioceses, to use the same, when all should have ratified it.

"(5) They surrendered the right of making, separately, any Alteration in the great Compact or Charter of Union.

"These things, as it seems to us, were done by the proposed Constitution of A. D. 1785.

"It underwent much discussion, and finally, on the 8th of August, A. D. 1789, the Constitution was formally adopted, and became the Fundamental Law of the Protestant Episcopal Church in the United States." Hawks' Cons. & Can. pp. 11, 12.

Q. What further right of the State (or Diocesan) Conventions does Bishop White affirm was " surrendered " and abandoned in A. D. 1789?

A. The right of a voice in the Ratification of the Articles of the General Constitution.

Bishop White says, " The mode in which the proposed Constitution of A. D. 1785 should be ratified was *subsequently changed.* For though this Constitution had been declared to be fundamental " when ratified by the Church in the different States," yet such a system appeared to the General Convention of A. D. 1786, so evidently fruitful of discord and disunion that *it was abandoned from this time.*" Mem. of Ch. pp. 123, 124. Wilson's Mem. Bp. White, pp. 134, 135.

" On the review of the Constitution, the Eleventh Article (on Ratification and Amendments) was altered so as to require a ratification 'by the Church in a majority of the States assembled in General Convention, with sufficient power for the purpose of such ratification.'" Jour. Gen. Conv. A. D. 1786, p. 42.

At the General Convention of A. D. 1789, the Deputies from the several States appeared with sufficient powers for that object, and a General Constitution was then adopted and finally ratified, *without being submitted to the State Conventions.*" Wilson's Mem. Bp. White, pp. 135, 136.

The Constitution thus " formally adopted and become the Fundamental Law in August 8th, A. D. 1789," was amended in its 3d Article in General Convention, October, 2, A. D. 1789, by virtue of the " powers delegated to this Convention," without reference to the State Conventions for any ratification by them, and thus evinced itself to be the SUPREME, as well as FUNDAMENTAL LAW OF THIS CHURCH. Jour. Gen. Conv. A. D. 1789, p. 95. See *post*, on the "Constitution."

II. THE POWERS AND AUTHORITY OF THE GENERAL CONVENTION.

Q. WHAT is the relation of the GENERAL CONVENTION to the Diocesan Conventions?

A. It is that of a *Supreme Legislature*, whose Constitution is the Fundamental Law of the Protestant Episcopal Church in the United States, and whose Canons either overrule or sanction the Canons of the several Diocesan Conventions.

<small>Historical Facts.</small> *Q.* State the facts to prove the Supremacy of the General Convention of the Protestant Episcopal Church in the United States.

A. (1) The first General Convention came together in A. D. 1785, and framed a Constitution which was referred to the Conventions of the several States for approval.
<small>1785.</small>

(2) The next fact is the Resolution of the General Convention, June 24, A. D. 1786, which recommended that the several State Conventions authorize and empower their Deputies to the next General Convention, after we shall have obtained a Bishop or Bishops in our Church, to confirm and *ratify* a General Constitution, respecting both the doctrine and discipline of the Protestant Episcopal Church in the United States of America. Hawks & Perry's ed. Jour. Gen. Conv. A. D. 1786, p. 42.
<small>1786.</small>

(3) Bishop Seabury was Consecrated in A. D. 1784. Bishops White and Provoost were Consecrated in A. D. 1787. Thus the one condition was fulfilled.
<small>1787.</small>

SUPREMACY OF THE GENERAL CONVENTION. 63

(4) At the General Convention in August, A. D. 1789, — the first Convention after obtaining the Episcopate, — "the Deputies declared themselves authorized and empowered by their respective Conventions to ratify a Constitution; and it was referred to a Committee of One from each State to consider the Constitution proposed in A. D. 1786. It underwent much discussion, and finally, on the 8th August, A. D. 1789, the Constitution was formally signed and ADOPTED." It was afterwards amended, *without recourse to the Dioceses*, in an Adjourned Meeting of General Convention, October 2, 1789. Jour. Gen. Conv. A. D. 1789, pp. 69, 83, 96. Wilson's Mem. Bp. White, p. 135. Hawks' Cons. & Can. p. 12. Hoff. L. C. pp. 97–101.

_{1789.}

The Constitution was thus established, ratified, adopted, and amended *by the whole Church assembled in General Convention.*

Q. Was there required any *subsequent* ratification of the General Constitution by the State Conventions before it should become "the Fundamental Law of the Protestant Episcopal Church in the United States"?

A. No. The Constitution was complete and Sovereign on the 8th of August, A. D. 1789. It was amended in General Convention, October 2, A. D. 1789, in order to admit Bishop Seabury and the Eastern Churches into Union, by its own inherent authority, and without reference to the State Conventions. See Hoff. L. C. p. 101. Jour. Gen. Con. A. D. 1789, p. 26.

Q. Did the State Conventions take action on the subject?

A. In several of the original States a recognition or ratification, *pro forma*, took place. South Carolina, October 19, A. D. 1790; New York, November 4, A. D. 1789; Maryland, A. D. 1790; New Jersey, A. D. 1790; Virginia, the Constitution was read and laid on the table May 1, A. D. 1790; Pennsylvania, the Constitution was read in Convention, June, A. D. 1790, and notice was given of a proposed amendment. The Constitution was recognized as binding, of its own authority. No formal ratification took place. The proceeding of Pennsylvania is specially important, because Bishop White, who assisted in framing the Constitution, is a contemporaneous witness that the General Constitution, being established by the Church in General Convention, required no ratification by the Dioceses, and " was not submitted to the State Conventions for ratification." Wilson's Mem. Bp. White, pp. 134–136. Delaware, no action is recorded.

Q. What are the just inferences from these various actions of the State Conventions?

A. (1) "That the Deputies to the General Convention of A. D. 1789 regarded themselves, and were treated by their associates and constituents as vested with full power to form a Constitution for the Church."

(2) That this authority was generally recognized by the State Conventions, and by the Clergy and Laity of the Parishes in the several Churches in the original Dioceses, the members of which were the Constituency represented in General Convention.

(3) That the General Constitution derived its power and authority as the controlling and Supreme Law of the Church, simply and solely from the votes of the Deputies in General Convention in A. D. 1789.

(4) Those Dioceses which approved, gave their positive recognition of the sufficient authority of their delegates; those which were silent signified thereby their acquiescence.

, In either case, however, the opinion of the Dioceses was not necessary to the validity of the General Constitution of the Church. Hoff. L. C. pp. 101–104.

Q. Was it within the powers of the original State Conventions to claim authority to ratify the Constitution before it should have force, or to refuse their consent to the action of their Deputies in the premises?

A. No. The first Constitution was framed by the first General Convention in A. D. 1785, and was specially referred to the State Conventions for ratification. The General Convention of A. D. 1786 again referred the Constitution with the Resolution before recited, that the State Conventions would " *authorize and empower their Deputies to the General Convention of* 1789 *to confirm and ratify a General Constitution.*" The Deputies to the Convention of A. D. 1789 appeared accordingly with plenipotentiary powers, " declaring themselves authorized by their respective Conventions to ratify a Constitution. Hawks' Cons. & Can. p. 12. The Constituency bound themselves thereby to accept, and to be governed by, the Constitution ratified by the Deputies to the Convention of A. D. 1789. Besides, there would have been endless confusion if the question of the expediency, authority, and supremacy of the Constitution of A. D. 1789 was permitted to oscillate between the General Convention and the State Conventions. Wilson's Mem. Bp. White, pp. 134–136. The State Conventions which were duly represented, were accordingly bound by the acts of their Representatives, and it was not in their power to refuse their assent. See Hoff. L. C. p. 104.

Q. Is this question historically mooted ?

A. No. None of the State Conventions claimed any authority to ratify the General Constitution, nor refused assent and obedience ; all approved, or acquiesced, and submitted.

Q. What was the authority of the Constitution (as amended in General Convention, October, A. D. 1789) in those States which had not sent Deputies, or which had not "empowered" them to "confirm and ratify a General Constitution " ?

A. As to Connecticut, the powers of the Deputies were specially limited, in consequence of the objection made in that Church to the Article of the Constitution (of August, A. D. 1789) restricting the Bishops from *originating* any measure in their separate House, and from *negativing* the Acts of the other House. These modifications were duly made in General Convention, October 2, A. D. 1789. Bishop Seabury and the Deputies from Connecticut, Massachusetts, and New Hampshire testified their assent as follows: "We do hereby agree to the Constitution of the Church, as modified this day in Convention," and signed the Constitution. And because the Deputies had not, like the other Deputies, been clothed with full powers, it was deemed necessary and proper to refer the Constitution of October A. D. 1789, thus amended, to the Church in Connecticut for ratification: which was done in Convocation A. D. 1790, and by the Parishes A. D. 1790-92. With regard to the other Northeastern States, Massachusetts, Rhode Island, and New Hampshire, their representative — the Rev. Dr. Parker (afterwards Bishop of Massachusetts) — having signed the Constitution, but with "no competent power delegated," it was also necessary and proper to refer the Constitution to those States for definite ratification. In A. D. 1790-91 the Churches of Massachusetts, New Hampshire, and Rhode Island, being separately organized, united themselves in a Diocese or Province, with a distinct Convention. The Convention met in May, A. D. 1791, when it "took into consideration the General Constitution agreed on in Philadelphia in October, A. D. 1789, which was read and considered by paragraphs, and after some debate the question was put, "Shall the said Constitution be adopted?" The vote was in the affirmative, "three Churches to one." Accordingly the Churches of Massachusetts, Rhode Island, and New Hampshire, came into the Union by virtue of the Act of their Convention of A. D. 1791, "in like manner as any other Diocese has subsequently come in, by acceding to the General Constitution by a positive Act." Hoff. L. C. p. 104.

Q. What further argument may be adduced to prove the Supremacy of the General Convention, in respect of Amendments to the Constitution?

A. The Ninth Article of the Constitution of October, A. D. 1789, providing for its *amendment*, requires every alteration to be proposed in the General Convention, and the proposed amendment " *to be made known* " to the several Diocesan Conventions, but confers no power on a Diocesan Convention to refuse its assent and obedience to the Constitution, when amended in the ensuing General Convention. The great Council of the Church in General Convention is, therefore, supreme in making amendments; admitting no coördinate authority, whether in one or in all the Dioceses, separately acting, nor otherwise than by their Deputies, being assembled in General Convention and representing the whole Church.

Q. Let us examine this point more particularly. Recite the words of the Eleventh Article of the Constitution as proposed to the State Conventions in A. D. 1785.

A. Article XI.: " This General Ecclesiastical Constitution, when ratified by the Church in the different States, shall be considered as fundamental, and shall be unalterable by the Convention of the Church in any State." Hawks & Perry's Ed. Jour. Gen. Conv. A. D. 1785, p. 23.

Q. Recite the Eleventh Article of the Constitution, as proposed to the State Conventions in A. D. 1786.

A. Article XI.: " The Constitution of the Protestant Episcopal Church in the United States of America, when ratified by the *Church in a majority of the States assembled in General Convention, with sufficient power for the purpose of such ratification, shall be unalterable* by the Convention of any particular State which hath been represented at the time of such ratification." Hawks & Perry's Ed. Jour. Gen. Conv. A. D. 1786, p. 42.

Q. Where is " the Church " affirmed to be, for the purpose of Ratification ?

A. " Assembled in General Convention," " in a majority of the States," by Deputies, " with sufficient power."

Q. Recite the Ninth Article of the Constitution, as passed in General Convention, October, A. D. 1789; being the same as now existing (except the word "States," changed into Dioceses in A. D. 1838).

A. Article IX.: " This Constitution shall be unalterable, unless in General Convention, by the Church, in a majority of the States which may have adopted the same; and all alterations shall be first proposed in one General Convention, and made known to the several State Conventions, before they shall be finally agreed to or ratified in the ensuing General Convention." Jour. Gen. Conv. A. D. 1789. Digest.

Q. By whom may the Constitution be altered?

A. "By the Church, in a majority of those Dioceses which have adopted the same."

Q. Where must the action of the Church, by such majority, be expressed?

A. "In General Convention."

Q. Where must alterations be proposed?

A. "In General Convention."

Q. Where must *proposed* alterations be finally agreed to, or ratified?

A. "In the ensuing General Convention."

Q. What must be done with the proposed alterations in the Interim?

A. They must be "made known" to the several Diocesan Conventions.

Q. For what purpose?

A. That the Church in the Dioceses may be duly informed of the proposed amendment, and so to send such Deputies to the next General Convention, as may duly represent the Church in their Diocese, in the making of the alterations in the Constitution of the whole Church.

Q. State the views and testimony of Bishop White on this point?

A. "The interfering instructions" (from the Conventions of the States in A. D. 1786, on agreeing to the "Pro-

SUPREMACY OF THE GENERAL CONVENTION. 69

posed Book" of Common Prayer) "proved ultimately beneficial, because they manifested the necessity of a well-constituted Legislative Body for the whole Church, and the futility of subjecting their measures to the review and authoritative judgment of the State Conventions. And such a system appeared so evidently fruitful of discord and disunion, *that it was abandoned from this time.*" Mem. of Ch. pp. 123, 124. Accordingly "a General Constitution, in A. D. 1789, was adopted and finally ratified without being submitted to the State Conventions. In order to give stability to it, by preventing hasty changes, it was also provided that the Constitution should be unalterable, unless in General Convention; and that the alterations should be first proposed in one General Convention, and made known to the several State Conventions before they should be finally adopted." Wilson's Mem. Bp. White, pp. 135, 136.

Q. If a majority of the Dioceses, in their respective Conventions, dissent from the proposed alterations, should the General Convention alter the Constitution against such expression of dissent.

A. The only Constitutional mode, whereby the General Convention can take knowledge of the dissent of the Church in the Dioceses to a proposed alteration of the Constitution, is by *the votes of their Deputies in General Convention* on the question.

Q. How are the Votes of the States (Dioceses) on Amendments to the Constitution expressed in General Convention?

A. The Votes in General Convention on a change of the Constitution, must be by "Dioceses and Orders;" each order of Clergy and Laity of a Diocese having one vote; and the concurrence of a majority of both orders being necessary to constitute a Vote of the Convention. Hence it follows that a Vote of the General Convention on the question of altering the Constitution, is the voice of "the

Church in the majority of the Dioceses," in exact conformity with the Constitutional requirement; or — as expressed in the Constitution of A. D. 1786 — it is the Vote of "the Church in a majority of the States *assembled* in General Convention;" or the equivalent article in the Constitution of A. D. 1789: "In General Convention, by the Church, in a majority of the States." The judgment of the States (Dioceses) can be not otherwise constitutionally uttered.

Q. What adverse inference has been drawn by Dr. Hawks from the language of Article IX. of the Constitution, as to the relation of the Conventions of the Dioceses to the General Convention?

<small>Adverse Arguments.</small>

A. An argument has been made by Dr. Hawks on the hypothesis that "the Constitution was made by the State Conventions," and therefore that all alterations of the Constitution, according to the provisions of Article IX. "are to be made *by* the State (Diocesan) Conventions" to whom the proposed Amendment is directed to be "made known." Hawks' Cons. & Can. pp. 49-58.

Q. What answer to the hypothesis on which this conclusion is postulated, does the History of the Constitution of A. D. 1789 furnish?

A. The facts of history contradict the postulate that "the Constitution" of A. D. 1789 "was made by the State Conventions."

(1) The Constitution was made by Representatives of the whole Church, coming together with full powers to frame and establish a General Constitution, which was finally and completely done in the General Convention, without recourse to the State Conventions for their ratification. See *ante*, and *post*.

(2) Another fact of history which contradicts the hypothesis of Dr. Hawks is this; namely, that the Third Article of the Constitution of August, A. D. 1789, upon the Report of a Committee of General Convention on October

SUPREMACY OF THE GENERAL CONVENTION. 71

2, A. D. 1789, was altered in that General Convention, and " so modified as to declare explicitly the right of the Bishops, when sitting in a separate House, to originate and propose acts for the other House of Convention, and to negative such acts proposed by the other House as they may disapprove." "After some debate the Third Article was so modified." Jour. Gen. Conv. October, A. D. 1789, p. 96. The views of that General Convention respecting their own Supreme powers to make alterations and amendments, without recourse to the Church in the States for ratification, is stated in the Resolution of the Committee of the Whole, on October 1, A. D. 1789, as follows: " Resolved, that for the better promotion of a Union of this Church with the Eastern Churches, the General Constitution established at the last session of this Convention is yet open to amendment and alterations, by virtue of the powers delegated to this Convention." Ibid. p. 95.

(3) A third fact is, that the Constitution was *not* "made by the *State Conventions* duly assembled for that purpose," as Dr. Hawks says (Cons. & Can. p. 41).

The General Convention is composed of the Representatives of the members of the " Church in each Diocese."

The State Conventions were themselves not an original power, but only Representatives, and the medium whereby the *Members of the Church*, in each State, delegated full powers to their Deputies in the General Convention. Hoff. L. C. pp. 97, *et seq.*

Q. What further argument does Dr. Hawks urge against the Supremacy of the General Convention ?

A. He asks, "*Where* is the change to be made ? The Article says, at its close, it may *finally* be agreed to or ratified *in*, not *by*, the General Convention. But what is to be agreed to, what to be ratified ? Men agree to something that *has been done* by others ; they ratify commonly some act which others, not themselves, *have* performed. *Ex vi termini*, therefore, it would seem that action somewhere else than *in* the General Convention is presupposed. Where is this previous action? The article directs that all alterations shall be first proposed in one General Convention, and made known to the several *Diocesan Conventions before* they shall be finally agreed to! The previous action, then, if anywhere, must be in the several Diocesan Conventions. They made the instrument originally, of which, by some alteration, it is now proposed to make a new or additional part." Hawks' Cons. & Can. p. 42.

Q. What answer does Article VIII. of the Constitution, providing for the Amendment of the Book of Common Prayer, furnish to this interpretation and argument of Dr. Hawks?

A. Article VIII. establishes the Book of Common Prayer, and provides for its Amendment in these words: —

"No alteration or addition shall be made in the Book of Common Prayer, or other offices of the Church, or the Articles of Religion, unless the same shall be proposed in one General Convention, and by a resolve thereof made known to the Convention of every Diocese, and ADOPTED AT the subsequent General Convention."

The Book of Common Prayer is established by the Constitution, and the provision for the Amendment of the Prayer Book is by an amendment of the Constitution. The authority to alter the Prayer Book is evidently reposed in the General Convention alone, and not in the Dioceses, for two reasons:

(1) The language of Article VIII. does not use the word ratified, but "adopted." And the word to adopt signifies "to take as one's own" (Webster). In law, "to pass upon finally." Moreover, the power to *make*, confessedly implies the power to *alter and amend*, which is "making a new or additional part." Hawks' Ibid. p. 42. Hence the language of Article VIII. construes the phrase "finally agreed to or ratified," as in Article IX. to be equivalent to the word "adopted." Moreover Article IX. itself uses the word "adopted."

It says, " This Constitution shall be unalterable, unless in General Convention, by the Church, in a majority of the Dioceses which may have ADOPTED the same." Art. IX. Cons. Dig.

This is the same word as is used in Article VIII. expressly as to the *Amendment* of the Constitution, when it says that the amendment shall be " *adopted at* the subsequent General Convention." And therefore, the power that *made* is the power that "*alters*" the Constitution, which power, in either case, is expressed by the word "*adopt.*" Hence, the argument that the phrase "finally agreed to or ratified" implies previous authoritative action in the Dioceses, is upset, on the principle that "every law should be so construed as to make it consistent with itself;" and therefore the Constitution *adopted* by the Convention is to be *amended* by the Convention alone.

(2) Article VIII. still further confutes the argument respecting the *place* where amendments are to be made, and answers Dr. Hawks' question, " *Where* is the change to be made ?" The *place where* is stated in Article VIII. to be " AT the subsequent General Convention;" and, therefore, is *not* at the Diocesan Convention.

Q. What further argument for "diocesan independence" does Dr. Hawks allege ? Ibid. pp. 42, 43.

A. He demands, "*By* whom, *in* the General Convention, is a change to be made ? The Article answers, By the Church, in a majority of the Dioceses. What does it mean by ' the Church ?' Is it simply the members of the General Convention ? Perhaps, it may be replied, a mere numerical majority was not meant, but a majority of Dioceses. *Admit it ;* it then proves that all votes in General Convention, on proposed changes in the Constitution, *must* be by *Dioceses ;* and this we believe ; but it also proves, we think, that States, quasi States, or Dioceses, are alone competent to alter the instrument at all. This helps us," he goes on to say, "to interpret the words in the Article, 'by the Church in a majority of the Dioceses.' It means a majority of the several Dioceses of the Protestant Episcopal Church in these United States. And on any other interpretation, the latter clause of the Article, while it affects to respect, in truth mocks at diocesan *independence*."

Q. What answer is to be made to this argument?

A. None at all. It concedes the whole question. The Dioceses act " in the General Convention," by a vote of " Dioceses and Orders " in amending the Constitution. Dr. Hawks " admits it." And this conceded place and method, whereby " the Church in a majority of the Dioceses " may alter the Fundamental Law, being admitted to be " in the General Convention," excludes all other places and methods of diocesan action, and " mocks at diocesan independence."

Q. What is the upshot and practical conclusion which Dr. Hawks infers from his hypothesis of " diocesan independency ? "

A. Twofold. He says (1), " As Dioceses, it is the right of each, if it pleases, to make known in some mode by a vote, or if they see fit, by instructing their Delegates to the General Convention, what the Diocesan Convention thinks of any proposed alteration of the Constitution or Book of Common Prayer."

(2) "And if a majority of such Diocesan Conventions should make known that they disapprove, we do not think that it was designed under this Article to permit the General Convention to make the alteration. We say we do not think *it was designed*. The reason is, it presents an anomaly without precedent or parallel in this country of constitutions." Hawks' Cons. & Can. p. 45.

Q. What have you to say to this twofold conclusion of the argument against the Supremacy of the General Convention ?

A. The *first* branch of the conclusion is undoubtedly

SUPREMACY OF THE GENERAL CONVENTION. 75

true, and is not disputed. The Diocesan Conventions may make known their thoughts on any proposed alteration of the Constitution, " if they see fit."

The *second* branch of the conclusion is not true, neither by the logic of the argument, nor by the practical test of interpretation under the historic action of the Dioceses and the General Convention. The vote by Dioceses and Orders in the General Convention is acknowledged to be the accepted way to make known the voice of the Church in altering the Constitution.

The argument of Dr. Hawks *finally* betrays its political origin, by its reference to "this country of constitutions," and by an evident bias towards the political theory of State Sovereignty, which Dr. Hawks goes on to maintain. Ibid. pp. 46–55.

Any discoverable political analogy is beside the question of our Ecclesiastical Polity, and ought not to be admitted to prejudice the judgment.

Q. State what has been the practice, or the precedent, in the mode of altering the Constitution.

A. The first change in the Constitution, after it had been published to the Dioceses and was become the Fundamental Law under which the General Convention met from July 28 to August 8, A. D. 1789, and enacted Canons, which are now extant and binding, was made at the adjourned session, September 29 to October 16, A. D. 1789. The Convention was a single House until October 2, and changed the Third Article of the Constitution by a vote of the House upon " special motion." Whether the vote was taken by Dioceses and Orders the record does not inform us. Jour. Gen. Conv. A. D. 1789, p. 26.

Dr. Hawks has enumerated the occasions of alterations as follows : —

" An alteration was made in A. D. 1804, by a vote taken in the usual mode of legislation and not by Dioceses."

" In A. D. 1808 a change was made of importance, giving

an absolute negative to the House of Bishops. A vote by Dioceses does not appear to have been called for; but the vote was by Dioceses, as if it were a matter of course."

"In A. D. 1811 an addition of entirely new matter to the Eighth Article was before the House, when it simply *Resolved*, that the addition be agreed to. The vote was taken in the common mode."

"In A. D. 1823 a change was made in the first Article, and the vote was taken by Dioceses."

"In A. D. 1829 the Eighth Article was altered, and it seems to have been done by a simple Resolution."

"In A. D. 1826 Bishop Hobart proposed certain changes in the Liturgy. These were made known to the several Diocesan Conventions. A message from the Bishops, in the Convention of A. D. 1829, that 'it was inexpedient to make the change,' was concurred in by the House, so that no other vote was taken."

Dr. Hawks calls special attention to the fact that "Bishop White, in his Memoirs, commenting on this transaction, uses this language, 'The alterations of this Book, proposed by the last General Convention, were not acted on by the present, having been found unacceptable to the major number of the Diocesan Conventions.'" Hawks' Cons. & Can. pp. 47, 48.

The succeeding alterations were made in the General Conventions of A. D. 1838, 1841, 1844, 1856, in which the vote was taken by Dioceses and Orders. All of them had been "made known to the several Diocesan Conventions."

Q. What does this historical enumeration of the amendments exhibit?

A. (1) It exhibits the acknowledged constitutional Supremacy of the General Convention. (2) It exhibits the *influence* of the Diocesan Conventions on a question of the expediency or inexpediency of any proposed action of the General Convention, of which either House is the independent judge. (3) It gives no color to the hypothesis

SUPREMACY OF THE GENERAL CONVENTION. 77

of the "independency of Dioceses," while it evinces their equality one with another, through votes by Dioceses and Orders.

Q. Will you again quote Bishop White on the question of the Supreme Authority of the General Convention under the Constitution of the Church ? <small>Confirmatory Argument.</small>

A. Bishop White, speaking of the effects of the provision of the General Constitution of A. D. 1785, *referring it to the several State Conventions for ratification* (see Art. XI. Cons. A. D. 1785, and Journal, p. 23), says as follows : —

"The mode in which the proposed Constitution should be ratified was subsequently changed in the General Convention assembled in June, A. D. 1786. The interfering instructions given by the State Conventions to their Deputies in the General Convention, relative to some of the proceedings of the last Convention, and the rejection of the proposed Liturgy in some States, and the use of it in others, manifested the necessity of a well-constituted Legislative Body for the whole Church, and the futility of subjecting their measures to the review and authoritative judgment of the State Conventions by whom the Deputies to it were appointed. And such a system appeared so evidently fruitful of discord and disunion, that *it was abandoned from this time.*"

"The Constitution thus framed in A. D. 1786, was acted under, although not ratified until the Convention of A. D. 1789, at which the Deputies from the several States appeared with sufficient powers for that object, as was recommended by the preceding Convention. And a General Constitution *was then adopted,* and *finally ratified without being submitted to the State Conventions.*" "In order to give stability to it, by preventing hasty changes, it was also provided that the Constitution should be unalterable, unless in General Convention ; and that the alterations should be first proposed in one General Convention, and made known to the several State Conventions, before they should be finally ratified." Mem. of Ch. pp. 123, 124. Wilson's Mem. Bp. White, pp. 134–136.

This testimony of Bishop White admits of but one interpretation, — proving the Supremacy of the General Convention over the Diocesan Conventions, and the reasons of it, as derived from the experience of the evils of coördinate jurisdiction.

It explains that " the presupposed previous action which is 'ratified,' 'finally agreed to,' and 'adopted,' " is the action, *not of Diocesan Conventions, but of the previous General Convention,* and that the place where, and the body by whom amendments are established, is at the next General Convention, by the Church, through Deputies coming fresh from their constituents in the Dioceses, to whom the proposed alterations have been " made known."

Recapitulation. *Q.* Recapitulate the facts which demonstrate the paramount authority of the General Convention.

A. (1) The evils experienced under the Constitution of A. D. 1785 in allowing the State Conventions coördinate jurisdiction and legislative powers.

(2) The Resolution of the General Convention of A. D. 1786, recommended the several State Conventions to " *authorize and empower* delegates," to " *confirm* and *ratify* a General Constitution." Jour. Gen. Conv. A. D. 1786.

(3) Having obtained Bishops in our Church, the Deputies from seven States appeared in General Convention, in A. D. 1789, declaring themselves " authorized by their respective Conventions to ratify a Constitution." Jour. Gen. Conv. A. D. 1789.

(4) The Constitution was accordingly "adopted" without recourse to the Dioceses, yet with the approval or acquiescence of the whole Church practically evinced.

(5) Those States (Dioceses) which had not sent Deputies "authorized and empowered" or none at all, came into union by acceding to the General Constitution as

SUPREMACY OF THE GENERAL CONVENTION. 79

already adopted and amended at the General Convention. Jour. Gen. Conv. A. D. 1789.

(6) The Constitutional provisions for *Amendments* lodge the Supreme and Sole Authority in the General Convention. Articles VIII., IX.

(7) Adverse arguments in favor of "diocesan independency" and of a coördinate authority in the Diocesan Conventions in amending the Constitution, are either groundless or illogical, being contradicted by historical facts, or by sound reasoning.

(8) Contemporary testimony evinces that the Supremacy of the General Convention, under the Constitution, was deliberately established, after an experience of some of the evils of the coördinate authority of the Conventions of Dioceses; and that the whole Church, at the time, and ever since A. D. 1789, have acquiesced in the principle of dutiful subjection to the Supreme Authority of the Constitution and Canons of the General Convention.[1]

Q. What further confirmation of the Supremacy of the General Convention, may you derive from the enactment of Canons by the General Convention of A. D. 1789? Hoff. L. C. pp. 104–106. Argument from the Canons

A. The General Convention of A. D. 1789, on August 7, adopted and ordered to be signed by the President and Secretary ten Canons, entitled, "Canons for the government of the Protestant Episcopal Church in the United States of America, agreed on and ratified in the General Convention of said Church, held in the city of Philadelphia," etc. Hawks & Perry's Jour. Gen. Conv. p. 79.

These Canons were adopted and engrossed, and ordered to be signed, *before the adoption of the Constitution in* A. D. 1789. Articles VIII., IX. of the *Constitution* were "con-

---

[1] The elaborate argument of Judge Hoffman, sustaining the supremacy of the General Convention, may be studied in *Hoffman's Law of the Church*, pp. 172–178. Dr. Hawks, *Contra*, in Hawks' *Cons. & Can.* p. 39–58.

sidered, and amended and agreed to" and ordered to be engrossed subsequently, on the same day, and signed by the Convention on the day following, August 8, A. D. 1789. Ibid. p. 82. These Canons do not, therefore, derive their authority from the Constitution, but from the whole Church assembled in Convention; nor from the Diocesan Conventions, for they were not referred to the Dioceses; nor was any other body called on "to agree to and ratify" them; but they were (as stated in the preamble) "agreed on and ratified in the General Convention of August, A. D. 1789.

Neither did they derive authority from the members of the General Convention, otherwise than from their plenipotentiary and original powers of legislation with which they were invested by the members of the Church. Hence the Church in General Convention evinced its Plenary Powers as acquiesced in ever since.

The conclusion, therefore, is that the General Convention had the Authority in the premises, as being the whole Protestant Episcopal Church in the United States, in Council assembled.

The first of these Canons is this, "In this Church there shall always be three Orders in the Ministry, namely, Bishops, Priests, and Deacons." The others are of cognate importance to the being and well-being of the Church.

The acquiescence of the Church in these Canons demonstrates, that THE GENERAL CONVENTION *possesses the acknowledged power of Supreme Legislation, as a corollary to the Supreme and Sole Authority to make, and to alter the Constitution of the Protestant Episcopal Church in the United States.*

III. THE CONSTITUTION OF THE CHURCH.

ARTICLE 1. "There shall be a General Convention of the Protestant Episcopal Church in the United States of America, on the first Wednesday in October, in every third year, from the year of our Lord one thousand eight hundred and forty-one; and in such place as shall be determined by the Convention; and in case there shall be an epidemic disease, or any other good cause to render it necessary to alter the place fixed on for any such meeting of the Convention, the Presiding Bishop shall have it in his power to appoint another convenient place (as near as may be to the place so fixed on) for the holding of such Convention; and special meetings may be called at other times, in the manner hereafter to be provided for; and this Church, in a majority of the Dioceses which shall have adopted this Constitution, shall be represented, before they shall proceed to business; except that the representation from two Dioceses shall be sufficient to adjourn; and in all business of the Convention freedom of debate shall be allowed." _{General Convention. Change of Place. Special Meetings. Quorum. Freedom of Debate.}

Q. State, in brief, the origin of this Article.
A. In the "Fundamental Articles" proposed _{Origin.} as the basis of Union of the Church, by a voluntary Convention in New York, October, A. D. 1784, the first was this, namely: "There shall be a General Convention of the Episcopal Church in the United States of America." In pursuance of this fundamental article, the Convention

of A. D. 1785 proposed the First Article of the Constitution, substantially, as it now stands.

Q. Who prescribes the place of meeting of the Triennial Conventions?

A. "The Convention," by the concurrent vote of the House of Bishops and the House of Clerical and Lay Deputies.

<small>Change of time and place of meeting.</small> *Q.* Name the amendments in reference to the time and place of meeting of the General Convention.

A. Originally, the time of meeting was the "third Tuesday in June." The Constitution was revised in A. D. 1786, when the time of meeting of the Convention was changed to "the fourth Tuesday in July." In August, A. D. 1789, the Deputies, being come together "with full powers to adopt a Constitution," substituted "the first Tuesday in August." At an adjourned meeting of the Convention in October, A. D. 1789, the time of meeting was again changed to "the second Tuesday in September;" and again, in A. D. 1804, to the "third Tuesday in May." In A. D. 1823, it was left to each Convention to determine the time and place of the next triennial meeting. The General Convention of A. D. 1841 fixed the time of meeting on "the first Wednesday in October in every third year" thereafter, and put the First Article of the Constitution into its present form.

Practical experience has confirmed the expediency of the present arrangement, as it respects both the convenience and the health of the Deputies. In September, A. D. 1798, the Convention could not meet in Philadelphia, owing to the prevalence of yellow fever. At that period the Bishops had authority, only when requested by "a Standing Committee of the General Convention," to summon the Convention to meet at another time; who, accordingly, called it together in June, A. D. 1799.

Q. By whom may the place of meeting of the General

Convention be changed, when good cause renders it necessary?

A. The Presiding Bishop is empowered, by the First Article of the Constitution, "to appoint another convenient place, as near as may be to the place fixed on by the Convention."

Q. How are Special Meetings of the General Convention regulated? *Special Conventions.*

A. The First Article of the Constitution provides for Special Meetings of the Convention, yet remits the manner of calling them to a future provision. By a *Resolution* of the General Convention, the power was confided to the Presiding Bishop, and was once exercised by him. Hawks' Cons. & Can. p. 391. It was ten years after the adoption of the Constitution, before the power of calling Special Conventions was regulated by Canon Law. Canon 1, A. D. 1799.

Q. Recite the terms of the Canon which regulates the right of calling "*Special* General Conventions."

A. "The right of calling Special Meetings of the General Convention shall be in the Bishops. This right shall be exercised by the Presiding Bishop, or, in case of his death, by the Bishop who, according to the rules of the House of Bishops, is to preside at the next General Convention: *Provided,* that the summons shall be with the consent, or, on the requisition, of a majority of the Bishops, expressed to him in writing." [1] § I. Canon 1, Title III. Dig.

Q. Where shall Special Conventions be held?

A. In the place fixed on by the preceding General Convention for the meeting of the next General Convention, unless changed, for good cause, by the Presiding Bishop. [2] § I. Canon 1, Title III. Dig.

Q. What Deputies shall compose a Special General Convention?

A. The Deputies elected to the preceding General Convention, unless other Deputies be chosen, in the mean time, by any of the Diocesan Conventions; in which cases such other Deputies shall represent, in the Special Convention, the Church of the Diocese in which they were chosen. Hoff. L. C. p. 139.

Presiding Bishop.   *Q.* Who is "the Presiding Bishop" mentioned in this Article I. of the Constitution?

A. He who, according to the rules of the House of Bishops, presided over the House of Bishops at the last General Convention; or, in case of his death, he who, by the same rules, is to preside at the next General Convention. [1] § I. Canon 1, Title III. Dig.

Q. State what the Rules of the House of Bishops have been, in reference to the Presiding Bishop.

A. At the first meeting of the Bishops in a separate House, Monday, October 5, A. D. 1789, in Philadelphia; present, the Rt. Rev. Samuel Seabury, D. D., and the Rt. Rev. William White, D. D., among the rules "agreed on and established for the government of this House" was this, namely: (1st) "The Senior Bishop present shall be the President; seniority to be reckoned from the dates of the Letters of Consecration." Bishop Seabury, consequently, took the chair, and presided until the adjournment on the 16th October. Both Bishops authenticated the acts of the House: "Samuel Seabury, Bishop of Connecticut, President;" "William White, D. D., Pennsylvania;" agreeably to the 2d Rule adopted, namely: "This House will authenticate its acts by the signing of, at least, the majority of its members." Journal House of Bishops, A. D. 1789, p. 123.

The next General Convention met in Trinity Church, New York, September 11, A. D. 1792, and after prayers, Bishop Seabury, the only Bishop present, adjourned the House "till 10 o'clock to-morrow morning."

On Wednesday, September 12th, the members met; Bishop Seabury (presiding); Bishop Provoost, of New

York, Bishop White, of Pennsylvania, Bishop Madison, of Virginia, present. The House attended Divine Service, and afterwards proceeded to business. On the next day, Thursday, September 13th, " The Bishops met, and attended prayers in the House of Clerical and Lay Deputies. The first rule for the government of the House of Bishops, as agreed on at the last Convention, was reconsidered, and it was *Resolved*, " That the said Rule be rescinded, — that the following be adopted instead thereof, namely : The Office of President of this House shall be held in *rotation*, beginning from the North ; reference being had to the Presidency of this House in the last Convention. In consequence of the above Rule, the Rt. Rev. Dr. Provoost took the chair. Adjourned." Ibid. A. D. 1792.

On the last day of this Session, the House of Bishops received a Message from the House of Clerical and Lay Deputies, " as to the mode of authenticating the Acts of the Convention ; " whereupon, the Bishops proposed that " the acts be authenticated by the signatures of the Presidents of the respective houses." The acts of the House of Bishops were accordingly signed, " Samuel Provoost, *President*." Ibid. p. 168.

The first example of the Title of *Presiding Bishop* is found in the Journal of the House of Clerical and Lay Deputies, in A. D. 1792, where it was " Ordered, that the Presiding Bishop be requested to forward to his Grace the Archbishop of Canterbury, thirty copies of the Journal," etc. Ibid. p. 158.

The General Convention of A. D. 1795 met in Philadelphia, September 8th, Bishop White alone present, of the Bishops. On the day following, September 9th, the record says, " The House met. Present: The Right Rev. Bishop White, of the State of Pennsylvania, *who, by the rules of the House, made at the last meeting, presided* : the Right Rev. Bishop Provoost, of the State of New York ; the Right Rev. Bishop Madison, of the State of Virginia." Bishop

White authenticated the Acts of the House, signing, " William White, *Presiding Bishop.*" Jour. Gen. Conv. A. D. 1795.

The next General Convention, June 11th, A. D. 1799, was a Special Convention; Present: Bishop White, Bishop Provoost, and Bishop Bass, of Massachusetts, of the House of Bishops. The Record of the Meeting of June 12th is as follows: " This being a Special Meeting, and the Bishop whose turn it would have been to preside, agreeably to the rules of this House, not attending, Bishop White, the President of the last Convention, was requested to preside." Jour. H. of Bishops, A. D. 1799. Canon 1 of A. D. 1799, authenticated the Title of " Presiding Bishop."

The General Convention of A. D. 1801 met in Trenton, New Jersey. The House of Bishops assembled on September 9th. Present: Bishop White, Bishop Claggett, of Maryland, and Bishop Jarvis, of Connecticut. The Journal recites that " Some doubt arising in regard to the meaning of the Rule of this House, in the year A. D. 1792, — substituted in the place of the 1st Rule of this House in A. D. 1789, — *Resolved*, That until the same shall be considered and explained by this House, the Right Rev. Bishop White be requested to preside at the present session." Ibid. A. D. 1801.

The General Convention met in A. D. 1804 in New York. The Journal of the House of Bishops, September 12th, records that " The House met. Present: The Right Rev. Bishop White, of Pennsylvania, the Right Rev. Bishop Claggett, of Maryland, and the Right Rev. Bishop Moore, of New York. *Resolved,* — That it be a standing Rule of this House, that the Senior Bishop *present at the opening of any Convention* shall preside. The Right Rev. Bishop White, in consequence, took his seat *as Presiding Bishop.*" Ibid. A. D. 1804.

The next General Convention, May 17th, A. D. 1808, met in Baltimore. Present, in the House of Bishops, " the

Right Rev. Bishop White, and the Right Rev. Bishop Claggett, of Maryland." Bishop White took his seat as "Presiding Bishop," by virtue of the Resolution of A. D. 1804, as "Senior Bishop *present at the opening of the Convention.*" The Resolution of the House of Clerical and Lay Deputies in A. D. 1792, and the Canon 1 of A. D. 1799, together with the Resolution of the House of Bishops in A. D. 1804, recognizing the title of "Presiding Bishop;" and the invariable habit of Bishop White in signing himself as "Presiding Bishop" (which office he held continuously until his death, July 17th, A. D. 1836), has led to the adoption of this title in the Constitution since A. D. 1841.

Q. Has the title of "Presiding Bishop" invested him with *superior rank or authority?*

A. No. It has not invested the Bishop presiding with any superior Episcopal authority, nor any rank above that of his colleagues.

Q. Is there any Rule of the House of Bishops fixing and establishing the priority of right to preside?

A. No. The House of Bishops may make any rule which they deem expedient, and may alter it at pleasure, in accordance with the examples adduced.

Q. What is the Law of the Church in England in respect of dignity and rank?

A. The Archbishop of Canterbury enjoys the first rank, next to the throne, and has the Title of "Primate of all England." The Archbishop of York is next in rank in the Church, with the Title of "Primate of England." They preside in their respective "Convocations" of the Provinces of Canterbury and York, *ex officio*.

Q. What is the Law of the Church in Scotland?

A. "Anciently no Bishop in Scotland had the style of Archbishop, but one of them had a precedency, under the style of *Primus Scotiæ Episcopus*. And after the Revolution of A. D. 1688 (during which many Bishops, both in

England and Scotland, were deprived of their Sees by the Civil power (because they refused to swear allegiance to William the Third), the Scots Bishops returned to their old style which they still retain; one of them being entitled *Primus*, to whom precedency is allowed and deference paid in the Synod of Bishops." See List of Succession of Scots Bishops, attested with the Deed of Consecration of Bishop Seabury. Appendix to Jour. Gen. Conv. A. D. 1789, pp. 140, 141.

Q. What constitutes a Quorum?

Quorum.

A. "A majority of each House shall constitute a Quorum to do business; but a smaller number may adjourn from day to day." This is the universal Rule, unless specially ordained otherwise. Constitution United States, Art. I. sec. 5. Cushing's Rules, p. 18. Jefferson's Manual, p. 26. The requisites of a quorum are made by Canon to conform to this general rule of deliberate bodies. In all cases, "A majority of the members, the whole having been duly cited to meet, shall be a Quorum: and a majority of the Quorum so convened, shall be competent to act, unless the contrary is expressly required by the Canon." Canon 7, Title III. Dig.

Q. What is the language in this Article I. of the Constitution?

A. "This Church, in a majority of the Dioceses which shall have adopted this Constitution, shall be represented, before they shall proceed to business; except that the representation from two Dioceses shall be sufficient to adjourn."

Q. What constitutes a representation of a Diocese in order to proceed to business?

A. "A Diocese shall be considered as duly represented by such Deputy or Deputies, as may attend, *whether Lay or Clerical.*" Art. II. Constitution.

Q. What constitutes a representation of a *Majority* of the Dioceses, in order to proceed to business?

A. A majority of the Dioceses must be represented in order to constitute a quorum; and each Diocese is sufficiently represented *for this purpose,* if one Clerical, or one Lay Deputy be present in Convention.[1]

Q. Is a Diocese duly represented for the purpose of a Quorum, if only the Clerical Deputies are present; or if only the Lay Deputies are present?

A. Yes. There must be either Clerical or Lay Deputies (one or more), to represent the Church in each Diocese for this purpose.

Q. What then is "a majority of the Dioceses" represented, in order to proceed to business?

A. A majority of Clerical Deputies, or a majority of Lay Deputies, representing a majority of the Dioceses, by one or more of either order. These are a Constitutional Quorum: "except that the representation from two Dioceses are sufficient to adjourn."

Q. What is meant by Freedom of Debate?

A. Freedom of Debate is the right of every member of the Convention to utter his thoughts on any question before the House, "in accordance with that order, decency, and regularity, which must be preserved in a dignified public body." 2 Hatsel, Rules of Parliament, p. 149. Jefferson's Manual, p. 14. *(Freedom of Debate.)*

Q. Specify the authoritative restraints of Rules of Order on the Freedom of Debate.

A. "Besides the Code of Rules, which may be specially ordered, no person is to speak impertinently, or beside the question; nor superfluously, nor tediously."

---

[1] This question was referred to the Committee on Canons in the General Convention of A. D. 1844. Journal, p. 105. At the next General Convention the Committee reported "that a majority of the Dioceses must be represented in order to constitute a quorum, and that each Diocese should be sufficiently represented for that purpose, if One Clerical *and* One Lay Deputy be present in Convention. Journal, A. D. 1847, p. 107.

In the MSS. Report of the Committee, the phrase is "*or* one Lay Deputy," and, likewise, in the printed Report. The conjunctive form "*and* one Lay Deputy" is no doubt a clerical error, and in a note of the Chairman of the Joint Committee, Bishop Hopkins, of Vermont, he so treats it. See Hoff. L. C. p. 140.

"No person is to use indecent language against the proceedings of the House, unless he means to conclude with a motion to rescind a prior determination."

"No person, in speaking, is to mention a Member, then present, by his name, but to describe him by his seat in the House; or as the member who spoke last on the other side of the question, etc.; nor to digress from the matter to fall upon the person; nor by uttering reviling or unmannerly words against a particular member. The consequences of a measure may be reprobated in strong terms; but to arraign the motives of those who propose or advocate it, is a personality, and against order."

"It is a breach of order in debate, to notice what has been said on the same subject in the other House, or the particular votes or majorities on it there; because the opinion of each House should be left to its own independency, not to be influenced by the proceedings of the other; and the quoting them might beget misunderstanding between the two Houses." See Jefferson's Manual, pp. 38-43, where authorities are cited. Cushing's Rules, c. xii.

Q. Does Freedom of Debate include a right to discuss a motion to enter a Protest in the Journal?

A. No. It has been the uniform practice of the Houses of General Convention to deny the right of Protest. Hence, a motion, which it is out of order favorably to entertain, it is out of order to debate. Policy restricts freedom in this respect; for if one person may enter a Protest, or debate the motion, then the whole disaffected minority might do the same; and the debate would be endless, or the Journal burdened with extraneous and inconclusive matter.

Q. How long since has it been a settled Rule to deny a claim to enter a Protest in the Journal?

A. Ever since the General Convention of A. D. 1795, and confirmed in General Conventions of A. D. 1862 and A. D. 1865. (See Appendix to Journal.) In A. D. 1865, a motion to enter a Protest by the present writer, was not received nor entered on the Journal. Bishop White reports that "three very respectable lay gentlemen, who were of a remarkably conciliatory character, pressed for permission to enter their Protest in the Journal of A. D. 1795. It was not granted; and as this has been the only instance, in which the question of a right to protest has undergone discussion, the recording of the denial of the right," he says, "falls in with the design of the present work." Mem. of Ch. p. 222.

ARTICLE 2. "The Church in each Diocese shall be entitled to a representation of both the Clergy and the Laity. Such representation shall consist of not more than four Clergymen, and four Laymen Communicants in this Church, residents in the Diocese, and chosen in the manner prescribed by the Convention thereof; and in all questions when required by the Clerical and[1] Lay representation from any Diocese, each Order shall have one Vote; and the majority of suffrages by Dioceses shall be conclusive in each Order, provided such majority comprehend a majority of the Dioceses represented in that Order. The concurrence of both Orders shall be necessary to constitute a Vote of the Convention. If the Convention of any Diocese should neglect or decline to appoint Clerical Deputies, or if they should neglect or decline to appoint Lay Deputies, or if any of those of either Order appointed should neglect to attend, or be prevented by sickness or

_{House of Clerical and Lay Deputies.}

_{Qualifications of Deputies.}

_{Vote by Dioceses and Orders.}

---

[1] Probable typographical error for "or." See *post*.

any other accident, such Diocese shall nevertheless be considered as duly represented by such Deputy or Deputies as may attend, whether Lay or Clerical. And if, through the neglect of the Convention of any of the Churches which shall have adopted or may hereafter adopt this Constitution, no Deputies, either Lay or Clerical, should attend at any General Convention, the Church in such Diocese shall nevertheless be bound by the acts of such Convention."

<small>What constitutes a Representation of a Diocese.</small>

<small>Dioceses not represented are bound.</small>

HOUSE OF CLERICAL AND LAY DEPUTIES.

Q. How are the Deputies to the General Convention chosen?

A. They are "Chosen in the manner prescribed by the Convention" of the Dioceses which they represent. Cons. Art. II.

Q. May a Diocesan Convention, by Canon or otherwise, delegate the right and power of choosing Deputies *prospectively*, either to the Bishop, or a Committee, or any other person or persons?

A. Decidedly not. "A prospective general transfer of the right to choose representatives is scarcely consistent with the relation the Diocesan Convention is meant to bear to the General Convention, nor with the just construction of the Constitutional provision." Hoff. L. C. p. 144.

Q. What is the just construction of this provision of the Constitution?

A. "The Constitution contemplates an action by the Diocesan Convention, for each General Convention; and that the representation is to be of the *direct* appointment of the Diocesan Convention." Ibid. p. 143.

Q. May a Diocesan Convention delegate to the Bishop, or other person or persons, the power to fill a vacancy?

A. Yes. The General Convention of A. D. 1847, on the report of the Committee on Elections, " *Resolved,* As the sense of this House, that members appointed by authority of the Diocesan Conventions are, according to the practice of the House of Clerical and Lay Deputies, fully entitled to their seats." Jour. Gen. Conv. A. D. 1847, p. 29.

But the cases specified in the report of the Committee were all cases of a vacancy, by death, or resignation, of persons chosen by the Diocesan Convention for that General Convention, and whose places were supplied by the Bishop or others, by a Canon of the Diocese, or by a special resolution of the Diocesan Convention. Hoff. L. C. p. 143.

Q. Would a Canon of a Diocese delegating the power and duty of choice, entirely and prospectively, be valid?

A. No. The delegated power can apply only to a vacancy occurring in the existing deputation. Hoff. L. C. p. 143.

Q. What is a Vacancy?

A. A vacancy implies a vacating; and vacating requires an agent who vacates. The office must, therefore, be first occupied, or intended to be occupied, before a vacancy can occur. An original office, not yet filled, is simply *empty.* " A thing is empty when there is nothing in it: as an empty room, an empty noddle. *Vacant* adds the idea of a thing's having been filled, or intended to be filled and occupied: as a vacant seat at table, or a vacant succession in Law." Bouvier's Law Dictionary. Webster's Dictionary, " Vacant."

Q. Whom does the House of Clerical and Lay Deputies represent?

A. " The Church in each Diocese." Cons. Art. II.

Q. Does it represent the Diocesan Conventions?

A. No. They are themselves only Representatives of the Church in their respective Dioceses.

Q. Who are " the Church in each Diocese "?

A. The Clergy and people, or Congregations, who, by the law, secular and ecclesiastical, are represented in the Diocesan Convention.

Q. What is the relation between the Diocesan Conventions and the General Convention?

A. The Diocesan Conventions are the medium of authority and communication, between the General Convention and "the Church in each Diocese." The Diocesan Conventions simply choose the Deputies to the General Convention; they likewise receive the communications of the General Convention of proposed Alterations of the Constitution, and of the Book of Common Prayer, for the information of "the Church in each Diocese." Arts. VIII. and IX. Cons.

Q. Is the Constituency of the General Convention and the Constituency of the Diocesan Conventions, one and the same?

A. Yes. One and the same, being "the Church in each Diocese."

Q. Who are "the Church in each Diocese," represented in General Convention?

A. The Clergy and Laity, distributed in the Parishes or Congregations of each Diocese; for the whole system of the organization of the Protestant Episcopal Church in the United States is *representative;* except the Bishops, who, by virtue of Consecration (see Office of Consecration of Bishops), are "Bishops in the Church of God," and do not "represent" the Church in their Dioceses, in General Convention, but take their seats in the House of Bishops, *virtute officii.*

The Parish or Congregation, consisting of Minister and people, is the *organic* unit of representation of "the Church in each Diocese."

The members of the Church in the Parish are the Constituency according to Ecclesiastical Law; while the secular statutes include, also, persons in a parish who may be connected with it by secular bonds alone. These persons (as the rule of law may provide the qualifications to vote) elect the Vestries; the Vestries (commonly) elect the Delegates to the Diocesan Conventions, agreeably to the Constitution of the Dioceses respectively, and these Delegates elect the Deputies to the General Convention.

The system, from first to last, is representative of the original constituency, to wit: the Clergy and people of "the Church in each Diocese." Mem. of Ch. p. 73. Hoff. L. C. p. 88. Hawks' Cons. & Can. *contra*, p. 53.

Q. What are the Qualifications of the Deputies to General Convention? *Qualifications of Deputies.*

A. (1) "Not more than four Clergymen and four Laymen. (2) Communicants in this Church. (3) Residents in the Diocese. (4) Chosen in the manner prescribed by the respective Diocesan Conventions."

Q. What is the origin of the admission of Laymen into the Councils of this Church? *Origin of Lay authority in the Church.*

A. The second of the "Fundamental Articles" proposed in A. D. 1784, was in these words, namely: "That the Episcopal Church in each State send deputies to the Convention, consisting of the Clergy and Laity."

Article VI. is in these words, namely: "That the Clergy and Laity assembled in Convention shall deliberate in one body, but shall vote separately; and the concurrence of both shall be necessary to give validity to every measure." These articles are the basis of the Lay representation in the Protestant Episcopal Church in the United States. See *ante*, "Preliminary History."

Q. Is there an earlier origin claimed in this country for the plan of admitting the Laity into the Councils of the Church?

A. Bishop White claims to be the *author* of the plan of admitting the Laity as a coördinate power with the Clergy, in a pamphlet issued by him in A. D. 1782. And he defends the measure on principle, as agreeable to the pattern of the First Council, recorded in the 15th chapter of the Acts of the Apostles, and as conforming to the example of the British Church. Mem. of Ch. pp. 73–81. Wilson's Mem. Bp. White, p. 123.

Q. Does the Coördinate Authority of the Clergy and of the Laity in General Convention confer on each Order the right to join in making laws to regulate the other Order?

A. It does.

Q. Does this provision of Concurrent Majorities of the two Orders confer unusual Ecclesiastical powers on the Laity?

A. It does. The Councils of the Clergy alone have been accustomed to make all the Canons for the government of the Clergy; while, in Great Britain, the laws of the Church that concerned the Laity in spiritual matters, were passed or ratified in the Supreme Legislature — the Witan and the Parliament, — in which a representation of the Laity existed. See *ante*, on the "Common Law of the Church." Hoff. L. C. p. 52.

Q. Is the voice of the Laity, in making Canons for the government of the Clergy, a departure from the primitive Law of the Church?

A. It is.

Q. What was the ancient and invariable rule of the British and Anglican Church, as inherited by the Church of England?

A. Ecclesiastical Laws or Canons could not be established nor changed, except by a National Synod consisting of "Bishops and other learned men of the Clergy." Records are now extant of the existence and organization of the British Church, from the year of our Lord 200; and the Canons under the Saxon Kings, styled "Monumenta Ecclesiastica," are accessible, showing that the same fundamental rule prevailed in the Anglo-Saxon Church and in the British Church. Ecclesiastical Canons affecting the

CONSTITUTION OF THE CHURCH.   97

Laity, during the same periods, were ratified in the Witenagemote by the King, with the advice of his great men. Those controlling the Clergy are called "Institutions;" those which touched the Laity are styled "Laws." From these Laws and Institutions respecting the British and Anglican Church, we learn that "the Councils of the Clergy were sufficient for the government of the Clergy; and that when the Laity were concerned, the Laws of the Church must have been passed or ratified by the Witan, in which a representation of the Laity existed." "The Norman Revolution, A. D. 1066, made no change in this respect." Hoff. L. C. p. 52. At the Reformation, A. D. 1534, the principle was not revoked, though it was impaired in its operation under Henry VIII. by the submission of the Church to the Crown. The Synod of the Bishops and Clergy, in A. D. 1603, made the Canons of the Church of England, which were afterwards confirmed by Royal Authority, and by the Houses of Parliament, wherein the Laity are represented. See *ante* on the "Common Law of the Church."

Q. In this country, where there is no union of Church and State, how are the respective rights of Clergy and Laity protected under the Constitution of the Protestant Episcopal Church? <small>Vote by Dioceses and Orders.</small>

A. (1) By the vote "by Dioceses and Orders in General Convention," when required by the Clerical (*and*)[1] Lay representation from any Diocese, each Order having one vote, and the concurrence of both Orders being conclusive; so that the rights of the Clergy and Laity are, so far forth, under their own protection respectively.

(2) By the qualification that Lay members shall be "Communicants in this Church:" whereby, an added security obtains, that justice and spiritual intelligence will predominate among the Laity in the debates and the Canons of General Convention. But as the Constitution *now*

---

[1] Probably typographical error for "or." See *post*.

stands, if the Clerical or the Lay representation in every Diocese, should decline to unite in the call for a vote by Orders, their ability to protect their several rights is in abeyance.

Q. What error, on this point of a call for a Vote by Dioceses and Orders, has probably crept into the Constitution?

A. Vice-Chancellor Hoffman states that "In the Constitution, as twice published by Bioren in the Journals (pp. 61, 75), the requisition for a Vote by Orders may be made by either the Clerical OR Lay representation of any Diocese." Hoff. L. C. p. 149. Dr. Hawks testifies to the same point in "Church Review," July, A. D. 1859, p. 328. It is not certainly known how the conjunctive word "*and*" is become substituted for the disjunctive word "*or*." Judge Hoffman says that in the other copies of the Constitution which he has examined, the word is "*and*." Additional researches indicate that the error first occurred in the Journal, A. D. 1808. Accordingly, the practice under the Constitution, *as it now reads*, requires an *united* demand " of the Clerical *and* Lay representation of a Diocese " to a call for a vote by Orders.

A typographical error seems clearly to have crept into this important Article of the Constitution in A. D. 1808. The original power, therefore, ought to be restored, whereby either Order, Lay OR Clerical, of a Diocese, may demand a Vote by Orders; then, and not till then, the rights of each Order, being in its own keeping, might be perfectly protected, as *they were intended to be.*

On this point of *intention* we have the positive testimony of Bishop White. Bishop White states that " the Constitution of A. D. 1789 gives the right to a call for a vote by Dioceses and Orders to the Clergy OR Laity representing a State (Diocese) in General Convention." Mem. of Ch. p. 23. He also transcribes the Constitution, in which the clause reads thus: " In all questions, when required by the

Clerical OR Lay representation from any State, each Order shall have one vote." Ibid. p. 418. Dr. Hawks transcribes the Constitution of A. D. 1789 the same as Bishop White; in "Church Review," July, A. D. 1859.

The Constitution prefixed to the Journal of the State Convention of Massachusetts, in A. D. 1800, by the Committee, appointed in A. D. 1799, to obtain and publish a Standard copy of the General Constitution, contains the word "or" in the Second Article. The substitution of "and" for "or" is discovered to have been introduced in the printed Journal, and to be an error of the press, in A. D. 1808, as will appear from the certificate of the examiner, Judge W. H. Bell, of New York:[1]—

52 JOHN STREET, N. Y., *Epiphany week*, 1870.
MY DEAR PROFESSOR:

I have carefully examined the Journals from A. D. 1789 to the Convention of A. D. 1804, and do not find any attempt to alter this word "or" in Article 2 of the Constitution. But in passing through the Journal of A. D. 1801, pp. 265–275, I find this pernicious and mischievous Resolution passed by the two Houses as follows:

"*Resolved*, That it be recommended to the several State Conventions of this Church to cause as great a number as possible of the Constitution and Canons of the Protestant Episcopal Church in the United States, and of the Constitutions and Canons of their respective Churches, to be printed and distributed among their respective congregations."

You perceive here was no responsibility for accuracy reserved, and a general license for the possible propagation of errors.

I have not met with any published under this recommendation and license.

This same Convention, pp. 268–277, also passed a resolution appointing a Joint Committee to revise and publish the Journal, etc., of this Convention. Bishop Moore and Dr. Hobart were on this Committee. It is to be presumed that nothing more was done than to publish the Journal of that year.

The Convention of A. D. 1804, pp. 302–312, passed the following:

"*Resolved*, That the Committee appointed to publish the Journals be authorized to publish the Constitution and all the Canons of the Church in the order of their enaction, making a reference by asterisk at the end of every Canon to a note, pointing out the various other Canons which refer to the subject of that particular Canon."

The Constitution and Canons published by the above Committee, and the office of Induction, are to be considered as AUTHORIZED AND STANDARD COPIES. See Original publication of Journal under the supervision of Bp. Moore and Dr. Hobart, by T. & J. Swords, New York, A. D. 1804, pp. 14–22.

I also have the original publication of the "Constitution, etc., of the Church from A. D. 1789 to A. D. 1804 inclusive. New York: Printed by T. & J. Swords, No. 160 Pearl Street, A. D. 1805,"—

[1] A conclusive certificate from Dr. Perry is given on p. 190.

With the following certificate:

WHEREAS, the General Convention of the Protestant Episcopal Church in the United States, held in the city of New York, in the month of September, A. D. 1804, passed the following resolution, namely:—

"*Resolved*, That the Committee appointed to publish the Journals be authorized to publish the Constitution and Canons of the Church in the order of their enaction, making a reference by asterisk at the end of every Canon to a note pointing out the various other Canons which refer to the subject of that particular Canon."

"We, the undersigned, being the Committee appointed for that purpose, do hereby publish the Constitution and Canons of the Church agreeably to the foregoing resolution, and do certify that this present edition of the said Constitution and Canons is the Standard Copy.

"BENJAMIN MOORE, D. D.,
Bishop of the Prot. Epis. Church in the State of New York.

"ABRAHAM BEACH, D. D.,
An Assistant Minister of Trinity Church, New York.

"WILLIAM HARRIS,
Rector of St. Mark's Church in the Bowery, New York.

"JOHN HENRY HOBART,
An Assistant Minister of Trinity Church, New York."

In this standard copy, Article 2, line 5, are to be found the words, "Clerical *or* Lay representatives," same as in the original, 2d October, A. D. 1789, the same "as copied in the Book of Records, that was read and compared and signed by both Houses of the General Convention, on the 15th October, A. D. 1789," p. 109.

I have carefully looked through the proceedings, or rather Journal, of A. D. 1808, for an authority for changing this "or" into "and," as was done by this same house of T. & J. Swords, in A. D. 1808.

Hawks and Perry include the Journals of A. D. 1804 and A. D. 1808 in their 1st vol., but say nothing in their "historical notes and documents" of this publication in A. D. 1804 — no doubt, for want of space, as these documents go no further down than A. D. 1786.

The next General Convention met in Baltimore, May 17, A. D. 1808.

On the last day of the Convention, May 26, the following Resolution was passed by both Houses, pp. 349-359:—

"*Resolved*, That the Secretary of the House of Clerical and Lay Deputies prepare the Journals and other Acts of this Convention for publication: and that the said Secretary and the President of this House, and the Right Rev. Bishop Moore, be a Committee to publish the same, together with the sermon preached at the opening of this Convention, and the pastoral letter of the House of Bishops, and that the Book of Canons, and the office of Institution, published by said Committee, be authorized as Standard Copies." — pp. 17-26 of original print.

This Journal in my possession has the following imprint: "New York: Printed by T. & J. Swords, No. 160 Pearl Street, A. D. 1808."

Note at the end of the Journal of House of Bishops:

"N. B. — The Canons passed at this Convention are published with the Constitution of this Church in a distinct pamphlet."

The title-page to this "distinct pamphlet," mentioned in the above "N. B.," is as follows:—

"Canons for the Government of the Protestant Episcopal Church, &c., being the substance of various Canons adopted in General Conventions of said Church, held in the Years of our Lord 1789, 1792, 1795, 1799, 1801, 1804, and now set forth with alterations and additions in General Convention, A. D. 1808. To which is annexed the Constitution of the Church, the Prayer to be used at the meetings of Conventions, and the course of Ecclesiastical Studies. New York: Printed by T. & J. Swords, No. 160 Pearl Street, A. D. 1808."

On the back of this title-page is the following:

"We, the undersigned, being a Committee appointed by the General Convention of the Protestant Episcopal Church in the United States, held in Baltimore, in the month of May, A. D. 1808, to publish the Canons of the Church as set forth by said Convention, do hereby publish the same, and do certify that this present edition of the Constitution, Canons, etc., is the Standard Copy.

"BENJAMIN MOORE, D. D.,
Bishop of the Prot. Epis. Church in the State of New York.
" ABRAHAM BEACH, D. D.,
An Assistant Minister of Trinity Church, New York.
" JOHN HENRY HOBART, D. D.,
An Assistant Minister of Trinity Church, New York."

Yet, although published by the same persons who certified to the edition of A. D. 1804 being a "standard copy," with the word "or" in the 2d Article of the Constitution, yet the same "or" in the present "standard copy" is changed into "and." As there is no authority for this change to be found in the proceedings of the Convention of 1808, the change must be attributed to a typographical error, the same as "ye"—Act Apos. Ch. VI. v. 3 — was substituted for "we," may, etc. An error it must be admitted to be, — and the continuance of this error for years, and the Convention having acted under the change, cannot give it the force of law. The utmost that can be claimed for it is, that all acts done in pursuance of the error, without any knowledge to the contrary, must be considered as valid acts. But when the error has been pointed out and it is proved that there is no existing authority for it, all subsequent acts must be considered invalid.

I have not yet examined the proceedings of 1856, when this Article 2 was amended.

Sincerely yours,
WILLIAM H. BELL.

To the REV. PROFESSOR FRANCIS VINTON, D. D., D. C. L., *Trinity Church, N. Y.*

January 14th, 1870.

MY DEAR PROFESSOR: —

I promised you to continue my investigations relative to the altering of "or" into " and," between 'Clerical" and " Lay " on line 7, Article 2, of the Constitution, as published in the Digest of 1869.

In my last I pointed out to you that the word "or" was in the Standard Copy of the Constitution published in A. D. 1804, by order of the General Convention, following the original document, adopted 2d October, A. D. 1789. But that the copy published as a standard by the same authority in A. D. 1808, contained this typographical error of " and " for " or,"—I say typographical error, because I can find no authority for the alteration, and I cannot bring my mind to believe that Bishop Moore, Dr. Beach, and Bishop Hobart, would have countenanced the alteration had they known it, as they were the Committee appointed to superintend its printing.

In the General Convention of A. D. 1850, p. 40, a Resolution was passed, "That the Committee on Canons be instructed to inquire into the expediency of so altering the second article of the Constitution that none but communicants of this Church be elected to serve as Deputies in the General Convention thereof." The Committee on Canons were the Rev. Dr. Jarvis, W. C. Mead, A. H. Vinton, S. Seabury, Ed. Y. Higbee, Messrs. H. D. Evans, E. A. Newton, Judges Chambers and Jones (pp. 41, 66, 88), A. D. 1853, pp. 42, 51, 124, 230. This Committee reported to the Convention the desired alteration, only arranging the verbal construction of the sentence for the purpose of making it read correctly, and it was printed on a fly-leaf before the title-page of the Journal of that year, showing *in italics* the proposed changes, which do not include the word "and" in place of "or" between "Clerical" and "Lay" representation. 1st May, A. D. 1856, Dr. Howe, Secretary of the Convention, gave the Canonical notice to the Diocese of New York. See its Journal A. D. 1856, pp. 33, 34, 47, 48, Sept. 24. And the amended article, with others, was given to a Committee consisting of Rev. Dr. Hawks, Brown, and F. Vinton, Judge Oakley and F. J. Betts, who reported favorably. It was adopted and sent to the General Convention of that same year.

On the 3d day of October, A. D. 1856, (p. 29,) Dr. F. Vinton, of N. Y., called upon the Secretary of the General Convention to know if he had given the Canonical notice of the proposed alterations of the Constitution about to be presented to the Convention for adoption, and he replied in the affirmative. Journal General Convention, A. D. 1856, p. 29; also see N. Y. Journal, A. D. 1857, p. 33.

The amendment to the 2d Article, or rather addition, respecting the qualification of Lay Deputies, was adopted 14th October, A. D. 1856, p. 179. In this alteration or addition, *no allusion was made to the clause in the 2d Article containing the typographical error under consideration.* It is remarkable that in A. D. 1859, when the Digest was prepared, the compilers had not recourse to the Original Standard written document of 2d October, A. D. 1789, where this error would have been discovered.   Very sincerely yours, etc.,

WILLIAM H. BELL.

To the REV. FRANCIS VINTON, D. D., D. C. L., *Professor of Charles and Elizabeth Ludlow Professorship of Ecclesiastical Polity and Law, Gen. Theo. Sem.*

QUALIFICATION OF LAY DEPUTIES.

Lay Communicants in this Church. Q. When was the qualification of being a Lay "Communicant in this Church" introduced into the Constitution of the General Convention?

A. In the Convention of A. D. 1853, and ratified by the Church in the Convention of A. D. 1856. When this qualification became a Fundamental Law, certain Laymen, sitting in General Convention, who were not Communicants (and one who avowed himself to be unbaptized), resigned their office, and retired from the Convention, as being justly disqualified.

Q. What is meant by "Communicants in this Church," as a qualification of Lay Deputies?

A. That he should be a Communicant, under the cure of a Rector or a Minister in this Church, at the time of his election, in good standing, and not under Ecclesiastical censure.

Q. What Ecclesiastical censure would invalidate the qualification of a Layman?

A. That which is sometimes styled the "*lesser Excommunication*," or *Suspension* from the Holy Communion, according to the second Rubric before the Communion Service, and Canon 12, Title II. of the Digest.

Q. If a Layman should incur Ecclesiastical censure during his term of office, would he be qualified to sit as Lay Deputy?

A. No. Suspension from Holy Communion carries with it suspension from the functions and privileges of "a Communicant in this Church."

Q. What is meant by the clause " Residents in the Diocese," as a Qualification of Clerical and Lay Members? <small>Residents in the Diocese.</small>

A. It means "*Canonical Residence*," or Residence in the Diocese, in the Ecclesiastical sense; the Church speaks the Church's language.

Q. What judgment must the Secular Courts give on the question of Residence in a Diocese?

A. The Civil Courts, if called on to decide on the bounds of a Diocese and residence therein or removal therefrom, must refer to Ecclesiastical Law for the definition of the word "Diocese," and consequently for "Residence in the Diocese." In this country, the Legislature does not define Ecclesiastical boundaries, nor Ecclesiastical qualifications, as in England, where Church and State are joined under the Constitution.

Q. What is the Canonical Residence of a *Clergyman*? <small>Clerical Residence.</small>

A. The Residence contemplated by the Canons of General Convention.

Q. State what the Canons on Residence of Clergymen require and enjoin.

A. (1) It is the duty of every Bishop of this Church to reside within his Diocese. § XII. Canon 13, Title I. Digest.

This Canon enjoins a Bishop to have his "See" and his Secular Domicile within the topographical limits of his Diocese.

(2) " Every Minister shall be amenable for offenses committed by him, to the Bishop, and if there be no Bishop, to the Clerical Members of the Standing Committee, of the Diocese in which he is Canonically Resident at the time of the Charge." § I. Canon 1, Title II. Dig.

This Canon of "Amenability" recognizes a Clergyman's residence to be Ecclesiastical Residence, under that Diocesan who has Ecclesiastical Jurisdiction over him, whatever his Domicile or Secular Residence may be.

(3) "It shall be the *duty* of all Ministers .... to obtain and present Letters Dimissory, whenever they remove from one Diocese or Missionary District to any other Diocese or Missionary District, whether Domestic or Foreign, and remain there for the space of six months."

This Canon expresses both the Duty and the Privilege of Clergymen, generally, to obtain and present Letters Dimissory from one Ecclesiastical and Diocesan Jurisdiction to another, and thus to change their Canonical Residence after six months' secular Residence, within the topographical boundaries of the Diocese to which they remove. An exception is made in this Canon in regard to "Professors in the General Theological Seminary, Officers of the Board of Missions, and Chaplains in the Army and Navy." These are Clergymen who are engaged in general Church work, stationary or diffusive. Of such Clergymen, no policy of the Church requires a change of their existing Ecclesiastical amenability or privilege; hence they are regarded, canonically, as continuing under the Jurisdiction of their respective Bishops, and as Members of their respective

Dioceses, wheresoever their secular residence may be. [4] § VII. Canon 12, Title I. Dig.

(4) " No clergyman *having a Parish or Cure in more than one Diocese*, shall have a seat in the Convention of any Diocese other than that in which he resides."

This Canon forbids a twofold Residence, Amenability, and Privilege. It confines the Clergyman to one Episcopal Jurisdiction.

The Ecclesiastical and Canonical Residence of the Clergyman is, by this Canon, furthermore declared to be with that one of the Congregations, in that Diocese, within the topographical "limits of which they dwell, and in which there is seated a church to which they belong."

He is under the exclusive Jurisdiction of *that* Bishop, and is entitled to sit only in *that* Convention, and has all the responsibilities and privileges of *that* Diocese, and not of the other Diocese.

His Canonical Residence, in this special case, is defined to be identical with his Secular domicile ; being that within the limits of which he and his congregation " dwell," and their Church is " seated." § I. Canon 5, Title III. Dig.

Q. What Canonical conditions prescribe the *time* when the privilege of Clerical Residence and Removal takes effect under Letters Dimissory ?

A. The *privilege* of Clerical Residence and Removal is insured to a Clergyman other than a Bishop, by his demanding and receiving Letters Dimissory from the Bishop, or other Ecclesiastical authority, within whose Jurisdiction he canonically resides, to be presented to the Ecclesiastical authority under whose Jurisdiction he removes.

But though a clergyman change his Domicile or Secular Residence, the Canons provide that : " No such Letter shall affect a Minister's Canonical Residence, until after having been presented according to its address, nor until it shall have been accepted, and notification of such acceptance given to the authority whence it proceeded. The *residence of the Minister, so transferred, shall date from the acceptance of his letter of transfer.* If not presented within three months after its date, it *may* be considered as void by the authority whence it proceeded: and *shall* be so considered, unless it be presented within six months. [1] [2] § VII. Canon 12, Title I. Dig.

Q. Is a Clergyman removing beyond the territorial limits of a Diocese into parts where there is no Bishop, required to maintain his Diocesan Residence?

A. Yes. The Canon, "Of a clergyman absenting himself from his Diocese, doubtless refers to a clergyman who removes into foreign parts, where there is no Bishop of this Church." It requires of him to give reasons for his absence, satisfactory to his Bishop, in writing, within a period of *five* years after his departure, on penalty of "suspension from the Ministry," unless he "renew his residence" afresh, after that interval of time. The time of absence, without reasons given or demanded, was extended from *two* to *five* years in A. D. 1862.

During all this time, the Clergyman is considered as "belonging to the Diocese," because in contemplation of Canon Law, he is under the jurisdiction of the Bishop thereof. Canon 7, Title II. Dig.

Q. To whom is a clergyman belonging to one Diocese, and charged with an offense committed in another Diocese, amenable?

A. He is, in the first place, amenable to the Bishop and Canons of that Diocese whence he came; being, in the language of the Canon, "Canonically resident" therein. Due notice is required to be given to the Bishop who has jurisdiction, by the Ecclesiastical Authority of that Diocese wherein the offense is alleged to have been committed. Due notice being given, and not heeded for the space of three months, the accused clergyman is then amenable to the Bishop and Canons of the Diocese in which the alleged offense was charged. § I. Canon 3, Title II. Dig.

Q. May the Ecclesiastical Authority of a Diocese refuse to accept Letters Dimissory presented by a Clergyman in good standing, who is called into the Diocese to take charge of a Parish?

A. No. When a Minister is called by a Vestry, or by other persons having the *quasi* right of Advowson, the Canons provide that: " If a Minister, removing into another Diocese, *who has been called to take charge of a Parish or Congregation, shall present a Letter Dimissory, it shall be the duty of the Ecclesiastical authority of the Diocese to which he has removed to accept it*," unless credible rumors prevail against the character of the Minister concerned, and when the Minister shall be duly exculpated from the said charges. [3] § VII. Canon 12, Title I. Dig.

This Canon defines a Clergyman's Residence to be, where the Parish which he serves is situated.

Q. What further interpretation on Clerical Residence do the Canons furnish?

A. A Clergyman ordained in a Foreign Country, by a Bishop in communion with this Church, may be "received into union with any Diocese," after certain prescribed preliminaries evincing his canonical fitness, according to the provisions of Canon 10. Title I.: but " before he shall be permitted to settle in any Church or Parish, or be received into union with any Diocese of this Church, as a Minister thereof, he shall produce to the Bishop " (or Ecclesiastical authority thereof) a Letter of Dismission, as provided for in Sect. VII. of Canon 12, Title I., which Letter of Dismission " shall be delivered within *six months* from the date thereof; and when such clergyman shall have been duly received, " he shall be considered as having passed entirely from the jurisdiction of the Bishop from whom the Letter of Dismission was brought to the full jurisdiction of the Bishop or Ecclesiastical Authority by whom it shall have been accepted, and become thereby subject to all the Canonical provisions of this Church;" *Provided*, that such

Minister shall not be entitled to settle in any Parish or Church, as canonically in charge of the same, until he shall have resided one year in the United States, subsequent to the acceptance of his Letter of Dismission. Canon 10, Title I. The Proviso of this Canon expressly distinguishes between Domicile or Secular Residence, and Ecclesiastical or Canonical Residence. Canon 10, Title I. Dig.

Q. What conclusion follows as to the meaning of the clause in Art. II. respecting Clerical Deputies, "Residents in the Diocese" which they represent?

A. The Church's laws are presumed to speak the Church's language, and when the Constitution and Canons speak of "Residents in the Diocese," they mean Ecclesiastical residence : and when Civil or Secular residence is meant, the context clearly defines it, or it is specially stated as distinct and exceptional, as in Canon 10, Title I. and Canon 5, Title III. Dig.

The Clergyman's residence in a Diocese, under the Constitution, as interpreted by the Canons, admits of no other interpretation than the being under the Episcopal Jurisdiction somewhere, and "subject to all the canonical provisions of this Church." He is amenable to the laws of that Diocese, and entitled to all the immunities and privileges appertaining to members of that Diocese of the Bishop who has jurisdiction over him. In other words: *His Bishop's jurisdiction over him defines the Diocese in which the Clerical Deputy canonically resides.*

By the Canons recited, the Bishop's See or Seat is within topographical limits: his Jurisdiction, however, over the Clergy of his Diocese, extends beyond the topographical and secular boundary of his District : it is a Jurisdiction over persons, — over Souls, — not merely a local Jurisdiction. The Bishop's Diocese, ecclesiastically, is coextensive with his Episcopal Jurisdiction, according to the Canons. His See or Seat is local. Diocesan Residence of a

Clergyman, other than a Bishop, according to the Canons, is dependent on Episcopal Jurisdiction. A Clergyman, removing out of the topographical limits of the Diocese, does not remove from his Bishop's Jurisdiction, and therefore not from the Diocese, until he shall have been received by another Bishop within his Diocese and under his Jurisdiction, by Letters Dimissory. "*And the residence of the Minister, so transferred, shall date from the acceptance of his letter of transfer.*"

But if the Clergyman withholds his Letter Dimissory three months, it is voidable by the authority whence it proceeded; if not presented within six months, it is void by the Canon law: in which cases the Minister is canonically resident in the Diocese *whence he came*, though no longer bodily there within its secular limits. The secular "domicile," beyond the topographical boundary of the Diocese, does not disturb his Diocesan residence under the Constitution and Canons of the Church.

It is, moreover, made the *duty* of every Clergyman removing to another Episcopal Jurisdiction "to obtain and present a Letter Dimissory within *six months*." If, after six months, he resides within the local boundaries of another Diocese, and neither obtains nor presents Letters Dimissory, he lives in defiance of this Canon Law; and, therefore, he may not enjoy the privileges of Members of the Diocese to which he has removed, nor of the Diocese whence he came, on the legal axiom that "no man may gain advantage from his own wrong." He is, accordingly, disqualified and ineligible as a Clerical Deputy in either Diocese after six months.

Q. What is the authority of the axiom that no man may take advantage of his own wrong?

A. "*Nullus commodum capere potest de injuria sua propria.*" It is a Maxim in Law. This is a rule of such binding force as to be held obligatory against the wrongdoer even as between himself and one cognizant or even participant of the wrong.

The Court of Errors of New York (4 Hill Rep. p. 457, A. D. 1842) says, "It is perhaps one of the most attractive features of the Law, that there are certain general principles which form prominent land-marks, not only to guide the jurist and lawyer, but which are of such obvious import, and so consonant with correct views of right and wrong, as to be recognized by the community generally as their rules of right action. They even become Maxims in Law; and just so far as we depart from them, so far are we pretty certain to depart from the safe paths of justice. Among them is that which declares that "No one shall be permitted to take advantage of his own wrong."

Q. What policy of the Church dictates the Constitutional and Canonical Residence of a Clergyman, as independent of Secular Residence or "Domicile"?

A. The policy of the Church is, that no Clergyman shall be vagrant; but he must have an *Ecclesiastical Domicile*, where he shall be amenable to the jurisdiction of some Bishop, and to the Canons of some Diocese. Therefore, his Canonical and Constitutional "Residence," or *Ecclesiastical Domicile*, is not affected by his personal removal into any State, District, or Diocese, until he shall have been duly received by the Bishop, or Ecclesiastical Authority, of the Diocese into which he has removed.

Q. Does the removal of a Clergyman into another State or District or Diocese, *ipso facto*, vacate his Ecclesiastical Domicile?

A. No. A personal removal into some other State, District, or Diocese, so far from changing his Ecclesiastical Domicile, *ipso facto*, his "Residence," under the Constitution and Canons of the Church, remains as it was; unless he present his Letters Dimissory within six months of their issue, and he be received by the Ecclesiastical Authority to whom his Letters are addressed, and the Ecclesiastical Authority that issued them shall have been duly notified of their acceptance. In failure of these conditions, a Clergyman continues to be a member of the Diocese whence he intended personally to depart.

Q. How is the principle that a Clergyman's Residence in a Diocese is determined exclusively by the fact of Episcopal Jurisdiction over him, and not by the laws of secular domicile, evinced by Article V. of the Constitution of the Church?'

A. Article V. of the Constitution provides for the Division of a Diocese in a State, into two (or more) Dioceses. Also, the Union of two (or more) Dioceses in contiguous States into one Diocese.

The Civil Courts, if called on to decide on the bounds of a Diocese and residence therein or removal therefrom, must refer to the Ecclesiastical law for the definition of the word "Diocese," and for the defining of its boundaries in any particular case. The Legislature in this country does not take original knowledge of Ecclesiastical boundaries, as in England, where the Church is established by law, and Church and State are joined under one Constitution. Nor does the Secular law recognize the Office of Bishop or Rector, or the establishment of a Diocese or Parish as original civil and secular Institutions.

Ecclesiastical *Corporations* are Civil Corporations established by the State under general laws, or by special Charter, as under the Common Law. But the *Corporators*, or persons who in the aggregate compose the Corporation, are simply Ecclesiastical persons appointed by Ecclesiastical rules, and holding office solely under Ecclesiastical tenure.

Suppose a State to be divided into five Dioceses (as in New York) by the exclusive legislation of the Church. The Judges of the Courts of the State must look to the Ecclesiastical laws for the bounds and limits of those Dioceses, and to find out what constitutes removal from one such Diocese to another, in that State. It is the same with regard to Parishes. The Secular Judges must resort to the Constitution and Canons of the Protestant Episcopal

Church, and not to secular Statutes, to discover what bounds and limits and definitions the Church has prescribed for Diocesan or Parochial Districts, Jurisdiction, Residence, or Removal.

Or again: A Diocese, by Article V. of the Constitution, may include two (or more) States, or parts of States. The Courts of Law, in either State, must look into the Ecclesiastical Constitution and Canons to judge of the rights and duties, the privileges and the amenability, of persons in that Diocese. For example, if Pennsylvania and Delaware were erected into one Diocese, the Courts of Pennsylvania could not decide that a person, changing his secular Domicile from Pennsylvania to Delaware, thereby changes his Diocesan Residence, or "Residence in his Diocese." The Constitution and Canons of the Church must govern the case at the civil tribunal of the secular Courts. See chapter xxiii. on "the Interposition of Civil Tribunals." Hoff. Ec. L. of N. Y. pp. 275–293. Hoff. L. C. pp. 467–479. Buck's Massachusetts Ec. L. pp. 213, *et seq*. "Ministers, Elders, and Deacons of the Ref. Prot. Dutch Ch. in the City of Albany *v.* Bradford, 8 Cowen, 457, A. D. 1826." Harmon *v.* Desher, Court of Appeals S. Carolina, 1 Spear's Equity Rep. p. 90 (A. D. 1843).

Q. What is the doctrine of the Canon of "Episcopal Residence?"

A. The Canon on the Residence of a Bishop defines Residence in analogy with secular definitions of "Domicile." It means that he shall reside in his See or Seat, which is a local habitation defined by topographical bounds. Under the law of the *State*, a citizen's Domicile is where he lives and sleeps in the State for a prescribed time. In New York, for example, a citizen's *civil* residence may be *anywhere* in the *State* of New York. But his Domicile or *political* residence is confined to some County, or other subdivision of the State, where he may vote. The State of New York is divided into *five* Ecclesiastical Districts or "*Dioceses.*" The Canon requires a Bishop to "reside within his Diocese;" that is, in that part of the State of New York defined by the local district and territorial boundaries of his Diocese, or where his See is.

This Canon evidently contemplates *Episcopal* Ecclesiastical Residence as not distinct from secular Residence, nor independent of it; but it is coincident with his political Residence or Domicile.

A Bishop of any one of the Dioceses in the limits of the State of New York must have his Ecclesiastical Residence in that part of the State where his Diocese is topographically defined; and he must, therefore, conform his Secular Domicile to his Ecclesiastical.

Q. Repeat what special immunity is accorded by Canon (in view of the rights of the Clergy and the *Laity*) to a Clergyman called to take charge of a Parish or Congregation?

A. It enjoins the Bishop to accept Letters Dimissory of a Minister *called to a Church* or *Congregation*, and to receive him into his Diocese, unless his character be credibly impugned, and on no other condition. In this case, the Minister's Ecclesiastical and Diocesan Residence is in the same Diocese as his Cure of Souls, and is determined by the location of the Church in which he ministers.

If, for example, a Clergyman has his civil and political Residence in Brooklyn, while his Cure is in the City of New York, his Canonical and Ecclesiastical Residence is not in the Diocese of Long Island, but in the Diocese of New York, and he sits in that Diocesan Convention, and he is eligible to represent the Diocese of New York (and no other Diocese) in General Convention, or elsewhere: while, if he had two Cures, one in New York and one in Brooklyn, his Ecclesiastical Residence is by Canon *specially limited* to that civil and political residence which coincides with that of the Congregation with whom he "dwells," and where the Church to which they belong is "seated." Canon 5, Title III. Dig.

Q. What is the conclusion of the question as to the meaning of the phrase "Residents in the Diocese," in respect of Clerical Deputies to the General Convention?

A. The conclusion is that, 1st, A Clergyman is "Resident in the Diocese" of that Bishop or Ecclesiastical Authority to whom he is amenable, independently of his civil or his political residence; and, on the principle that *amenability and privilege are correlative*, he is entitled to all the privileges to which any members of the Diocese, under the same Episcopal Jurisdiction, are qualified; unless there be special exceptions, applicable to particular cases, in the Canons of the Diocese, or of the General Convention.

2d. That such an exception prevails over such Clergymen as do not fulfill "the duty of all Ministers to obtain and present Letters Dimissory, whenever they remove from one Diocese to another Diocese, and remain there six months." They are ineligible, from their own fault, to represent either Diocese, after the six months' grace shall have expired. They may not represent the one Diocese, because the Law requires them to take measures to remove their residence from it; they may not represent the other Diocese, because they have not duly presented their Letters, and been duly received as resident therein. Yet if the one Bishop declines to give Letters Dimissory to a Clergyman removed from the local limits of his Diocese, or the other Bishop, within whose local Diocesan limits the Clergyman is come, declines to receive them, the Clergyman, from no fault of his, remains under the jurisdiction of the former Bishop, and is eligible, by that Diocese, as a Resident thereof, to its offices and its honors.

3d. That a Clergyman's secular or civil Residence is not, in any wise, contemplated in the phrase of the Constitution, "Residents of the Diocese:" because, the Canons specially distinguish civil Residence whenever it is meant.

If civil Residence were meant in this clause of the Constitution, — " Residents of the Diocese," — it would nullify the Canons, and destroy a Clergyman's Ecclesiastical amenability and privileges. For, until the Bishop had duly received him he would not be *amenable* to the Ecclesiastical authorities of the Diocese in which he had his secular "domicile," inasmuch as, by the Canons, he belonged to another Diocese by virtue of his *Canonical* obedience. Nor could he be eligible to any Ecclesiastical *office* in that Diocese where he dwells, because he belonged ecclesiastically to that other; so that if the phrase " Residents in the Diocese " does not signify, solely and exclusively, Canonical and Ecclesiastical Residence, determined by the Episcopal *Jurisdiction* over a Clergyman, he would be *ineligible* to any office in the Church; moreover, he would be even *disfranchised*. He would, canonically, be disfranchised for *non-residence* in any Diocese. But non-residence, by Canon, is impossible to Clergymen. The Canons of the Church require that her Clergy shall be resident *somewhere*, and not be vagrant — in some *Diocese*, and not *at large*. By Canon, the Episcopal Diocesan Jurisdiction follows him, and his Diocesan rights attend him, wherever he abides or travels. The Canons do not disfranchise, nor make ineligible any Clergyman on the score of non-residence, because non-residence is impossible under the Canons.

Hence the supposition in question — that the clause in this Article of the Constitution on *Clerical Residence*, means Civil Domicile only, and a removal from the local limits of a Diocese is deemed to disqualify a Clergyman belonging to a Diocesan Episcopal Jurisdiction from representing that Diocese in General Convention — would nullify and make void the Canons. Therefore, the clause " Residents in the Diocese " signifies, not secular but Ecclesiastical Residence.

4th. If Diocesan Residence be not independent of, and

distinct from, civil Residence or secular "Domicile," a Clergyman might have an Ecclesiastical Residence *nowhere*. For the argument for civil Residence, as the proper interpretation of this clause of the Constitution, presumes that when he removes from the local limits of the Diocese, he vacates his canonical Residence in that Diocese *ipso facto;* while his *Domicile*, beyond the local limits of the Diocese, does not by his removal confer canonical Ecclesiastical Residence. He is consequently deprived of Residence in a Diocese altogether; and being deprived of Diocesan Residence, he becomes discharged from Episcopal Jurisdiction, as well as from amenability and privilege; which, as before said, is contrary to the policy of the Church, and to good order, and to Canon Law.

Therefore, Diocesan Residence is distinct from, and independent of Secular Residence.

5th. That a Clergyman in good standing, having received and accepted a call to a Parish or Congregation in another Diocese, is entitled by the Canon to be received therein by the Ecclesiastical Authority thereof; and, therefore, no failure of the Ecclesiastical Authority to receive his Letters Dimissory shall deprive him of Residence in that Diocese into which he is called to serve a Parish; albeit his secular Domicile, in the neighborhood of his Parish, shall be beyond the local boundaries of the Diocese in which his Parish is situated. The fault and disobedience of the Ecclesiastical Authority, in not receiving the Clergyman in good standing and called to a Parish, shall not invalidate the right of the Congregations to call, nor the right of the Clergyman to accept the call, and to change his ecclesiastical Residence from the one Diocese into the other. In which case, his Residence, under the Canons, is in his Cure or Parish; and therefore, he is eligible to represent the Diocese *in which his Cure or Parish is.* The Bishop, or Ecclesiastical Authority, *must* receive him, because the Church has ruled, and equity demands, that her laws shall be obeyed. Neither tyranny, nor caprice, nor negligence of the Ecclesiastical Authority, may impair the canonical Rights either of the Laity or of the Clergy. The Ecclesiastical Authority is established to enforce the Canons, and not to break them. Hence, "Residents in the Diocese," means Canonical Residence, or Residence in the Ecclesiastical sense.

Q. When are Laymen "Resident in the Diocese" and qualified to represent it in the General Convention ? <small>Residence of Laymen.</small>

A. Lay representatives, by the Constitution, must be "Communicants in the Church." The Canon requires that "a Communicant removing from one parish to another *shall procure from the Rector* .... a certificate stating that he is a Communicant in good standing; and the Rector of the Parish or Congregation to which he shall remove, shall not be required to receive him as a Communicant, until such letter shall be produced. § I. Canon 12, Title II. Dig.

A layman, therefore, ceases to be a Resident in the Diocese, when he shall have removed into a Congregation under the Episcopal Jurisdiction of another Bishop, and shall have procured a certificate of good standing as a Communicant in this Church, and shall have presented it to the Rector of the parish into which he has removed.

Q. Suppose he fails to comply with the Canon ?

A. His failure to comply destroys his claim to eligibility to the General Convention from the Diocese into which he has removed; because he is not Canonically transferred to that Diocese, and, therefore, is not Canonically Resident in that Diocese. He is equally ineligible from the Diocese whence he came; because he has not complied with the Canon in that case provided. He has disqualified himself from election in either Diocese; because "no man may derive privilege or advantage from his own fault."

Q. Does the Canon contemplate a *dispensation* from the consequences of the Lay Communicant's negligence and fault in not procuring a Letter Dimissory ?

A. It does. The Canon says, the Clergyman " shall not be required to receive him as a Communicant, until such letter shall be produced."

If the Rector of the Parish, in the exercise of his Canonical discretion, receives the Lay Communicant from another Parish without a Letter Dimissory, such action of the Rector may be deemed a *dispensation;* and his receiving of the layman as a Communicant establishes his status as a Communicant in that Parish, in that Diocese.

<small>Manner of choosing Deputies.</small> *Q.* Repeat the provision in the Constitution for choosing Deputies.

A. In "the manner prescribed by the Convention of each Diocese." Art. II. Cons.

Q. Does this provision give color to the idea that the Deputies chosen by the Convention, represent the *Convention?*

A. No. It discountenances the idea, by specifying and limiting the power of the Diocesan Conventions, simply to the "manner" of election. The Deputies chosen "in the manner prescribed by the Convention," are, in the language of the Constitution, a "representation of the *Church* in each Diocese," not of the Convention. The *Congregation* is the corporate Unit of the Constituency, both of the Diocesan and of the General Convention. "The Church" represented, is the aggregate of the Congregations, wherein the primary elections are held; as for the Vestry, so also for the Delegates to the Convention of the Diocese. *Ante,* " Preliminary History."

<small>Vote by Dioceses and Orders, for a majority.</small> *Q.* What is a Vote by Dioceses and Orders?

A. Each Order in the Representation of a Diocese, has one vote, — that is, the Clerical Deputies of a Diocese who are present in Convention count one vote; and the Lay Deputies of a Diocese, present in Convention, count one vote, for that Diocese, in either Order. "And the concurrence of both Orders shall be necessary to constitute a vote of the Convention." Art. II. Cons.

Q. What number of votes in either order, is a Vote of that order?

A. " A majority of suffrages by Dioceses shall be conclusive in each Order, provided such majority comprehend a majority of the Dioceses represented in that Order." Art. II.

Q. Suppose the vote of either Order be divided, as two against two?

A. It is equivalent to a Blank Vote.

Q. What is the specific usage of the General Convention in regard to divided Votes?

A. The first record on the Journals of General Convention appears in the Journal of A. D. 1786, when the General Convention consisted of only one House. The question was, " Whether the words ' He descended into Hell,' should be restored in the Apostles' Creed." The English Bishops had demanded this restoration, as a condition precedent to the consecration of Bishops in this Church; and the Committee had reported that these words " shall be and continue a part of that Creed commonly called the Apostles' Creed."

The Ayes and Noes being called for, the votes were as follows: " New York (Clergy *Aye*, Laity *No*), *divided;* New Jersey, *Aye;* Pennsylvania (Clergy *Aye*, Laity *No*), *divided;* Delaware (Clergy *divided*, Laity *divided*), *divided;* South Carolina, *Aye.* And so the words are to be restored, there being two Ayes and no negative." Jour. Gen. Conv. A. D. 1786, pp. 59, 60.

Q. Were divided votes counted?

A. No. In this first instance of a recorded vote by Dioceses and Orders, on a question of paramount importance, the Divided Dioceses were not counted as Votes, leaving the decision to an apparent minority of the Convention; and because there was " no negative," the affirmative votes, though less than a majority of the Dioceses present, determined the matter before the House in the affirmative.

Q. State what Bishop White says on this Vote in A. D. 1786.

A. Bishop White says, " Whoever looks into the Journal will see that the result was not owing to the having of a majority of the Votes, but to the NULLITY of the Votes of those Churches in which the Clergy and Laity were divided." Mem. of Ch. p. 133. Comments of English Bishops, pp. 147, 148.[1]

Q. What was the Article of the Constitution under which the vote by Orders in A. D. 1786 was taken?

A. " There shall be a representation of both Clergy and Laity of the Church in each State, which shall consist of one or more Deputies, not exceeding four of each Order; and in all questions the said Church in each State shall have one Vote : and the majority of Suffrages shall be conclusive." Art. II. Cons. of A. D. 1785.

Q. How is this seeming *Plurality* Vote to be construed as that of the majority of Suffrages of the Church in each State represented?

A. On the rule that a " Divided Vote " is no " Suffrage," but is a *blank vote*, and does not count; and that the majority of *recognized votes* were for the measure. The *Call* of the House showed that five Dioceses were represented. Three were a Quorum ; the Two were a majority of a Quorum. This Quorum, however, was not manifest in the *Vote*. Yet Dioceses may be called and decline to vote. On this principle the " Divided Votes,"

---

[1] Bishop White reports the remarks of the English Bishops, seemingly touched with the spice of sarcasm, respecting the manner in which the Votes, touching the Creeds, appear in the Minutes: " His Grace, the Archbishop of Canterbury, said he did not like the manner in which the Votes of the Convention of A. D. 1786, touching the question of the Creeds, appeared on the Minutes; preferring the mode of business used in all the bodies with which he was acquainted, among whom it was customary to mention the business brought before them and the results of the debate, without specifying the votes of individual members." See Bishop White's Letter to the Committee of the Prot. Epis. Ch. in Pennsylvania. Mem. of Ch. pp. 147, 148. The English Bishops, however, acquiesced in the result. They made no further question as to the " manner " in which the result was attained.

on call of the House, simply indicated the presence of the Dioceses not voting. The three " Divided " Votes having been ignored, as the " Suffrages " of the Dioceses, only two Dioceses were " present and voting." The Vote was accordingly regarded as unanimous, — " two Ayes and no Negative."

Q. Is this example of the General Convention of A. D. 1786 followed by the Church in subsequent Conventions?

A. No. The Constitution was amended, and now requires that a Vote by Orders shall be conclusive not only by a majority of Suffrages *in each Order*, but, furthermore, that " *such majority shall comprehend a majority of the Dioceses represented in that Order.*"

Q. What is the Parliamentary Rule respecting Blank Votes in a balloting?

A. " In all ballotings Blanks shall be *rejected*, and not taken into the count in the enumeration of votes, nor reported by the tellers." Standing Rules of House of Rep. U. S. Rule 8. Jefferson's Manual, p. 136.

Q. Is a Divided Vote equivalent to a Blank Vote?

A. Yes; because neither of them is a " Suffrage."

Q. Is this Parliamentary Rule applicable to *Divided* votes under the Constitution of the General Convention?

A. It is; so long as no Canon exists which supersedes the Common Law of Deliberate Bodies.

Q. What is the proper mode of Counting a vote by Dioceses and Orders, under Article II. of the Constitution of the General Convention?

A. (1) " There must be a majority of Suffrages in each Order." If the vote of the four Clerical, or of the four Lay Deputies, be divided, — two Ayes and two Nays, — there is no *Suffrage* of that Diocese in that Order. It is equivalent to a *Blank Vote*, and is not to be counted nor reported.

(2) " The majority of Suffrages in each Order " must be " a majority of the Suffrages of all the Dioceses repre-

sented in that Order;" their presence being proved by the *Call* of the Dioceses and the answer of their Representatives. Hoff. L. C. pp. 149, 150.

Q. What principle in respect to the rank of Dioceses, and the Coördinate rights of Clergy and Laity, does the Vote by Dioceses and Orders establish?

A. It establishes Diocesan *equality*, and the right of the Laity to be considered an " Order in legislation." Bishop White has been heard by Dr. Hawks to say, that "on no other ground would the Dioceses ever have come into union." Notes to Historical Notes and Comments to Jour. Gen. Conv. p. 430. Hawks' Cons. & Can. p. 20.

Q. Is it true that " diocesan *independency*, in all matters not surrendered for the great end of union, is asserted" by the fact that "any Diocese may demand a vote by Dioceses?" Hawks' Cons. & Can. p. 20.

A. The argument is not obvious. "Parity of rank in our Dioceses," be they great or small, is quite distinct from the "independency of Dioceses." The demand of " *any Diocese* " for a vote by Dioceses proves *equality* among themselves, as represented in General Convention ; but it is no assertion of any independency of General Convention, and has no apparent relation to this idea. The hypothesis of diocesan "independence" is, moreover, contradicted by the subsequent provision of Article II. of the Constitution. See *post*.

Q. If the Convention of any Diocese appoint Lay Deputies, or Clerical Deputies, of whom some do not attend, what constitutes a Representation of the Diocese in General Convention, in a vote by Dioceses and Orders?

A. A Diocese is "considered as duly represented by such Deputy or Deputies as may attend, whether Lay or Clerical." Art. II. Cons.

Q. If only a Lay Deputy, or only a Clerical Deputy attend, does he, in a vote by Dioceses and Orders, represent the whole Diocese?

A. No. He represents his Order only of that Diocese. Hoff. L. C. p. 150. Hawks, *contra*, Cons. & Can. p. 21.

Q. If a Diocese " has but a single Deputy of either order, upon a call for a vote by Dioceses and Orders, has that Diocese a voice in that order that may chance to be present, equal to that of the largest Diocese with all its *eight* delegates?" See Hawks' Cons. & Can. p. 21.

A. No. If one Deputy only from a Diocese be present, his vote counts for *his order* in that Diocese, not for the other order; therefore, his one vote equals *four*, not eight votes, of any other Diocese fully represented. Hoff. L. C. p. 150.

Q. What is a Quorum of the House of Clerical and Lay Deputies, for a vote by Dioceses and Orders?

A. A Quorum for a Vote by Dioceses and Orders is, (1) A representation of *each order*. (2) Such a representation as admits of a *majority*. (3) A representation in one of the orders of a *majority of the Dioceses in Union*. Hoff. L. C. p. 151. Hence, a representation in one Order of a majority of the Dioceses; and a representation in the other order of three or more Dioceses, is a Quorum for the voting by Dioceses and Orders, in the House of Clerical and Lay Deputies.

Q. If the Convention of any Diocese should neglect or refuse to appoint Clerical and Lay Deputies; or if Deputies, Clerical or Lay, should not attend at any General Convention, would the Church in that Diocese be discharged from amenability to the Canons of that General Convention? [Dioceses unrepresented.]

A. No. On the contrary, " the Church in such Diocese shall, nevertheless, be bound by the acts of such Convention." Art. II. Cons.

Q. Does this clause of Article II. contradict the hypothesis of " diocesan independency?"

A. Undoubtedly it does, in regard to " any of the Churches which have adopted, or may hereafter adopt this Constitution." Art. II. See *ante*.

Q. What relation does this clause of Article II. establish between the General Convention and the Church in any Diocese?

A. It establishes the Supremacy of the General Convention, and the voluntary and permanent subjection to it of any Diocese which has adopted the Constitution.

ARTICLE 3. "The Bishops of this Church, when _{House of Bishops.} there shall be three or more, shall, whenever General Conventions are held, form a separate House, with a right to originate and propose acts for the concurrence of the House of Deputies composed of Clergy and Laity; and when any proposed act shall have passed the House of Deputies, the same shall be transmitted _{Negative upon the Lower House.} to the House of Bishops, who shall have a negative thereupon; and all Acts of the Convention shall be authenticated by both Houses. And in all cases, the House of Bishops shall signify to the Convention their approbation or disapprobation (the latter with their reasons in writing) within three days after the proposed act shall have been reported to them for concurrence; and in failure thereof, it shall have the operation of a law. But until there shall be three or more Bishops, as aforesaid, any Bishop attending a General Convention shall be a member *ex officio*, and shall vote with the Clerical Deputies of the Diocese to which he belongs; and a Bishop shall then preside."

HOUSE OF BISHOPS.

Q. How many Bishops of this Church form a House of Bishops?

A. Three or more.

Q. What are the powers of the House of Bishops?

A. They have a right to originate and propose Acts for the concurrence of the House of Deputies; they have also a negative on the Acts of the House of Deputies.

Q. Is this negative absolute and unconditional?

A. No. It is conditional: —

(1) The disapprobation of the Bishops must be signified within *three* days after the proposed Act shall have been reported to them for concurrence. (2) They must signify their *reasons* for their veto. (3) They must communicate their reasons in *writing*.

Q. What result follows from the failure of the House of Bishops in complying with these conditions, or either of them?

A. The proposed Act of the House of Deputies "shall have the operation of a law."

Q. Suppose the Act of the House of Deputies be reported to the House of Bishops for their concurrence within three days of the adjournment of the Convention?

A. If the Convention should adjourn within the space of three days, allowed to the Bishops for their consideration, the Act of the House of Deputies would fail (if not concurred in by the House of Bishops), and would *not* "have the operation of a law."

Q. What constitutes a Quorum of the House of Bishops?

A. Two Bishops. Canon 7, Title III. Dig.

Q. How is this manifest? State the History of the organization of the House of Bishops.

A. Originally, the General Convention consisted of only one House, namely, of Clerical and Lay Deputies.

The Constitution of A. D. 1785 admitted a Bishop to be a *member ex officio*, but made no special provision for his vote; that of A. D. 1786 allowed a Bishop to preside.

These Conventions, however, were held before the

Church had received Bishops, and their Presiding Officer was elected by vote of the Deputies. The Convention of July, A. D. 1789, met after the Consecration of William White and Samuel Provoost as Bishops, when "The Right Rev. Dr. White was President, *ex officio.*" Jour. Gen. Conv. A. D. 1789.

The acts of this Convention are authenticated under the Episcopal title prescribed in A. D. 1785 (Journal, p. 25), by "William White, Bishop of the Protestant Episcopal Church in the Commonwealth of Pennsylvania," and "President of the Convention." This Convention adjourned to September 29, A. D. 1789, "in order to meet the Bishop (Seabury) and Clergy of the Church in Connecticut, and the Clergy in the Churches of Massachusetts and New Hampshire, for the purpose of settling Articles of union, discipline, uniformity of worship, and general government among all the Churches in the United States." Preface to Jour. Gen. Conv. A. D. 1789.

Article III. of the Constitution, adopted at the previous session of the Convention (from July 29 to August 8th, A. D. 1789), was as follows: —

ARTICLE 3. The Bishops of this Church, when there shall be three or more, shall, whenever General Conventions are held, form a *House of Revision;* and when any proposed Act shall have passed in the General Convention, the same shall be transmitted to the House of Revision for their concurrence. And if the same shall be sent back to the Convention, with the negative, or non-concurrence of the House of Revision, it shall be again considered in the General Convention ; and if the Convention shall adhere to the said Act by a majority of *three fifths* of their body, it shall become a law to all intents and purposes, notwithstanding the non-concurrence of the House of Revision; and all acts of the Convention shall be authenticated by both Houses. And in all cases, the House of Bishops shall signify to the Convention their approbation or disaprobation, the latter with their reasons in writing, *within two days* after the proposed Act shall have been reported to them for concurrence, and in failure thereof, it shall have the operation of law. But until there shall be three or more Bishops as aforesaid, any Bishop attending a General Convention shall be a member *ex officio*, and shall vote with the Clerical Deputies of the State to which he belongs. And a Bishop shall preside." Jour. Gen. Conv. A. D. 1789.

Bishop Seabury, and the Clergy from the New England States, declined to unite in General Convention, unless "the Third Article of the Constitution be so modified as to declare explicitly the right of Bishops, when sitting in a separate House, to originate and propose Acts for the concurrence of the other House of Convention, and to negative such acts proposed by the other House, as they may disapprove."

The Committee of Conference, on the part of the Convention (Dr. William Smith, Chairman), recommended "a compliance with the wishes of their brethren, and that the Third Article of the Constitution may be altered accordingly." Report of Com. of Conference. Jour. Gen. Conv. A. D. 1789, October 2.

"Upon special motion the above Report was read a second time; whereupon the following resolution was proposed: *Resolved*, That the Convention do adopt that part of the Report of the Committee which proposes to modify the Third Article of the Constitution, so as to declare explicitly the right of the Bishops, when sitting in a separate House, to originate and propose acts for the other House of Convention, and to negative such acts proposed by the other House, as they may disapprove, *provided they are not adhered to by four fifths of the other House.*"

"After some debate, the Resolution *with the proviso annexed* was agreed upon, and the Third Article was accordingly modified." Jour. Gen. Conv. A. D. 1789, October 2.

On the same day, Bishop Seabury, and the Deputies from the Churches in the Eastern States, delivered the following testimony to their assent to the same, namely, "We do hereby agree to the Constitution of the Church as modified this day in Convention."

"After subscribing the above, the Right Rev. Bishop Seabury and the Clerical Deputies aforesaid took their seats as members of the Convention." Jour. Gen. Conv. October 2, A. D. 1789.

Bishop Provoost, of New York, was detained, and was not present in this Convention.

On the following day, October 3, A. D. 1789, it was on motion "RESOLVED, *That agreeably to the Constitution of the Church, as altered and confirmed, there is now in this Convention a separate House of Bishops.*" "The Bishops now withdrawing, the President's chair was declared vacant; whereupon the House of Clerical and Lay Deputies proceeded to the election of a President by ballot." Jour. Gen. Conv. October 3, A. D. 1789, Saturday.

On Monday, the 5th day of October, at the State House, in the City of Philadelphia, in the Committee Room of the Honorable House of Assembly, *the First House of Bishops met.* Present, the Right Rev. Samuel Seabury, D. D., and the Right Rev. William White, D. D.

These two Bishops constituted the House of Bishops, sitting, not as Representatives of their respective Dioceses, but *virtute officii.* Hoff. L. C. pp. 96, 97. Hawks' Cons. & Can. p. 21.

Q. Mention the subjects which engaged this House of Bishops.

A. The momentous subjects of the Faith, Worship, and Discipline of the Church, engaged their deliberations, as *the House of Bishops.*

October 8, A. D. 1789. "This House went into the consideration of the Litany, and of the other parts of the Service connected with Morning and Evening Prayer."

"The House then proceeded to the consideration of the Collects, Epistles, and Gospels, and from them to the Order for the Administration of the Holy Communion."

"October 9, A. D. 1789. The House went into a review of the Service for the Public Baptism of Infants, and prepared proposals on that subject."

"The House then went immediately into the consideration of the Tables of Lessons for Sundays and other Holy-days," laid before them by message from the House of Clerical and Lay Deputies, and "prepared some amendments of the same."

"October 10, A. D. 1789. The House completed the instrument of amendments of the Tables of Lessons, and sent the same by their Secretary to the House of Clerical and Lay Deputies. The House went into further consideration of the proposed form of Morning Prayer."

"October 12, A. D. 1789. Monday. The House prepared alterations of the Form of Solemnization of Matrimony, and of the Order for the Visitation of the Sick."

"October 13, A. D. 1789. The House of Bishops proceeded to prepare the Order how the Psalter is appointed to be read : the Order how the rest of the Holy Scriptures is appointed to be read; and the Order for the Burial of the Dead ; and proceeded to prepare a Commination Service, etc. ; the form and manner of setting forth the Psalms in metre ; tables of Movable and Immovable Feasts ; with tables for finding the Holy-days."

"October 14, A. D. 1789. The House originated Alterations in the Services for Private Baptism, and for the Baptism of Adults; Alterations of the Catechism, of the Order of Confirmation, and a Form of Family Prayer."

"October 15, A. D. 1789. The House of Bishops originated and proposed to the other House alterations of the Title-page; a form of Ratification of the Book of Common Prayer ; a Table of Contents ; a form or manner of printing the former Preface of the Church of England, and those called 'Of the Service of the Church;' and 'Of Ceremonies;' these, with the form of 'Thanksgiving of Women after Childbirth,' before prepared, and the amendments of the 'Occasional Prayers,' were sent to the House of Clerical and Lay Deputies."

"October 16, A. D. 1789. The House of Bishops acceded to *Canons* proposed by the other House, except the amendment of one, which was accordingly withdrawn."

They were engaged also in considering various amendments proposed by the House of Clerical and Lay Deputies. The House originated and proposed to the other House, "A Ratification of the Thirty-nine Articles, except in regard to the Thirty-sixth and Thirty-seventh Articles;" a "Form for the Communion of the Sick;" a "Form for the Visitation of Prisoners;" a "Form of Thanksgiving for the Fruits of the Earth;" and prayers to be inserted in the "Visitation of the Sick."

These proceedings, touching the Faith and Worship of the Church in the United States, after various amendments and conferences, occupied the General Convention of A. D. 1789, and were ratified in Convention by the Church there assembled; the Quorum of the House of Bishops being a majority of the House, — three Bishops constituting the House, and two Bishops being the Quorum. Extracts from Journal of House of Bishops, A. D. 1789.

Q. On what principle did the House of Bishops proceed in revising the Liturgy and Offices?

A. The House of Bishops took the "English Book as the ground of their proceedings," on the principle that the Protestant Episcopal Church possessed that Liturgy as an use and an inheritance. Their revision, therefore, consisted of alterations and amendments of the English Book, with additions such as conformed to the new state of things in this country. Wilson's Mem. Bp. White, p. 140. Mem. of Ch. pp. 175–179.

Q. Did the House of Deputies adopt the same *principle* — the revision of the English Book?

CONSTITUTION OF THE CHURCH. 131

A. No. They "proceeded as if the Church was destitute of any Institutions, until they were provided for by the authority of the Convention, and they appointed Committees to prepare *de novo* the several offices." See *post.* Wilson's Mem. Bp. White, p. 141. Jour. Gen. Conv. A. D. 1789. Mem. of Ch. 175–178.

Q. How does Bishop White account for the celerity in the dispatch of business in the House of Bishops?

A. From the "smallness of the number of Bishops, and a disposition in both of them to accommodate," as well as from their familiarity with the subject. Mem. of Ch. p. 179.

ARTICLE 4. "The Bishop or Bishops in every Diocese shall be chosen agreeably to such rules as shall be fixed by the Convention of that Diocese; and every Bishop of this Church shall confine the exercise of his Episcopal Office to his proper Diocese, unless requested to ordain or confirm, or perform any other act of the Episcopal Office, by any Church destitute of a Bishop." Jurisdiction of Bishops.

DIOCESES.

Q. What is a Diocese?

A. "Diocese signifies the circuit of a Bishop's Jurisdiction." Hoff. L. C. p. 158. Burns' Ec. Law, vol. ii. p. 157. Jurisdiction of Bishops.

Q. What is the derivation of the word Diocese?

A. It is derived from the Greek διοικέω, "to regulate or administer household affairs." Ibid.

Q. What is the historical Origin of Dioceses?

A. "In the first ages of the Church, the Bishops were accustomed to convene their clergy whenever matters of importance occurred for deliberation." Hoff. L. C. p. 130. Chapter of Van Espen (De Synodis Provincialibus) on Diocesan and Episcopal Synods.

"In course of time these Conventions came to be held twice a year." "When Provincial Councils were fixed to be held annually, the Episcopal Synods were annual also." "The See of the Bishop was in a City," and only one Bishop could be in one city. Bingham, Ecc. Antiq. book ii. § 13. 8th Canon Council of Nice.

"Chorepiscopi, or Bishops under the Bishop of the City, exercised special and limited jurisdiction in the rural districts, and were in the Diocese or jurisdiction of the Bishop of the City." Bingham, Ecc. Antiq. book ii. chap. 14.

The Church was thus organized on the basis of Diocesan Episcopacy. Epistles of St. Cyprian, *et al.* Mem. of Ch. p. 97.

The object and advantages of an annual meeting of the Bishop and the Clergy were "to discuss the affairs of the Church, and the welfare of souls." Hoff. L. C. p. 131. Van Espen, Supplement, vol. ii. Title 8, ch. 1.

"Some of the Laity were admitted at the opening of the meetings, but after certain prayers and ceremonies, they were excluded." Hoff. L. C. p. 130, note.

Q. What are the bounds of a Diocese by Canon Law?

A. "The bounds of Dioceses are to be determined by witnesses and records; but *more particularly by the administration of Divine Offices, in case of a dispute.*" Hoff. L. C. p. 158. Burns' Ecc. Law, vol. ii. p. 157. Gibson's Codex I. 133.

Q. How were the bounds of Dioceses determined in this Church?

A. When the Colonies became independent States, the Church in each State became a distinct Church.

The Constitutions of the General Convention of A. D. 1785 and of A. D. 1786 recognized the boundary of Dioceses as coextensive with States, and the Conventions thereof were styled "*State* Conventions."

Article VI. required that every Bishop shall confine the exercise of his Episcopal Office to his proper jurisdiction. Art. VI. Cons. A. D. 1785. Art. VI. Cons. A. D. 1786.

The Convention of A. D. 1789 changed the word "jurisdiction" to "*diocese* or *district.*" Art. IV. Cons. A. D. 1789.

The Convention of A. D. 1838 (after the division of the State of New York into two Dioceses) struck out the words "*or district;*" and for "*State,*" substituted "*Diocese*" wherever it occurred, leaving Article IV. of the Constitution as it now stands.

Q. How are the bounds of Dioceses now fixed?

A. The topographical boundaries are now fixed by the existing facts of "witnesses and records;" but further and more particularly, by "the administration of Divine Offices," according to the accustomed Jurisdiction of the Bishop, agreeably to the Canon Law as before mentioned.

New Dioceses, carved out of existing ones, are made by the concurrent act of the Bishop and Convention of the Diocese to be divided, and of the General Convention, under the provisions of Article V. of the Constitution, and of Canon 6, Title III. of the Digest.

Q. How may new Dioceses be formed in outlying Missionary districts?

A. By the appointment of Missionary Bishops to exercise Episcopal functions in States or Territories not organized into Dioceses within the United States, and in Foreign Countries where there is no Bishop. §§ VII., VIII., Canon 13, Title I. Dig.

Q. By what claim and authority does the Church appoint Domestic Missionary Bishops?

A. Because "the Jurisdiction of this Church extends in right, though not always in form, to all persons belonging to it within the United States." [4] § VII. Canon 13, Title I. Dig.

Q. By what authority does the Church appoint Foreign Missionary Bishops?

A. By the command of the LORD to his Apostles: "Go ye into all the world" .... "Make disciples or Christians of all nations" (marginal reading), "baptizing them in the

NAME of the FATHER, and of the SON, and of the HOLY GHOST; teaching them to observe all things whatsoever I have commanded you: and, lo, I am with you alway, even unto the end of the world. Amen." St. Mark xvi. 15, 16. St. Matt. xxvii. 19, 20.

Q. What is the relation of the Bishops of this Church to the Apostles to whom the Lord gave mission?

A. They are themselves Apostles in their day and generation, to whom the Lord gives the same command and promise as at the first.

Q. What are the bounds and limits of the Jurisdiction of Domestic and Foreign Missionary Bishops?

A. The local boundaries of their Dioceses are prescribed by the General Convention; and their apostolic Jurisdiction is limited to persons who are not within the Episcopal Jurisdiction or Diocese of some other Bishop of the "One, Holy, Catholic, Apostolic Church."

Q. Is it possible that in the same place there can be several different *Churches?*

A. "Unity of communion being the law of God, both in the Universal Church and in all the particular Churches in which it is arranged; *it is impossible that in the same place there can be several different Churches*, authorized by GOD and united to CHRIST." See Palmer on the Church, vol. i. p. 81, *et seq.*

Q. Is it possible that, by the law of God, there may be more than one *Apostle* or *Bishop* in the same place, without disturbing the Unity of Communion in the Church?

A. Yes. St. James, St. Peter, and St. John were Apostles to the Circumcision, while St. Paul and St. Barnabas were Apostles to the Uncircumcision. Gal. ii. 9. Both Apostles, St. Paul and St. Peter, were Bishops in Rome together, and "He that wrought effectually in Peter to the Apostleship of the Jews, the same was mighty in Paul toward the Gentiles." Gal. ii. 8.

"And it came to pass, also, that St. Barnabas and St.

Paul for a whole year assembled themselves at Antioch with the Church, and taught much people. And the disciples were called Christians first in Antioch." See Acts xi. 22–26.

Afterwards, "The HOLY GHOST said, Separate ME Barnabas and Saul, for the work whereunto I have called them." And they went, "being sent forth by the HOLY GHOST" with fasting and prayers and benediction of the Church in Antioch, and departed into Seleucia, and thence to Cyprus, preaching the Word of God in Salamis and Paphos, in the synagogues of the Jews, and to Jewish sorcerers, and to Roman Proconsuls and to other Gentiles. They pursued their mission in Iconium also, and in Lystra, and to Derbe, " ordaining Elders in every Church," and " confirming the souls of the disciples on their return to Antioch : " " where they abode long time with the disciples." See Acts xi.–xv.

Q. What do you gather from these examples of Holy Scripture respecting the original *Norm* or rule of Apostolic or Episcopal jurisdiction?

A. The original, normal jurisdiction of Bishops is over certain persons and classes of people ; who, though being distinctly separate, may yet be residing in the same place. The Jurisdiction or Diocese of different Bishops in communion with each other, and in communion with the One, Catholic, and Apostolic Church, may extend over these classes of people, in the same place, without conflict of jurisdiction.

The bounds of Episcopal Jurisdiction to a local or topographical limit is *not* normal and primitive, but is the canonical arrangement in subsequent, though early, times, for the sake of order and convenience. The true and original idea of Episcopal Jurisdiction is over *persons*, as St. Cyprian testifies, for the practice of his own time, namely: " All Bishops are so united in one body, that though they were many pastors, yet they had but one flock to feed, and *every one* was obliged to take care of *all the sheep of Christ,* which HE has purchased with HIS own Blood and Passion." Cyp. Ep. 68, ad Steph.

Bingham also recites instances during the Arian controversy, of Athanasius, of Eusebius of Samosata, of Epiphanius, ordaining within the *local* limits of various Dioceses of other Bishops; and when some of their adversaries objected that it was done contrary to Canon, Epiphanius vindicated his practice upon the strength of the principle which St. Cyprian maintained: "*Episcopatus unus est, cujus a singulis in solidum pars tenetur,*"—The Episcopate is one, each part of which is held by each one for the whole. Cyp. de Unit. Eccles. vol. i. p. 381; Edinburgh ed. A. D. 1868.

St. Chrysostom says (Hom. 17): "St. Paul had the whole world committed to his care, and every city under the sun;" "he was teacher of the Universe" (Hom. 6), and "presided over all Churches" (Hom. 17); which St. Chrysostom repeats in his usual hyperbole, in many places of his writings. And Bingham subjoins: "Nor was this prerogative so peculiar to the Apostles, but that every Bishop, in some measure, had a right and title to the same character." Bing. Ecc. Antiq. bk. ii. ch. 5.

Q. Does this Church legislate on the principle, that a Diocese is the Bishop's *Jurisdiction,* in its normal character, and is over persons and not defined by places?

A. Yes. By the Constitution, in Article V. as amended in A. D. 1856, "making Presbyters and Parishes," and not Territory, as formerly, the rule in the formation of New Dioceses; and also in the Canons on "Residence," and on "Episcopal Missionary Jurisdiction," and on "Congregations in Foreign Lands," and in other Canons. [4] § VII. Can. 13, Title I. Canons 10, 12, Title I. [1] § III. Can. 5, Title III. Dig.

Q. What is the force of the Limitation on the Bishop's Jurisdiction in this Article IV.?

A. The provision that "Every Bishop shall confine the exercise of his Episcopal office to his proper Diocese," enacts (1), That he shall not obtrude his jurisdiction over persons belonging to the jurisdiction of another Bishop, though they may chance to reside within the local limits of his own Diocese.

(2) Neither shall he himself pass beyond the local bounds of his Diocese into that of another Bishop to exercise any Episcopal jurisdiction or perform any Episcopal act.

Q. What is the Canon Law on this point?

A. "A Bishop may perform Divine offices, and use his Episcopal habit, in the Diocese of another without leave, but he may not perform therein any act of jurisdiction without permission of the other Bishop." Burns' Ecc. Law, vol. ii. p. 158. Gibson's Codex, pp. 133, 134.

Q. By what authority may a Bishop exercise his Episcopal office outside of the local limits of his own proper Diocese, according to Article IV. of the Constitution of this Church?

A. By the request of "any Church destitute of a Bishop." Art. IV. Cons.

Q. Does this Article prohibit the Bishop of the Diocese from inviting another Bishop to exercise his Episcopal functions in his Diocese?

A. It does: for it confines the authority of inviting another Bishop into a Diocese "to the request of any *Church destitute of a Bishop.*"

Q. How can a Bishop of a Diocese justify his own invitation to another Bishop to exercise the Episcopal office in his Diocese?

A. Only by falling back on English and Catholic Canon Law.

Q. What further does this Article contemplate?

A. It contemplates the office of a Bishop as necessarily connected with some field in which he is to exercise his jurisdiction.

Hence, it was argued that a Bishop might not resign his jurisdiction; for the American Church does not tolerate a vagrant Bishop, or Bishop at large.

A Canon accordingly has been passed enabling a Bishop to resign his Episcopal jurisdiction, but not his Episcopal office, which is indelible. § XVI. Canon 13, Title I. Dig.

Assistant Bishops.   *Q.* May an Assistant Bishop be consecrated without assurance of his continuance in some Episcopal Jurisdiction after the demise of his principal?

A. No. The election of Bishop Meade by the Convention of the Diocese of Virginia, in A. D. 1829, as Assistant to Bishop Moore, *without the right of succession*, led to a protest of the House of Bishops (Jour. Gen. Conv. A. D. 1829) against its being made a precedent; and the General Convention of that year enacted the Canon on "Assistant Bishops;" requiring, among other conditions, that "he shall in all cases succeed the Bishop in case of surviving him." § V. Canon 13, Title I. Dig. See Bingham, Ecc. Antiq. bk. ii. ch. 13. Hawks' Cons. & Can. pp. 111–121.

The Canon, likewise, forbids the election and consecration of a Suffragan Bishop and more than one Assistant Bishop in a Diocese at the same time. Ibid. Can. 13.

Q. What is a SUFFRAGAN Bishop?

Suffragan Bishops.   *A.* Anciently, Suffragan Bishops were all the Bishops of *Cities* of any Province under a Metropolitan; who were called his Suffragans, because they met at his command to bestow their *suffrages* or votes in giving council, assistance, or advice in a Provincial Synod. Bingham, Ecc. Antiq. bk. ii. § 14.

In England, as late as A. D. 1430 (according to Lyndwood), all the Bishops were Suffragans under their Archbishops or Metropolitans. Ibid. Lyndwood's Prov. Con. After the Reformation, by a Statute of 26 Henry VIII. ch. 14, every Archbishop and Bishop might have a Suffragan. Grey's Ec. Law, p. 39. Gibson's Codex, p. 135.

CONSTITUTION OF THE CHURCH. 139

Q. What were the duties of Suffragan Bishops in England?

A. They were empowered to discharge such Episcopal offices as were *purely Spiritual,*—such as Ordinations, Confirmations, Visitations,—" supposing the Bishop not wholly disabled." They were confined to the exercise of such Episcopal functions only as their Bishop committed to them from time to time. But they could not exercise any *Jurisdiction,* nor any Episcopal power, except such as the Bishop should authorize, for a fixed time, under his seal. 26 Henry VIII. ch. 14. Gibson's Codex, p. 136.

Q. What were the privileges of Suffragan Bishops?

A. They might enjoy two Benefices. They had a seat in Convocation, in the Lower House, as "*Dignitaries* of the Church." They were duly consecrated Bishops, but took their "Title" from certain towns, either within or beyond the Dioceses in which they officiated. Gibson's Codex, p. 136. Grey's Ec. Law, p. 40.

Q. How long have Suffragans been disused in England?

A. Since A. D. 1606, when Dr. Stern, Suffragan Bishop of Colchester, was suspended for not appearing in Convocation.[1] Gibson's Codex, p. 136. Grey's Ec. Law, p. 41.

Q. What was a COADJUTOR Bishop?

A. Coadjutor Bishops were persons appointed by the Archbishop, where the Bishop of the Diocese was *wholly disabled,* by reason of old age or bodily infirmities, from discharging the Episcopal Office. Being duly consecrated, the Episcopal Jurisdiction was vested in the Coadjutor Bishop, such as to collate to Benefices, to institute Clerks, to grant Commendams, etc. He succeeded the Bishop of the Diocese at his death. Gibson's Codex, p. 137. Grey's Ec. Law, pp. 41, 42.

Coadjutor Bishops.

Q. What relation does an Assistant Bishop in this Church bear to the Suffragan and Coadjutor Bishops of the Church of England?

[1] Suffragans are being revived in England, at this time, by virtue of the unrepealed Law of 26 Henry VIII.

A. He combines the powers and faculties of both; as appears from the inspection of the Canon 13, Title I. of the Digest. See Hawks' Cons. & Can. pp. 120, 121.

Organization of Dioceses under Catholic Canon Law. *Q.* Give a succinct statement of the organization of the Church under the Catholic Canon Law, which has been established or ratified by the Œcumenical Councils and received by the Church Universal.

A. The Roman Empire was divided by Constantine into four grand divisions, styled *Pretorian Prefectures*. Each Prefecture was divided into many Dioceses: each Diocese into many Provinces.

(1) The Prefecture of the EAST comprehended *Asia, Egypt, Libya,* and *Thrace*: five Dioceses: forty-eight Provinces.

(2) The Prefecture of ILLYRIA comprehended *Mœsia, Macedonia, Greece,* and *Crete:* two Dioceses: eleven Provinces.

(3) The Prefecture of ITALY comprehended *Italy,* a part of *Illyria,* and *Africa:* three Dioceses: twenty-nine Provinces.

(4) The Prefecture of GAUL comprehended *Gaul, Spain,* and *Britain:* three Dioceses: twenty-nine Provinces.

At the head of each Prefecture was placed a Prefect of the Pretorium, or Pretorian Prefect, being Commander-in-Chief. In the Dioceses, the Emperor sent to represent the Prefects, magistrates named Vicars (*vicarii*). Each Province was confided to a President, who bore the title of Proconsul or Rector (*rector provinciæ*). Ortolan, Histoire de la Legislation Romaine, p. 309.

The CHURCH was organized under Constantine according to this general outline, in the fourth Century. The Bishops of the several Cities had there each one his See, styled his " Parochia " or Parish. The Suburbs were served by Chorepiscopi, similar to Suffragans. The Clergy were usually itinerant, but generally dwelt with the Bishop. Hoff. L. C. p. 130.

The Bishops of the Province were subordinate to the Bishop of the Chief City in that Province, or the Metropolis, who was hence styled *Metropolitan*. The Metropolitans of a Province were subordinated to the Chief Bishop of the Diocese, styled *Patriarch*.

This arrangement of Ecclesiastical Government and Order was continued until the Papal usurpation in the tenth Century. The Emperor Justinian, A. D. 533, confirmed it, as a political safeguard of the Empire. He commands (in one of his Novels), "the Patriarch of each Diocese to publish the Code of Civil Laws in their respective Churches, and to make them known to the Metropolitans under him, — that so the Metropolitans might make the like publication, and make them known to the Bishops under them, — that so those Bishops might publish them in their Churches: and so none in the whole Empire be left ignorant of what he had enacted for the honor of the GREAT GOD, and our SAVIOUR JESUS CHRIST."

This Ecclesiastical organization was modified in the early British Church by the infusion of "the ancient British Liberties," until it crystallized into the two Provinces of the Archbishops, the Dioceses of the Bishops, and the Parishes of the Rectors. See Hoff. L. C. on "*Dioceses*," pp. 129-133. Van Espen, Supplement, vol. ii. Tit. 8, ch. 1. Kenneth's Ec. Syn. p. 180, edition A. D. 1701. See "Common Law of the Church," *ante*.

ARTICLE 5. "A Protestant Episcopal Church in any of the United States, or any Territory thereof, not now represented, may, at any time hereafter, be admitted on acceding to this Constitution: and a new Diocese, to be formed from one or more existing Dioceses, may be admitted under the following restrictions. *Admission of new Dioceses.*

142   MANUAL COMMENTARY.

"No new Diocese shall be formed or erected within the limits of any other Diocese, nor shall any Diocese be formed by the junction of two or more Dioceses, or parts of Dioceses, unless with the consent of the Bishop and Convention of each of the Dioceses concerned, as well as of the General Convention.

<small>Consent required.</small>

"No such new Diocese shall be formed which shall contain less than fifteen self-supporting Parishes, or less than fifteen Presbyters who have been for at least one year canonically resident within the bounds of such new Diocese, regularly settled in a Parish or Congregation, and qualified to vote for a Bishop. Nor shall such new Diocese be formed if thereby any existing Diocese shall be so reduced as to contain less than thirty self-supporting Parishes, or less than twenty Presbyters who have been residing therein and settled and qualified as above mentioned: *Provided* that no city shall form more than one Diocese.

<small>Limit of Presbyters and Parishes.</small>

"In case one Diocese shall be divided into two Dioceses, the Diocesan of the Diocese divided may elect the one to which he will be attached, and shall thereupon become the Diocesan thereof. And the Assistant Bishop, if there be one, may elect the one to which he will be attached; and if it be not the one elected by the Bishop, he shall be the Diocesan thereof.

<small>Rights of the Diocesan and the Assistant Bishop.</small>

Whenever the division of a Diocese into two Dioceses shall be ratified by the General Convention, each of the two Dioceses shall be subject to the Constitution and Canons

<small>Constitution and Canons of new Dioceses.</small>

CONSTITUTION OF THE CHURCH. 143

of the Diocese so divided, except as local circumstances may prevent, until the same may be (sic.) altered in either Diocese by the Convention thereof. And whenever a Diocese shall be formed out of two or more existing Dioceses, the new Diocese shall be subject to the Constitution and Canons of that one of the said existing Dioceses to which the greater number of Clergymen shall have (sic.) belonged prior to the erection of such new Diocese, until the same may be (sic.) altered by the Convention of the new Diocese." <small>Consolidation of two or more Dioceses.</small>

ADMISSION OF NEW DIOCESES.

Q. How may a New Diocese be admitted into union with the other Dioceses and with the General Convention?

A. By "*acceding*" to the "Constitution of the Protestant Episcopal Church in the United States."

Q. Does the act of "acceding" to the Constitution imply the right of any Diocese to *secede* from the union established by the Constitution?

A. No. Dr. Hawks says, "The several Dioceses surrendered "— (1) " Such an exercise of independency as would permit them to withdraw from the union at their own pleasure, and without the assent of the other Dioceses." Hawks' Cons. & Can. p. 11.

Q. State the other powers of "independency", which Dr. Hawks says the Dioceses "surrendered?"

A. (2) "They surrendered the right of having the Bishop whom they might elect, consecrated without the assent of the Church at large."

(3) "They surrendered the right of sole and unrestricted legislation for themselves, in the Dioceses alone; but consented that part of those laws should be made in a General Legislature of which they were members."

(4) "They surrendered the right of framing their own Liturgy, and agreed through all the Dioceses to use the same."

(5) "They surrendered the right of making separately any alteration in the great compact or Charter of Union." Hawks' Cons. & Can. pp. 11, 12.

Q. What supreme function of "diocesan independency," does Bishop White say, was *abandoned* by the State Conventions, under the Constitution of A. D. 1789?

A. The right of the different States to ratify the Articles of the Constitution (and by parity of reasoning to amend them), being found "fruitful of discord and disunion, *was abandoned from this time,*" A. D. 1786; and "the Constitution was so altered as to require a ratification by the Church in a majority of the States *assembled in General Convention.* The General Constitution of A. D. 1789 was adopted and finally ratified without being submitted to the State Conventions." Mem. of Ch. p. 123. Wilson's Mem. Bp. White, pp. 135, 136. See *ante,* on the "History of the Constitution."

Q. What is the process by which a Church in any of the United States is admitted into Union?

A. The application for admission into union, together with a copy of the Constitution of the Diocese, is presented to the House of Clerical and Lay Deputies, and referred to a Committee.

The Committee examine the Constitution of the Diocese, and finding that the Church in that Diocese declares its accession to the General Constitution and Canons of the Church, they recommend that the Church applying, be admitted into union with the General Convention of the Protestant Episcopal Church in the United States.

If the House adopt the recommendation by a Resolution, it is sent to the House of Bishops. The House of Bishops signifying their concurrence, the names of the Deputies of the new Diocese are called, and they take their seats in the House of Clerical and Lay Deputies.

The Bishop of the new Diocese takes his seat in the House of Bishops, not as representing his Diocese, but *ex officio*. Hoff. L. C. pp. 161, 162.

Q. What is the process by which a "New Diocese, formed from one or more existing Dioceses," is admitted into union?

A. By the provisions of Canon 6, Title III. of the Digest.

Q. What are the Constitutional Restrictions on the dividing of an existing Diocese?

A. (1) The consent of the Bishop and Convention of the Diocese must first be given to the division of the Diocese.

(2) The consent of the General Convention, in both Houses, must concur with the prayer of the Diocese for division.

Q. Into how many Dioceses does this Article of the Constitution contemplate the Division of a Diocese?

A. Into two Dioceses, and no more, at the same time.

Q. What was the interpretation of this Article whereby the Diocese of New York, in A. D. 1868, was divided into *three* Dioceses with the consent of the General Convention of that year?

A. The argument of the Diocese of New York was this: "The use of the singular number does not exclude the idea of plurality, but denotes a severalty, signifying that what is required for one new Diocese shall be equally required for every other. But, even if the Constitution were supposed to prohibit the formation of more than one new Diocese at a time, the prohibition would easily be satisfied *by successive acts of legislation* which should erect the several new Dioceses one by one."

"Even, therefore, if the Constitution" (of the General Church) "be understood as requiring a separation in time between the erection of two new Dioceses, yet that separation need be only the time required for two separate acts of legislation" of the parent Diocese. Report of a Sub-Committee, Journal N. Y. Conv. A. D. 1867, p. 82.

The Committee and the Convention adopted the principle " that there is nothing in the Constitution or Canons of the Church forbidding the erection, at this time, of more than one new Diocese within the Diocese of New York." " When the Convention shall have erected one new Diocese, its action, so far as the Diocese of New York is concerned, is complete and final; and it may then proceed to legislate for the formation of a second." Journal N. Y. Conv. A. D. 1867, p. 73.

The General Convention, on the Report of the Committee on New Dioceses, established this interpretation of Article V. of the Constitution, and ratified the action of the Diocese of New York in erecting two new Dioceses at the same Convention. Jour. Gen. Conv. A. D. 1868, pp. 47, 54. H. of Bishops, p. 197.

Q. What is the further restriction on the erection of New Dioceses?

A. (1) Every new Diocese shall contain not less than fifteen self-supporting Parishes, nor less than fifteen Presbyters who have been for at least one year canonically resident within the bounds of such new Diocese, regularly settled in a parish or congregation, and qualified to vote for a Bishop.

(2) That the old Diocese shall not be reduced by division, so as to contain less than thirty self-supporting Parishes, nor less than twenty Presbyters, who have been residing therein, and settled and qualified as above mentioned.

(3) That no City shall form more than one Diocese.

Q. What is the principle adopted and published in these " restrictions," respecting the definition of a Diocese?

A. The principle, that, a Diocese is defined by the Presbyters and persons, in Parishes, contained therein (and not by local bounds and limits), under the Bishop's Jurisdiction.

CONSTITUTION OF THE CHURCH. 147

Q. When was Article V. put into its present form?

A. In the General Convention of A. D. 1856.

Q. What was the principle of the old Fifth Article respecting the defining of Dioceses, which is now superseded?

A. The former principle, now superseded by amendment, was the defining of a Diocese by *Topographical boundaries*, as "Eight thousand square miles in one body," for the "bounds of a new Diocese;" and not less than "eight thousand square miles" for the existing Diocese.

The primitive and normal rule, that a Diocese is defined by a Bishop's Jurisdiction over "the sheep of Christ," as St. Cyprian witnesses, was restored in A. D. 1856, and is made the Fundamental Law of this Church.

Q. What is the right of Jurisdiction of the Bishop when his Diocese is divided? <small>Diocesan Rights of the Bishops and the Assistant Bishops.</small>

A. He has the right to elect which one he shall be the Diocesan of.

Q. What is the right of Jurisdiction of the Assistant Bishop?

A. He may elect to be the Diocesan of any one of the New Dioceses to which the Bishop does not choose to be attached.

Q. What is the Fundamental Law of New Dioceses? <small>The Fundamental Law of new Dioceses.</small>

A. The Constitution and Canons of the parent Diocese, when applicable, and until altered by the respective Conventions of the New Dioceses.

Q. May two or more Dioceses be united into one Diocese?

A. Yes. This article of the Constitution provides for the Consolidation of Dioceses.

Q. What is the fundamental Law of the Consolidated Diocese?

A. It is the Constitution and Canons of that one of the Dioceses to which the greater number of Clergymen

148 MANUAL COMMENTARY.

have belonged prior to the erection of such new Diocese, and until the same shall have been altered by the Convention of the Consolidated Diocese.

ARTICLE 6. "The mode of trying Bishops shall be provided by the General Convention. The Court appointed for that purpose shall be composed of Bishops only. In every Diocese, the mode of trying Presbyters and Deacons may be instituted by the Convention of the Diocese. None but a Bishop shall pronounce sentence of admonition, suspension, or degradation from the Ministry, on any Clergyman, whether Bishop, Presbyter, or Deacon."

<small>Ecclesiastical Court and Trial of Bishops.</small>

<small>Diocesan Courts, Trials, and Sentences.</small>

COURT AND TRIAL OF BISHOPS.

Q. What is the mode of trying Bishops?

A. The mode is provided by the General Convention, in Canon 9, Title II. Dig.

<small>Court and trial of Bishops.</small>

Q. Who may constitute the Court for the trial of Bishops?

A. The Court shall be composed of Bishops only.

Q. What was the corresponding article of the Constitution of A. D. 1785?

A. Article VIII. of the General Constitution of A. D. 1785 was as follows: "Every clergyman, whether Bishop, or Presbyter, or Deacon, shall be amenable to the authority of the *Convention in the State* to which he belongs, so far as relates to suspension or removal from office; and the Convention of each State shall institute rules for their conduct, and an equitable mode of trial." Art. VIII. Cons. A. D. 1785.

This Constitution of the Church was submitted to the

Bishops of the Church of England, together with the proposed alterations of the Liturgy, when the Church applied for the Episcopal Succession.

Q. What comment on this Article was made by the English Bishops?

A. In reply to the letter of the Committee of General Convention, the Archbishops of Canterbury and York, after objecting to certain proposed alterations in the Creeds and Liturgy, used this language: "We should be inexcusable, too, if, at the time when you are requesting the establishment of Bishops in your Church, we did not strongly represent to you that the Eighth Article of your Ecclesiastical Constitution appears to us to be a degradation of the Clerical, and still more of the Episcopal character. We persuade ourselves, that, in your ensuing Convention, some alteration will be thought necessary in this Article before this reaches you, or, if not, that due attention will be given to it, in consequence of our representation." Jour. Gen. Conv. A. D. 1786, p. 53.

Q. What comment does Bishop White make on this portion of the communication from the English Bishops?

A. Bishop White says, " The Bishops further declare their disapprobation of an Article in the proposed Constitution, which seemed to them to subject future Bishops to a trial by the Presbyters and Laymen, in the respective States."

" This, however, does not seem to be the meaning of the Article alluded to, which expresses no more than that Laws for the trial of Bishops should be made, not by the General, but by each State Ecclesiastical representative." Mem. of Ch. p. 16.

Q. What is the further comment of Bishop White on the remonstrance of the English Bishops?

A. He says, " The Archbishops of Canterbury and York complained that the Eighth Article was " a degradation of the Clerical, and, much more, of the Episcopal character." " The foundation of this complaint was rather in omission, than in anything positively declared. For the Bishop's being amenable to the Convention of the State to which he belonged, does not necessarily involve anything more than that he should be triable by laws of their enacting, himself being a part of the body; and it did not follow that he might be deposed or censured, either by Laymen or Presbyters. This, however, ought to have been guarded against; but to have attempted it, while the Convention were in their excited temper, would have been to no purpose." Mem. of Ch. pp. 94, 95.

Q. On what legal and equitable principle did the English Bishops object to the provision for the Trial of the Clergy?

A. On the principle of personal security under every just law, that "the accused shall be tried by his Peers," and that "where there is no authority to confer power, there can be none to disannul it. Wherever, therefore, the power of ordination is lodged, the power of deprivation is lodged also." Bishop Seabury's Letter to Dr. Smith, August 15, A. D. 1785. Mem. of Ch. p. 345.

Q. What modification did the General Convention of A. D. 1786 make in Article VIII. of the Constitution?

A. The General Convention of A. D. 1786 added these words, namely: "At every trial of a Bishop, there shall be one or more of the Episcopal Order present, and none but a Bishop shall pronounce sentence of deposition or degradation from the ministry on any Clergyman, whether Bishop, or Presbyter, or Deacon." Art. VIII. Cons. A. D. 1786.

Q. Does this amendment remove the objection of the remonstrance of the English Bishops?

A. Partially, but not on just ecclesiastical Principles. It still allowed Presbyters and Laymen to compose, in part, a Court for the trial of Bishops.

Q. How did the General Convention of A. D. 1786 treat the remonstrance of the English Bishops?

A. On the question, " Shall the Eighth Article of the Ecclesiastical Constitution remain as proposed and published by the late Convention ? (of 21st June, A. D. 1786,) it was unanimously determined in the affirmative." Jour. Gen. Conv. A. D. 1786, p. 60.

Q. How long did Article VIII. remain in the Constitution unchanged ?

A. It was modified in A. D. 1789, as follows: " In every State, the mode of trying Clergymen shall be instituted by the Convention of the Church therein."

" At every trial of a Bishop, there shall be one or more of the Episcopal Order present; and none but a Bishop shall pronounce sentence of deposition or degradation from the ministry on any Clergyman, whether Bishop, Priest, or Deacon." Jour. Gen. Conv. A. D. 1789, p. 84.

This modification did not change the underlying false principle. But, in A. D. 1841, the first two sentences were added to it, namely, " The mode of trying Bishops shall be provided by the General Convention. The Court appointed for that purpose shall be composed of Bishops only." Jour. Gen. Conv. A. D. 1841. Appendix to Constitution and Digest.

Q. What notable advance towards Catholic Canon Law was made by the Amendment of A. D. 1841 ?

A. (1) The law that Bishops are amenable to the whole Church of God. (2) That they are entitled to trial by their Peers in the Province or National Church with which they are connected. Apos. Can. 74. 1 Council of Constantinople, Can. 6. Council of Antioch, Can. 4, 12, 13, 14.

Q. What further change was made in this Article respecting the trial of Presbyters and Deacons ?

A. The Article, in A. D. 1841, confined the power to the Dioceses, of enacting the mode of trying Presbyters and Deacons, in these words: " In every Diocese, the mode of trying Presbyters and Deacons *shall* be instituted by the Convention of the Diocese." <small>Diocesan Courts and Trials.</small>

In 1848, the word "*shall*" was stricken out, and the word "*may*" was substituted, as in Article VI. of the Constitution, recited above, giving to the Dioceses a permissive power to make penal laws, only so long as the General Convention shall abstain from enacting them. Hoff. L. C. pp. 164–166.

Q. What advance towards Catholic Law was made by this Amendment of A. D. 1848?

A. Such an advance as (1) That it made it possible to enact uniform laws for the Clergy of the whole Province or National Church, to which all the Clergy alike should be amenable. (2) That the Representatives of the Clergy, in General Convention, by the vote of Dioceses and Orders, might have power to protect the rights of Clergy.

Imperfection of the Judiciary. *Q.* Is the equal amenability of the Clergy of this Church established by the provision for Diocesan Courts and Canons?

A. No. That which is made an offense by the Canons in one Diocese may not be, and frequently is not, an offense in another; neither is there an uniform mode of Trial for the same offense, whether against Diocesan Canons, or against the Canons of the General Convention of the whole Church.

Q. What remedy does this Article provide?

A. It provides for an uniform Code of Jurisprudence, and the organization of Courts for the whole Church, by authority of the General Convention, so soon as the General Convention had adopted a Canon on the subject. Hoff. L. C. pp. 164, 165.

Q. Would the Canon of the General Convention supersede an existing Diocesan Canon, on the trial of Presbyters and Deacons?

A. The Article, as it now is to be interpreted, confers *permissory* power on the Diocesan Conventions, whereby "they could act until the General Convention acted." But when the General Convention had adopted a Canon on the subject, that Canon would be supreme and exclusive in all points which it reached." Hoff. L. C. pp. 165, 166.

Q. Has the General Convention exercised its constitutional and inherent prerogative in providing a Code of Laws, and a system of Judicial Proceedings?

A. No. The comprehensive and thoughtful Canons proposed by Judge Murray Hoffman in the General Convention of A. D. 1856 and A. D. 1859, failed. The history of this Article of the Constitution demonstrates that, from the beginning, the Legislation of the Church on this subject is fragmentary, slow, suspicious, and unjust.

Q. What crying enormity prevails, for lack of just and wise General Canons for the trial of Presbyters and Deacons?

A. Besides the inequality and uncertainty in regard to offenses in different Dioceses and the modes of trial, there is no *Court of Appeal* made possible to Clergy convicted by Diocesan Courts.

Q. Why is the denial of the power of Appeal so enormous a wrong?

A. Because the Right of Appeal belongs to the meanest of human beings. In every civilized country it is fundamental. It was guaranteed by the pagan Roman Law to every citizen, and St. Paul availed himself of it. It is sacred under the Civil Law of Justinian. It is a portion of British Liberties which we have inherited from the Church and the State. It is a right under the Constitution of the United States, and is incorporated in the "Bill of Rights" in every State. It is a right under the Law of God to the Elder Church, and is confirmed to the Universal Church of Christ by the New Testament, by Catholic Canons, and by the uninterrupted consent of Councils, of Fathers, of Judges, and of Courts of Law. The Presbyters and the Deacons who suffer the misfortune of being convicted, after trial by Ecclesiastical Courts in a Diocese in the Protestant Episcopal Church, are the only men on the face of Christian Civilization who are deprived of the human Right of Appeal.

Q. What Commentary does Dr. Hawks make on this Article?

A. He says: "This is the only clause in the Constitution relating to the important subject of the Judiciary. At the time it was adopted, had the effort been made to leave the subject in the hands of the General Convention, it would have produced strong feelings of opposition to union. Uniformity of judicial proceeding and judicial decision is, of course, not to be expected under such an arrangement as leaves them with the Dioceses; and yet both are of great importance to the Church. In fact, the weakest and most defective part of our whole ecclesiastical system is in the department of the Judiciary." Hawks' Cons. & Can. p. 34.

"In vain will any one ask, What is the Law? No man can say. The convict of a Diocese, doubting, as well he may, under such circumstances, the propriety of his intended punishment, would fain APPEAL to some tribunal competent to adjust these conflicting interpretations. But where is such a tribunal? *Nowhere in the Church.*" "We need a Court of *Appeals*, with power authoritatively and finally to settle the true interpretation of Constitution and Canons, *ut sit finis litium.*" Hawks' Cons. & Can. p. 57.

Q. What is the view of Judge Hoffman?

A. He argues and pleads the necessity of the establishment of a Judicial System, and rests the power and the responsibility on the "inherent power of the General Convention prior to, and not derived from, a grant in the Constitution." Hoff. L. C. p. 166.

Sentences. *Q.* What Sentences may an Ecclesiastical Court pronounce?

A. "Admonition, Suspension, or Degradation from the Ministry." Art. VI. Cons.

Q. What is Admonition?

A. Admonition is either private or public, at the discretion of the Bishop.

Q. What is Suspension?

A. Suspension is a "penalty inflicted on a Bishop, Priest, or Deacon in this Church to cease on terms, or at a certain time, to be specified in the sentence." § I. Can. 10, Title II. Dig.

Q. Is there such a Sentence known to Canon Law as "Indefinite Suspension?"

A. No. It is contradictory in terms, and has never been pronounced or inflicted in the Catholic Church in any age or country, outside of the United States. See "The Law of Suspension in the Primitive Church," in a Discourse of Ignotus. Pamphlet: Phil. 1855: Printed by C. Sherman & Son.

Q. What is Degradation?

A. Degradation is the Sentence of Ecclesiastical Law, whereby, in this Church, a Minister is deposed from the Ministry entirely, and not from a higher to a lower Order of the same. [1] § II. Can. 10, Title II. Dig.

Q. Does the Sentence of Degradation, Deposition, or Displacement (equivalent terms in the Canons), take away the *office* of a Minister in this Church?

A. No. It deprives him of the *exercise* of his Office in this Church.

Q. May a deposed Minister be restored to the Exercise of his Office?

A. Yes, under conditions provided for in the Canons. Proviso of § II. Can. 6, Title II. Dig.

Q. Must he be ordained again, if restored?

A. No.

Q. What notice shall be given to the Church when a Clergyman is sentenced to "Degradation?"

A. "The Bishop who pronounces the Sentence shall without delay give notice thereof to every Minister and

Vestry in the Diocese, and also to all the Bishops of this Church, and when there is no Bishop, to the Standing Committee." [2] § II. Can. 10, Title II. Dig.

In the case of a Bishop deposed, the Sentence shall be communicated by the Court to the Ecclesiastical Authority of every Diocese in this Church; and it shall be the duty of such authority to cause such sentence to be made known to every Clergyman under his jurisdiction." [10] § VI. Can. 9, Title II. Dig.

Q. Who alone may pronounce a Sentence?

A. None but a Bishop. Art. VI. Cons. Can. 122 of A. D. 1603, Ch. of Eng.

Q. Under what Solemnities shall a Bishop pronounce a Sentence?

A. They are prescribed in [10] § VI. Can. 9, of Title II. on "The Trial of Bishops." Can. 8, Title II. on a "Bishop abandoning the Communion of the Church." §§ I. and V. Can. 5, Title II.; § II. Can. 6, Title II.; Can. 7, Title II. on "Trial of Presbyters and Deacons." Dig.

ARTICLE 7. "No person shall be admitted to Holy Orders, until he shall have been examined by the Bishop, and by two Presbyters, and shall have exhibited such testimonials and other requisites as the Canons, in that case provided, may direct. Nor shall any person be ordained until he shall have subscribed the following Declaration:

Requisites for Ordination.

"'I do believe the Holy Scriptures of the Old and New Testament to be the Word of God, and to contain all things necessary to Salvation; and I do solemnly engage to conform to the Doctrines and Worship of the Protestant Episcopal Church in the United States.'

Declaration.

"No person ordained by a foreign Bishop shall

CONSTITUTION OF THE CHURCH. 157

be permitted to officiate as a Minister of this Church, until he shall have complied with the Canon or Canons in that case provided, and have also subscribed the aforesaid Declaration." *Admission of Foreign Clergy.*

Q. What was the origin of this Article?

A. In many places in this country, Divine Services were kept up during the war by zealous Laymen. The caution of due examination and direction, in respect to *Lay Readers*, was first proposed in a Resolution of a voluntary Convention of Clergy and Laity from Massachusetts, Rhode Island, Connecticut, New York, New Jersey, Pennsylvania, Delaware, and Maryland, in the City of New York, 7th October, A. D. 1784 (Hawks & Perry, Hist. Notes, etc. Gen. Conv. p. 375); and it was incorporated into the first Constitution of the Protestant Episcopal Church by the General Convention of A. D. 1785, in regard to *Candidates* for Holy Orders. *Origin.*

The Article consisted only in the requirement of subscription to the Declaration of belief in the Holy Scriptures as the Word of God, containing all things necessary to Salvation; and in the engagement to conform to the Doctrines and Worship of the Protestant Episcopal Church, as settled and determined in the Book of Common Prayer. Jour. Gen. Conv. A. D. 1785, p. 23.

The General Convention of A. D. 1786 added the requirement that the Candidate for Holy Orders should be examined by the Bishop and two Presbyters, and should exhibit testimonials of his moral conduct for three years last past. Jour. Gen. Conv. A. D. 1786, p. 42.

The General Convention of A. D. 1789 put the Article precisely into its present form. Jour. Gen. Conv. A. D. 1789, p. 84. Hawks' Cons. & Can. p. 36. Hoff. L. C. p. 166.

Q. What are the foremost requisites for Ordination? *Requisites for Ordination.*

A. The requisites for Ordination first named in this Article of the Constitution, are (1) that the Candidate shall have been examined by the Bishop and two Presbyters. (2) That he shall have exhibited such testimonials and other requisites as the Canons in that case provided may direct. Art. VII. Cons.

Q. What Canons provide the regulations for Candidates for the Holy Order of Deacons?

A. Canon 2, "Of the Admission of Candidates for Holy Orders." Canon 3, "Of Admitted Candidates." Canon 4, "General Provisions and Requisites for Ordination." Canon 5, "Examination and Testimonials for Deacon's Orders and Ordination." Title I. Dig.

Q. What Canons provide the regulations for Candidates for the Holy Order of Priests?

A. Canon 6, "Of Deacons." Canon 7, "Of Candidates for Priest's Orders and their Ordination." Title I. Dig.

<small>Declaration.</small> *Q.* What is the next condition precedent to Ordination into the Ministry of this Church?

A. The person to be ordained must first subscribe the following Declaration: — "*I do believe the Holy Scriptures of the Old and New Testaments to be the Word of God, and to contain all things necessary to Salvation; and I do solemnly engage to conform to the Doctrine and Worship of the Protestant Episcopal Church in the United States.*"

Q. Why is not a subscription to the "Articles of Religion" required, as in the Church of England?

A. Because the subscription to the *Declaration* was deemed to be a sufficient subscription to the Articles of Religion; and hence the further subscription to the Articles would be superfluous.

Q. State the authority for this answer, from the records of the General Convention in A. D. 1804?

A. "A proposed Canon concerning subscription to the Articles of the Church was negatived, under the impression that a sufficient subscription of the Articles is already required by Article VII. of the Constitution." Jour. Gen. Conv. A. D. 1804, p. 301.

"The subscription to the *Declaration*, prescribed in the Constitution of the American Church, had so far acquired the approbation of the English Prelates, as to be thought sufficient, without subscriptions to the Articles, on the part of those who came to them for consecration from America." Mem. of Ch. p. 28.

Q. What is the force of the Declaration that the Holy Scriptures "*contain* all things necessary to Salvation"? <small>Container of the Faith.</small>

A. The force and meaning of the Declaration are explained and evinced by the Sixth Article of Religion. "Holy Scripture containeth all things necessary to Salvation; so that whatsoever is not read therein, nor may be proved thereby, is not to be required of any man, that it should be believed as an Article of the Faith, or be thought requisite or necessary to Salvation." Article of Religion VI.

Q. Do you distinguish between "The Faith" and the Doctrines, contained in the Holy Scriptures of the Old and New Testaments?

A. The distinction is radical. The FAITH is what is requisite to be believed as necessary to Salvation. The Doctrines of Christianity, are beside the Faith, — such as Election, Predestination, Free Will, on which subjects good men may differ without peril of damnation.

Q. Does this Declaration, as interpreted by this Article of Religion, affirm that the Holy Scripture *teaches* what is the Faith?

A. No. Both the Declaration and the Article are explicit in confining the sufficiency of the Holy Scriptures of the Old and New Testaments to the "*containing*" of the Faith; and not as *teaching* what the Faith is.

Q. What would be the effect of the dogma that the Holy Scripture is the only or the foremost *Teacher* of the Faith?

A. The effect would be to allow every man to select for himself out of the Scriptures, what to believe, *as of the Faith,* and what to reject, according to his private judgment; and so authorize and justify as many Sects of Christianity as there are opinions.

Q. Whence do we derive the Holy Scriptures of the Old and New Testaments?

A. We derive the Old Testament from the testimony and tradition of the Elder Church of the Jews: We derive the New Testament from the testimony and tradition of the Catholic Church from the Apostolic times.

Q. What are the tokens and demonstration of the Truth of the testimony and tradition of the Church?

A. That which has been witnessed to and handed down, always, everywhere, and by all — " *quod semper, ubique et ab omnibus,*" — has the marks of authenticity and credibility, as Truth derived from one Original. The Bible possesses these Infallible Marks of its origin and authority, as God's inspired Word written.

<small>Teacher of the Faith.</small> *Q.* Where is the TEACHER OF THE FAITH to be found?

A. "The Church hath authority in controversies of Faith," and is the " Witness and Keeper of Holy Writ." Articles of Religion XX.

Q. Where is the " Faith " taught?

A. In the Creeds, — in the one commonly called the "Apostles' Creed," — and in the other, styled the " Nicene Creed," as published by the first Council of the Universal Church at Nicæ in Bithynia, A. D. 325, and by the second Council of the Universal Church at Constantinople, A. D. 381.

Q. Is the particular Church, as of Jerusalem, of Alexandria, of Rome, of England, of the United States of America, liable to err?

A. Yes; not only in their living, but also in matters of Faith. Art. of Religion XIX.

Q. What limitation is there on the Authority of a particular or national Church?

A. "It is not lawful for the Church to ordain anything that is contrary to God's Word written."

"Neither may it so expound one place of Scripture that it be repugnant to another:" "nor decree anything against the same." "Nor beside the same, ought it to enforce anything to be believed for necessity of salvation." Art. of Religion XX.

Q. Is this Limitation of Authority applicable to the Church Universal?

A. In theory it is; although the proposition implies an impossibility in fact.

Q. May not the Church Universal err?

A. No; neither in the Faith, nor in expounding the Scriptures, nor in its teaching of Christian Morality. For, otherwise, the proposition would be true, that "always, everywhere, and by all," the teachings on the same subject would be "contrary" and "repugnant" to each other; which is absurd and impossible.

Q. What is the visible Church?

A. "The visible Church of Christ is a congregation of faithful men, in which the pure Word of God is preached, and the Sacraments be duly administered in all those things that of necessity are requisite to the same." Art. of Religion XIX.

Q. What is meant by "faithful men"?

A. That congregation who profess the Catholic Faith as taught in the Creeds.

Q. Are the Creeds to be received as Symbols of the Faith, simply because they are put forth by the witness of Œcumenical Councils of the Church?

A. No. The Creeds possess the double witness of the Church and the Bible. "They ought thoroughly to be received and believed; for they may be proved by most certain warrants of Holy Scripture." Art. of Religion VIII.

<small>Extent and Limitation of Private Judgment.</small> *Q.* Is there, then, both a Limitation and a Latitude of private judgment?

A. Yes. A person is, first of all, to "hear the Church" *propound the Faith*, — this is the Limitation; and afterwards he has Latitude of judgment, like the Bereans, to "search and see whether these things be so." St. Matt. xviii. 17; St. John vi. 39; Acts xvii. 11.

Q. What, then, is the final or ultimate Rule of Faith?

A. The Holy Scriptures of the Old and New Testament.

Q. What if a Searcher of the Scriptures disagree with the testimony of the Church, as to the Faith?

A. "To his own *Master* he standeth or falleth." Romans xiv. 4.

Q. May a *Minister* of this Church have any Latitude of private judgment, in matters of the Faith, Doctrine, Sacraments, or Discipline of CHRIST?

A. No.

Q. What is the authority for this answer?

A. (1) At the ordination of every Priest, the Bishop demands " Will you give your faithful diligence always so to minister the Doctrine, Discipline, and Sacraments of CHRIST, as the LORD hath commanded, and *as this Church hath received the same, according to the commandments of* GOD, so that you may teach the people committed to your cure and charge with all diligence to keep and observe the same?" — to which he answers, "I will so do, by the help of the Lord."

(2) He subscribes the Declaration in Article VII. of the Constitution of the Protestant Episcopal Church in the United States: which includes the profession of his faith in the Holy Scriptures, and his agreement with the Articles of Religion, and his engagement to conform to the Doctrine and Worship of this Church.

Q. What if the Priest teaches contrary to the Faith, Doctrine, Sacraments, or Discipline of this Church?

A. He is to be presented, tried, and, by just judgment, admonished, suspended, or deposed.

Q. Repeat the words of the engagement of Conformity, in the Declaration?

A. " I do solemnly engage to conform to the Doctrines and Worship of the Protestant Episcopal Church in the United States." Art. VII. Cons.

Q. Where are to be found the Doctrines and Worship of the Protestant Episcopal Church, to which the Clergymen of this Church engage to conform?

A. In the Book of Common Prayer; which is required to be used in those Dioceses which have adopted the Constitution of the Protestant Episcopal Church in the United States. Art. VIII. Cons.

Q. Where are the directions for Divine Worship in this Church to be found?

A. In the Rubrics of the Prayer Book, and in the Canons of General Convention.

Q. Does the Clergyman engage to conform to the Rubrics and Canons?

A. Yes. " The Prayer Book is the formula of worship; and the Rubrics, being a portion of it, are equally binding as the rest." Hoff. L. C. p. 318.

Q. What is the Canon Law on conformity to the Worship of this Church?

A. (1) " Every Minister shall, before all sermons and lectures, and on all other occasions of public worship, use the Book of Common Prayer, as the same is or may be established by the authority of the General Convention of this Church; and in performing such Service, no other prayers shall be used than those prescribed by the said Book." Can. 20, Title I. Dig.

(2) The Bishop of each Diocese may compose " Forms of Prayer or Thanksgiving for extraordinary occasions,"

which "the Clergy in those Dioceses may use;" and also, "Forms of Prayer to be used before Legislative and other Public Bodies." § XIV. Canon 13, Title I. Dig.

Q. What duty do these Canons enjoin?

A. The duty of using no prayers in the public worship of this Church besides those which are prescribed by authority of the Prayer Book, or by the Bishop, by way of neither addition, nor omission, nor alteration.

Q. In the interpretation of these Canons, confining the use of prescribed prayers in "*public worship*" and "*before all sermons,*" may a Clergyman *after* the sermon use any other prayers or services than those which are prescribed?

A. "The letter of the Canon would seem to justify such a proceeding." Hawks' Cons. & Can. p. 377.

Q. May a Clergyman use other prayers or services before the Public Worship shall have commenced?

A. "The letter of the Canon would seem to justify such a proceeding," by parity of reasoning.

Q. Are Processional and Recessional Hymns allowable, on the literal interpretation of these Canons?

A. Undoubtedly, by the same reasoning.

Q. May Clergymen, during Public Worship, neglect or omit to use, any part of the prescribed Form of Prayer.

A. "It is a violation of the Constitution and Canons, and presentable, of course." Hoff. L. C. p. 318. Hawks' Cons. & Can. p. 377.

Q. What is the duty of a Clergyman in officiating in Missionary work, or where the Prayer Book is unknown?

A. If we "know and remember what this meaneth, I will have mercy and not sacrifice, we would not condemn the guiltless." (St. Matt. xii. 7.) The Clergyman would have no canonical right to violate the rubrics, and must seek for justification or pardon in the law of "mercy" to the ignorant and the perishing. Yet, he must preserve, as far as possible, the Liturgic order and spirit of the Church's worship.

Dr. Hawks, in his Commentary, asks the question (implying its own answer), "Might it not be well to provide a proper service by authority, to be used where the Prayer Book is not known." Hawks' Cons. & Can. p. 378.

A printed Missionary Service is used by Bishops and Clergymen to meet the emergency; which, however, lacks Canonical Authority, and will rest only on usage, or "the Common Law of the Church," until the General Convention shall give its sanction.

Section XIV. Canon 13, Title I. would, meanwhile, authorize the Bishop of each Diocese to compose a Form of Prayer for missionary purposes in his Diocese, as "for extraordinary occasions."

Q. Would the Publication of opinions tending to the derogation or depraving of the Prayer Book, be a violation of the Clergyman's subscription and promise of Conformity to the Doctrines and Worship of the Protestant Episcopal Church?

A. "Whether such a publication would be presentable has not been judicially settled in any case in our Church." Hoff. L. C. p. 318.

Judge Hoffman refers to the Law of the Church of England in the case of Sanders *v.* Head, 3 Curteis' Rep. 565. The accused published in a newspaper a letter, etc., "in which it was openly affirmed and maintained, that the Catechism and the Order of Confirmation in the Book of Common Prayer, contain erroneous and strange doctrines; and wherein were also openly affirmed and maintained other positions, in derogation and depravation of the said Book of Common Prayer."

The learned Judge decided, that, "By the general Law, every Clergyman is bound to conform to the Book of Common Prayer, under his subscription and the Canon Law of the Church; and that a Clergyman could, after this, publish anything he saw fit against the Liturgy or Prayer Book, *would be a monstrous proposition.*" Hoff. L. C. p. 319, note.

Admission of Foreign Clergy.   *Q.* Recite the clause in Article VII. touching the admission of Foreign Clergy into the Protestant Episcopal Church in the United States.

A. "No person ordained by a Foreign Bishop shall be permitted to officiate as a Minister of this Church, until he shall have complied with the Canon or Canons in that case provided, and have also subscribed the aforesaid DECLARATION."

Q. What are the Canons in that case provided?

A. Canon 9, Title I. entitled, "*Of the admission of Ministers ordained by Bishops not in communion with this Church.*"

Canon 10, Title I. entitled "*Of Ministers ordained in Foreign Countries by Bishops in Communion with this Church.*"

Canon 11. Title I. entitled "*Of Persons not Ministers in this Church, officiating in any Congregation thereof.*" Dig.

ARTICLE 8. "A Book of Common Prayer, Administration of the Sacraments, and other Rites and Ceremonies of the Church, Articles of Religion, and a Form and Manner of making, ordaining and consecrating Bishops, Priests, and Deacons, when established by this or a future General Convention, shall be used in the Protestant Episcopal Church in those Dioceses which shall have adopted this Constitution. No alteration or addition shall be made in the Book of Common Prayer, or other Offices of the Church, or the Articles of Religion, unless the same shall be proposed in one General Convention, and by a resolve thereof made known to the Convention of every Diocese, and adopted at the subsequent General Convention."

HISTORY OF THE BOOK OF COMMON PRAYER.

Q. What is the History of the Compilation of the Book of Common Prayer of the Protestant Episcopal Church in the United States?

A. The important principle of the *Identity of the Church in this Country with that of England*, asserted in every Church in the Colonies, and by the Church in the States after the Declaration of Independence, induced, at first, changes in the English Prayer Book in accustomed use, only so far as the new political allegiance demanded.

The prayers for the King and the Royal Family were omitted; and that for Parliament was altered and accommodated for the prayer for Congress, — and such like appropriate emendations. These changes were made directly after the Declaration of Independence, and by each separate Congregation whose minister remained with the people.

Such was the condition of the Liturgy until the voluntary Convention of October 6th and 7th, A. D. 1784, in New York; as is witnessed by many of the old, mutilated English Prayer Books, now extant as curiosities in our libraries.

1784.

That Meeting proposed six Fundamental Articles of union, to be laid before a General Convention of the Church, summoned in a seventh Article or resolution of that Meeting.

The fourth of the Fundamental Articles was as follows: "That the said Church shall maintain the Doctrines of the Gospel as now held by the Church of England; and shall adhere to the Liturgy of said Church, as far as shall be consistent with the American Revolution and the Constitutions of the several States." Preface to Jour. Gen. Conv. Ed. of Hawks & Perry, p. 10.

Q. What was done by the next Convention of A. D. 1785, on this subject?

A. The next Convention assembled in September, A. D. 1785, in Christ Church, Philadelphia, when the following Resolutions were passed: "Ordered, that the proceedings of a former Convention, at New York, be again read; which being done, and the different Articles considered, —

1785.

"*Resolved*, That the first, second, and third Articles proposed as Fundamental, are approved of. The fourth Article being read, it was, on motion, *Resolved*, That a Committee be appointed, consisting of one Clerical and one Lay Deputy from the Church in each State, to consider of and report such alterations in the Liturgy as shall render it consistent with the American Revolution, and the Constitutions of the several States; *and such further alterations in the Liturgy as it may be advisable for this Convention to recommend to the consideration of the Church here represented.*"

The need of more latitude in the revision of the Prayer Book was here first publicly intimated.

On Saturday, October 1, A. D. 1785, the Committee reported, "that they had prepared a draft of the alterations to be made in the Liturgy." From day to day, the Committee reported progress in making "the further alterations." On the 5th October, A. D. 1785, the Convention finished the work, and it was "Ordered, that the transcribed copy of the 'Alterations in the Liturgy, to render it consistent with the American Revolution and the Constitution of the respective States,' be read and considered by paragraphs; which being done, *Resolved*, That the Liturgy shall be used in this Church, as accommodated to the Revolution, agreeably to the alterations now approved of, and ratified by this Convention."

"On motion, *Resolved*, That the Fourth of July shall be observed by this Church forever, as a day of Thanksgiving to Almighty God for the inestimable blessings of religious and civil Liberty, vouchsafed to the United States of America."

"On motion, *Resolved*, That the first Tuesday in November, in every year forever, shall be observed as a day of general Thanksgiving to Almighty God, for the Fruits of the Earth, and for all other blessings of His merciful Providence."

It was then, in the evening session of the same day, October 5, 1785, "*Resolved*, That the said alterations be proposed and recommended to the Protestant Episcopal Church, in the States from which there are Deputies to this Convention." Jour. Gen. Conv. A. D. 1785, pp. 18-24.

Q. What notable alterations in the Symbols of the Faith were made in the "Proposed Book" of A. D. 1785?

A. The Article on the "Descent into Hell" was stricken out of the "Apostles' Creed."

The "Nicene Creed," and the "Athanasian Creed" were wholly omitted.

Q. What notice of the alterations in the Faith did the English Bishops take?

A. They remonstrated, and demanded the restoration of the Creeds, in a letter to the committee of General Convention, in A. D. 1786; expressing their "grief that two of the Confessions of our Christian Faith have been entirely laid aside; and that even in that which is called the Apostles' Creed, an Article is omitted which was thought necessary to be inserted, in view to a particular heresy in a very early age of the Church;" and they earnestly exhorted the Convention to restore to its integrity the Apostles' Creed, and to give the other two Creeds a place in the Book of Common Prayer. See communications from the Archbishops of Canterbury and York: Mem. of Ch. pp. 363, *et seq.* Jour. Gen. Conv. A. D. 1786, pp. 51-53.

Q. What heresy do the English Bishops refer to, as contradicted by the Catholic Church, in the Article in the Apostles' Creed, on the "Descent into Hell?"

A. The Apollinarian heresy, in the fourth century,

against the proper Humanity of Christ, and which denied a human soul to the Saviour; maintaining that His Divine Nature supplied its place. Mem of Ch. p. 190.

Q. What else was done in the premises, by the Convention of A. D. 1785?

A. A Committee of Publication was appointed, on October 7, A. D. 1785, with power to "make verbal corrections, and also a Calendar of Proper Lessons, and reading and singing Psalms, while the Prayer Book was in passing through the press; and to sell the Copyright for the benefit of the several Corporations for the relief of the widows and children of deceased Clergymen."

The final action of this General Convention in the premises, was a vote of thanks to the Rev. Dr. William Smith, of Maryland, Chairman of the Committee, "for his exemplary diligence and the great assistance he rendered this Convention in perfecting the important business in which they have been engaged." Jour. Gen. Conv. A. D. 1785, pp. 28, 29. Read the letters between the Committee — Revs. Dr. White, and Dr. Wharton, and Dr. Smith — in Hist. Notes to Jour. of Gen. Conv. Hawks & Perry.

Q. What was done in General Convention, in A. D. 1786, in respect to the restoring of the Creeds in their Integrity?

A. The letter of the Archbishops of England was referred to a Committe of a Clerical and a Lay Deputy from each State, in the Convention of A. D. 1786, who reported, *First,* That in the Creed commonly called the Apostles' Creed, these words, "He descended into Hell," shall be and continue a part of that Creed. *Second,* That the Nicene Creed shall also be inserted in the said Book of Common Prayer, immediately after the Apostles' Creed, prefaced with the Rubric (" or this "). Jour. Gen. Conv. A. D. 1786, pp. 58, 59.

The second Resolution, restoring the Nicene Creed, was passed unanimously. The first Resolution, on the Article in the Apostles' Creed, was passed " after a warm debate," by a vote of two Dioceses in the affirmative, three divided, — "two Ayes and no Negative." Ibid. p. 60. Bishop White says, "Had the issue been different, there could have been no proceeding to England for consecration at this time." Mem. of Ch. p. 133.

Q. What was done with the Athanasian Creed?

A. On motion "that the Athanasian Creed be admitted in the Liturgy," it was decided in the negative, — three Dioceses Nay, two Dioceses Divided. In the General Convention, A. D. 1789, the House of Bishops (Seabury and White) proposed to insert the Athanasian Creed, with a rubric *permitting* the use of it; but the Amendment was negatived in the lower House. Mem. of Ch. pp. 179, 180.

Q. What do you observe in this sketch of the History of the Compilation of the "Proposed Book" of Common Prayer?

A. (1) We observe the introduction of the Laity into the Committee of Revision, as the first instance in Ecclesiastical History in which Laymen were empowered with authority to assist the Clergy in determining the Faith, and in regulating the Divine Worship of the Church.

(2) We notice the gradual weaning of the Church from the idea of adhering closely to the Liturgy of the Church of England.

(3) We are impressed with the exhibition of gratitude for the Independence of the Country; and of loyalty to the Constitutions of the States; and with the recognition of the Hand of GOD in political affairs.

Yet Bishop White expresses the opinion, that, the obligation of the Service for the Fourth of July was "the most injudicious step taken by the Convention," and was reprehensible, for the reason that it endangered a cordial union, "because of the lingering opinions of many of the Clergy who still regarded the American Revolution as unjustifiable." Mem. of Ch. p. 105.

(4) The Convention was evidently satisfied with their work, deeming it worthy of universal acceptance and of use " forever."

(5) They anticipated the profitable sale of " the Proposed Book;" appropriating, beforehand, the profits to a charitable purpose.

Q. Were these expectations realized?

A. No. The Churches differed as to the merits of the " Proposed Book," some ratifying, and some rejecting it; and no bookseller would undertake its publication at his own risk. Mem. of Ch. pp. 114, 118.

Bishop White further states that " in this whole business there was encountered a prejudice entertained by many of the Clergy in other States, who thought that nothing should be done towards the organizing of the Church until the obtaining of the Episcopacy." Mem. of Ch. pp. 95, 102, *et seq.*

"It is strange to tell that the Rubric, held to be intolerable in Virginia, was that of allowing the Minister to repel an evil liver from the Communion.". . . . " It was objected that there should be any provision of the kind, or power exercised to the end contemplated." Mem. of Ch. p. 118.

Q. What was done in the next General Convention in A. D. 1786.

A. The next General Convention assembled June 20, A. D. 1786, in Christ Church, Philadelphia; and another " adjourned " meeting in Wilmington, Delaware, October 10, A. D. 1786.

"The Convention, assembled in A. D. 1786 in Philadelphia, bore strong appearances of a dissolution of the Union in this early stage of it. The interfering instructions from the Churches in the different States, the embarrassment that had arisen from the rejection of the " Proposed Book " in some States, and the use of it in others, were prognostics of falling to pieces, in the opinions of some." Mem. of Ch. p. 123.

CONSTITUTION OF THE CHURCH. 173

But these "interfering instructions," Bishop White says, "were silenced by the motion — *recorded as his own on the Journal* — for referring them to the first Convention which should meet fully authorized to determine on a Book of Common Prayer. The instructions, far from proving injurious, had the contrary effect; by showing as well the necessity of a duly constituted Ecclesiastical Body, as the *futility of taking measures to be reviewed, and authoritatively judged of, in the bodies of which we were Deputies. Such a system appeared so evidently fruitful of discord and disunion that it was abandoned from this time.*" Mem. of Ch. pp. 123, 124.

Q. How did this motion of Bishop White settle the question of the Supreme Authority of the General Convention, and prevent all future interfering instructions from the Dioceses?

A. The motion of Bishop White, creating the obligation to the use of the Book of Common Prayer, as set forth by the sole authority of the General Convention, was *incorporated into the Constitution* of A. D. 1786, and was made the Fundamental Law of the Church. In taking away from the Conventions of the Church in each State (Diocese) the right of "reviewing and authoritatively judging" of the Acts of the General Convention, it confined their relations to the Supreme Council of the Church to the sending of Deputies thereto, clothed with full powers to make and to alter the Constitution and to enact Laws for the whole Church. The *Coördinate* Authority of the Church in the States, or in Diocesan Conventions, Bishop White says, "*was abandoned from that time.*" See "Supremacy of General Convention," *ante*.

Q. Repeat the Article of the Constitution, introduced by Bishop White, and the Article for Amendments, adopted by that General Convention at its first Session in June, A. D. 1786.

A. Art. IX. " Whereas, it is represented to this Convention to be the general desire of the Protestant Episcopal Church in these States, that there may be further alterations of the Liturgy than such as are made necessary by the American Revolution, — therefore, 'The Book of Common Prayer, and Administration of the Sacraments, and other Rites and Ceremonies, as revised and proposed to the use of the Protestant Episcopal Church, at a Convention of the said Church in the States of New York, New Jersey, Pennsylvania, Delaware, Maryland, Virginia, and South Carolina,' may be used by the Church in such of the States as have adopted, or may adopt, the same in their particular Conventions, till further provision is made, in this case, by the first General Convention which shall assemble with sufficient power to ratify a Book of Common Prayer for the Church in these States."

Art. XI. " The Constitution of the Protestant Episcopal Church in the United States of America, when ratified by the Church in a majority of the States assembled in General Convention, with sufficient power for the purpose of such ratification, shall be unalterable by the Convention of any particular State, which hath been represented at the time of such ratification." Cons. Gen. Conv. A. D. 1786.

Q. What became of " the Proposed Book " ?

A. It was in voluntary use until superseded by the Book of Common Prayer, established by the General Convention of A. D. 1789. Wilson's Mem. Bp. White, p. 139.

Q. State the proceedings of the General Convention of A. D. 1789, in regard to the Book of Common Prayer.

A. This General Convention opened with one House only. The Deputies were duly vested with full powers to make and ratify the Constitution, which they proceeded at once to do. On the acceding to the Constitution by Bishop Seabury and the New England Deputies, the House of Bishops became a separate House under the Constitution; whereupon the Convention pro-

CONSTITUTION OF THE CHURCH. 175

ceeded to make provision for, and to ratify a Book of Common Prayer.

Q. On what principle did the Convention proceed?

A. No sooner had the Convention divided into two Houses, " when Dr. Parker, of Boston, proposed that the English Book should be the ground of proceedings to be held, without any reference to that Book set out and proposed in A. D. 1785. This was objected to by some, who contended that a Liturgy ought to be formed without reference to any existing Book, although with liberty to take from any whatever the Convention should think fit. The issue of the debate was the wording of the Resolves as they stand on the Journal, in which the different Committees (composed of Clergy and Laity) are appointed, ' to *prepare* a Morning and Evening Prayer;' ' to *prepare* a Litany;' ' to *prepare* a Communion Service;' and the same in regard to other departments; instead of its being said, *to alter the Services*, which had been the language in A. D. 1785." Mem. of Ch. p. 176. [Principle of Revision of the House of Deputies.]

Q. What was the opinion of the Bishops?

A. The Bishops thought this principle " very unreasonable, because the different Congregations of the Church were always understood to be possessed of a Liturgy *before* the consecration of her Bishops, or the existence of her Conventions." The principle affirmed in the House of Clerical and Lay Deputies implied " that there were no Forms of Prayer, no Offices, and no Rubrics, until they should be formed by the Convention now assembled." That House of Clerical and Lay Deputies (of A. D. 1789) " would not allow that there was any Book of Authority in existence;—a mode of proceeding in which they have acted differently from the Conventions before and after them, who have recognized the contrary principle." [Principle of Revision of the House of Bishops.]

" If that adopted by the majority of the House of Clerical

and Lay Deputies had been acted on by the Clergy, and by the individual Congregations, on the taking place of the civil Revolution, it would have torn the Church to pieces." Mem. of Ch. pp. 175–178.

Q. Whose words are you reciting?

A. The words of Bishop White in his "Memoirs of the Protestant Episcopal Church."

Q. What does Bishop White say of the Rubric allowing the *omission* of the Article in the Apostles' Creed on the "Descent into Hell," as printed in the Prayer Book of A. D. 1789?

<small>Rubric on allowing Churches to omit the Article on the Descent into Hell.</small>

A. He protests against that Rubric as "not being authorized by the House of Bishops," but "printed by the Committee on Printing of the lower House, *without leave of either House,*" and *unjustifiably.* He gives seven statements, showing the bad consequences of the action of that Committee in "altering the body of the Creed;" and allowing "Churches" to omit this Article. And, moreover, he contends, justly, that the license to omit this Article "does not square with (his) ideas of good faith," by reversing the action of the Convention of A. D. 1786, and by being "contrary to the pledge given to the English Bishops by the Convention of October, A. D. 1786," to restore and use it, as the condition of their consecration of our Bishops. Letter to Bishop Seabury, Philadelphia, December, A. D. 1789. Mem. of Ch. pp. 194–198.

Q. Recite the Resolution of the House of Deputies of A. D. 1789, appointing the Committee on printing the Prayer Book.

A. "Friday, October 16, A. D. 1789. *Resolved,* That Dr. William Smith, Rev. Dr. Magaw, Rev. Dr. Blackwell, Mr. Hopkinson, and Mr. Coxe, be a Committee to superintend the printing of the Book of Common Prayer, as set forth by this Convention, and that they advise with any person or persons who shall be appointed by the House of Bishops for the same purpose."

CONSTITUTION OF THE CHURCH.   177

"A message was received from the House of Bishops" (on the same day) "with the information that the Right Rev. Bishop White consents to advise with the Committee appointed by this House to superintend the printing of the Book of Common Prayer." Jour. Gen. Conv. p. 112.

Q. What was done by Bishop White when he discovered the unauthorized interpolation of that part of the Rubric allowing the *Omission* of the Article in the Apostles' Creed on "the Descent into Hell"?

A. He annexed to the Record "a declaration that his signing of the Morning Prayer is not to be con- <small>Protest of Bishop White.</small> strued as involving an acknowledgment of the consent of the House of Bishops to that matter." Mem. of Ch. p. 197.

He further avers that "a copy for the printer *from the papers prepared by the Convention* would not contain the license to *omit* the Article, but only the amendment, of the House of Bishops, explaining the meaning of the Article: and the Members might truly declare they never meant to give a license to omit it. And, moreover, it would appear in full proof that the (Committee's) amendment was never read to the House." Ibid. p. 193.

Q. How was the Prayer Book compiled?

A. The House of Clerical and Lay Deputies acted on the principle of "preparing" a New Book of <small>Method of Proceeding.</small> Common Prayer, through its Committees of Clergy and Laity as a matter *originating with them*, referring their Acts to the House of Bishops for their concurrence. The House of Bishops (consisting of Bishops Seabury and White) adapted the English Service, as their principle of action, acknowledging the old Forms (except the political parts) as of existing obligation, until altered; yet introducing original matter on various heads, or deriving it from extant and ancient Liturgies. Mem. of Ch. pp. 182, 183, 194, 230. Wilson's Mem. Bp. White, pp. 140, 141.

Each House sent its productions to the other for concurrence or amendment, and finally authorized the Book of Common Prayer as it is now used by the Protestant Episcopal Church in the United States; without any recourse to the Churches in the several States for Ratification.

Q. What is the characteristic of the change, or growth of sentiment, as evinced in this History of the Compilation of the Prayer Book?

A. A growing sense of Ecclesiastical Independence of the Church of England, corresponding with that which obtained in political relationships, yet without trenching on the historic facts of the Continuity of the Church, through the fresh Branch which God had established in the Vine. The same which the Church of England did at the Reformation, the Protestant Episcopal Church in the United States did in the Convention of A. D. 1789, in the "preparing" of a Book of Common Prayer, for public worship, suited to the times and institutions of the land, while adhering to, and maintaining, the purity and integrity of the Catholic Discipline and Doctrine.

<small>Analogy of the Reformation.</small>

Q. What intimation have we that the Church regarded her Polity as completed and fixed in A. D. 1789?

A. "Some Canons had been passed in the preceding Session; but they were reconsidered and passed with sundry others, which continue to this day substantially the same." Mem. of Ch. p. 24.

<small>Articles of Religion.</small> *Q.* Were the Articles of Religion adopted at the Convention of A. D. 1789?

A. No: they were proposed, but postponed. Neither the Articles, nor Offices (as of Ordinations, and Administration of the Sacraments), nor Hymns, are strictly parts of the Book of Common Prayer. They may be set forth, and printed separately. Cons. Article VIII. Jour. Gen. Conv. A. D. 1792.

Q. When were the Articles of Religion established by the General Convention?

A. They were "Established by the Bishops, the Clergy, and Laity of the Protestant Episcopal Church in the United States of America, in Convention, on the twelfth day of September, in the year of our Lord 1801;" as appears in the caption in the Prayer Book." Jour. Gen. Conv. A. D. 1801.

Q. Is there any force in the assertion of some persons, that the Articles of Religion were not "adopted" by the General Convention of A. D. 1801, but only "set forth"?

A. The assertion is contrary to the record. The Articles of Religion were "set forth" and "established," etc., and the certificate of their being "adopted" is as follows: —

"Adopted by the House of Bishops.
  WILLIAM WHITE, D. D., *Presiding Bishop.*
Adopted by the House of Clerical and Lay Deputies.
  ABRAHAM BEACH, D. D., *President.*"
Appendix to Jour. Gen. Conv. of A. D. 1801, p. 279; also, Jour. Gen. Conv. pp. 264, 266, 273, 276.

Q. Are the Articles of the same authority as the Book of Common Prayer?

A. The same (as above indicated), and also are protected against change, by the same Article of the Constitution of the Church. Art. VIII. Cons.

Q. Why was the establishment of the Articles postponed?

A. Because they were previously existing as a "Bond of Union." Moreover, when it was proposed in succeeding sessions to "establish them" by General Convention, there appeared an evident reluctance to commit the Church to the Articles of the Church of England. At last, a Committee of the Convention of A. D. 1799, in the House of Clerical and Lay Deputies, *prepared* and reported a series of heterodox opinions, in the shape of seventeen New Articles. See House Clerical and Lay Dep. Jour. Gen. Conv. A. D. 1799.

The Convention postponed the further consideration of

them, until the next General Convention. The Churches in the Dioceses, meanwhile, elected, for the most part, different Deputies to the next General Convention. On Wednesday, September 9, A. D. 1801, the House of Bishops took the initiative, and adopted and set forth the Articles of Religion as they now stand, after the model of those of the Church of England. The House, unanimously, concurred in adopting them, on Friday, September 11, A. D. 1801.

Q. What account does Bishop White give of the Articles?

A. Bishop White says, that "after repeated discussions and propositions, it had been found that the Doctrines of the Gospel, as they stand in the XXXIX. Articles of the Church of England, with the exception of such matters as are local (and of the Athanasian Creed), were more likely to give general satisfaction, than the same Doctrines in any new shape that might be devised. The former were, therefore, adopted by the two Houses of Convention in A. D. 1801, without their altering of even the obsolete diction in them." Mem. of Ch. p. 28.

Q. When were the other Offices of the Church compiled?

A. The Bishops reviewed the "Ordinal" and proposed a few alterations, which were adopted in the Convention of A. D. 1792. The Convention of A. D. 1795 adopted the "Office for the Consecration of a Church or Chapel," substantially the same with a Service composed by Bishop Andrews in the Reign of James I. The Convention of A. D. 1798 was prevented by the prevalence of yellow fever in Philadelphia, but was summoned in A. D. 1799, when the review of the Articles of Religion was moved. The Convention of A. D. 1801 adopted the Articles, and thus "perpetuated the principles of the Church of England." The Convention of A. D. 1804 framed and ordered to be used the "Office of Induction." The Convention of A. D. 1808 changed "the Office of Induction" to "the Office of Institution," and rested it on recommendation, not on requisition, as before. Thirty Hymns were added. The first pastoral Letter was delivered and published. The Convention of A. D. 1817 appointed a Committee to effect the establishment of the General Theological Seminary. Mem. of Ch. pp. 24–42.

Q. What is the difference between "Induction" and "Institution"?

A. Induction is an Act which instates the Incumbent in full possession of the Temporalities of his Cure. It is purely of a temporal nature, and is cognizable only in the temporal Courts. In the Canon Law, Induction is styled "Corporal possession."

Institution is the Act of the Bishop or Ordinary, or some one deputed by him, admitting the Clerk, as Rector of the Parish, to have there the Cure of souls. Institution is, therefore, purely an Ecclesiastical and Spiritual investiture, and is exclusive against all persons, save the King. Title BENEFICE: Gibson's Codex, pp. 804–815. Burns' Ecc. Law, vol. i. pp. 167–176. Degge's Parson's Counsellor, part i. ch. 2.

After Institution, the incumbent is formally Inducted to the Benefice by the Archdeacon, or such other person as the Bishop may appoint: or by the Dean and Chapter, but not by the Patron. The ceremony of Induction is performed by the delivery of the ring of the Church door, or the latch of the Church gate: or by the delivery of the bell-rope to the new-instituted Clergyman, who tolls the bell as notice to the parishioners and others.

Q. Why was the title "Induction" changed by General Convention in A. D. 1808 to "Institution"?

A. Because the Clergy usually receive no Benefice, but chiefly spiritual Cure and Jurisdiction. While Institution is evidently the more appropriate title, yet our Office combines both ideas.

Q. What ought our emotions to be in view of this History?

A. Devout thanksgiving to the HOLY GHOST, the LORD and GIVER of Life, the Inspirer of all Truth, from whom all holy desires and all good works do proceed, that our Fathers were enabled to establish a Book of Common Prayer, and Offices, and Articles of Religion, in which the Faith and Worship and Discipline of God is set forth and fixed, as it was first delivered to the Saints, whole and undefiled.

<small>Use of the Book of Common Prayer.</small> *Q.* How does this Article VIII. distinguish the Book of Common Prayer?

A. It distinguishes the BOOK OF COMMON PRAYER from the Offices of "Administration of Sacraments, and other Rites and Ceremonies of the Church, Articles of Religion, and the Form and Manner of making, Ordaining, and Consecrating Bishops, Priests, and Deacons."

Q. May the Offices be printed in a separate Book?

A. Yes. The Ordinal was ordered to be printed in a separate book by the General Convention of A. D. 1792, as appears from the Journal, pp. 157, 165. The other Offices, and the Articles of Religion, may be included, being distinct from the Prayer Book.

Q. What is the authority for the use of the Book of Common Prayer, the Offices, and the Articles of Religion?

A. The Supreme authority of the General Convention.

Q. To what extent is the use of the Book of Common Prayer, and the Offices enjoined?

A. In " the Protestant Episcopal Church in those Dioceses which shall have adopted this Constitution " (Art. VIII.), and in all other Dioceses which shall have acceded to it.

Q. What is the obligation due from Clergy and Laity to the Articles of Religion?

A. The obligation of the Clergy to accept, *ex animo*, the

Doctrines of the Protestant Episcopal Church, as set forth in the Articles of Religion, is subscribed by them, virtually, in the "Declaration" required of every person prior to his Ordination. Jour. Gen. Conv. A. D. 1804, p. 301. And, over and above this "Declaration," the Articles of Religion are a part of the Constitution of the Protestant Episcopal Church, which every Layman, as well as every Clergyman, is bound to obey, *in foro conscientiæ*.

Q. What is the advantage of the Common Prayer Book, Offices, and Articles of Religion?

A. One uniform Worship, Faith, and Discipline, whereby "the unity of the Spirit" in the bond of peace, is witnessed and maintained, in fellowship with the Catholic Church.

Q. How are Alterations and Amendments made? <small>Alterations and Amendments of the Book of Common Prayer.</small>

A. Alterations and amendments "must be proposed in one General Convention, and by a resolve thereof made known to the Convention of every Diocese, and adopted at the subsequent General Convention." Art. VIII. Cons.

Q. Why are proposed alterations "made known" to the Conventions of every Diocese?

A. In order that no hasty change may be made without the knowledge of the Church in every Diocese; and that the Church in every Diocese may send Deputies to express their views of a proposed alteration in the subsequent General Convention where the alteration is to be "adopted." Wilson's Mem. Bp. White, pp. 134, 136.

Q. Are the Deputies bound by their Instructions?

A. The better opinion is that they are not bound, and that it would be unwise to trammel their free and independent judgment, whereby they may "profit by the light of other minds." Hoff. L. C. p. 178. Hawks' Cons. & Can. p. 45.

Q. How is the Alteration to be made in the Book of Common Prayer, and the Offices, and the Articles?

184   MANUAL COMMENTARY.

A. By Vote in the House of Clerical and Lay Deputies, with the concurrence of the House of Bishops. The Vote in the House of Deputies must be taken by Dioceses and Orders.

Q. Does this Article of the Constitution specify the necessity of voting by Dioceses and Orders?

A. No. But the alteration of the Prayer Book, etc., being an alteration of the Constitution, the rule obtains of a Vote by Dioceses and Orders, according to Article IX., which requires a Vote of the "majority of the Dioceses." Art. IX. Cons.

Q. What do approved Commentators say on this point?

A. (1) Dr. Hawks says, " That in all questions of Constitutional or Liturgic changes, the Vote in the House of Clerical and Lay Deputies *must* be taken by Dioceses." Hawks' Cons. & Can. p. 51.

(2) Judge Hoffman says, "The Dioceses act in General Convention through their delegates:" "there must be a majority of the Dioceses in union to effect a change in the Constitution." Hoff. L. C. p. 175.

ARTICLE 9. "This Constitution shall be unalterable, unless in General Convention, by the Church, in a majority of the Dioceses which may have adopted the same; and all alterations shall be first proposed in one General Convention, and made known to the several Diocesan Conventions, before they shall be finally agreed to, or ratified, in the ensuing General Convention."

<small>Alterations of this Constitution.</small>

ALTERATIONS OF THE CONSTITUTION.

Q. Where shall the Constitution be altered?

A. "In General Convention;" or, as Article VIII. expresses it, "*at* the General Convention." Hoff. L. C. pp. 172, *et seq.*

Q. By whom may the Constitution be altered?

A. "By the Church, in a majority of the Dioceses which may have adopted the same."

Q. How must the Voice of the Church in the Dioceses be expressed?

A. By a Vote in General Convention, by "Dioceses and Orders." Hoff. L. C. p. 175. Hawks' Cons. & Can. p. 51.

Q. What constitutes a majority of the Dioceses in General Convention?

A. A majority of the Clerical or a majority of the Lay Deputies, in their respective Orders, representing the Dioceses, — being, at least, one Clerical and one Lay Deputy from a Diocese (Art. II.), — and a number of the other Order (at least three) sufficient to make a majority on a division. Judge Hoffman states the Rule for a majority of Dioceses and Orders, as "a Representation in one Order of a majority of the Dioceses in union; and a Representation in the other Order of three or more Dioceses." Hoff. L. C. p. 151.

Q. Where must the Alteration be proposed?

A. "In the General Convention."

Q. Where, and by whom, must the Alteration be "finally agreed to or ratified?"

A. "In the ensuing General Convention, and by a majority of the Dioceses, voting by Dioceses and Orders.

Q. What is directed to be done with the proposed Alteration, in the *interim* between the two Conventions?

A. The proposed Alteration is to be "made known to the several Diocesan Conventions."

Q. For what purpose is the proposed Amendment "made known?"

A. The purpose is to acquaint the "Church in each Diocese" with the proposed Alteration, that they may not be taken by surprise, and may take action on the subject, if they see fit.

Q. What action in the premises may the Church in a Diocese take?

A. They may elect Deputies, with instructions or not, as they see fit; or they may acquiesce in silence.

Q. If a majority of Diocesan Conventions should oppose a proposed amendment, what then?

A. The General Convention ought to give due weight to their objections, but be not otherwise influenced by them. The Diocesan Conventions had no voice in the Making of the Constitution, and can have no voice in the Altering of it,— which is tantamount to making a new Article.

Q. What is the testimony of Bishop White?

A. Bishop White says that the Constitution was not submitted to the States for Ratification. Wilson's Mem. Bp. White, p. 136.

And, furthermore, that "the system of taking measures in General Convention to be reviewed and authoritatively judged of in the bodies of which they were Deputies, proved to be futile, and was so fruitful of discord and disunion that it was abandoned from that time" of the General Convention of A. D. 1786. Mem. of Ch. p. 123.

Q. What does Dr. Wilson, in his "Memoirs of Bishop White," say of the purpose of the clause of this Article, requiring the proposed alteration to be "made known" to the Diocesan Conventions?

A. He says the purpose was "to give stability to the Constitution by *preventing hasty changes*." Wilson's Mem. Bp. White, p. 136.

ARTICLE 10. "Bishops for Foreign Countries, on due application therefrom, may be consecrated, with the approbation of the Bishops of this Church, or a majority of them, signified to the Presiding Bishop; he thereupon taking order for the same, and they

Consecration of Bishops for Foreign Countries.

being satisfied that the person designated for the Office has been duly chosen, and properly qualified: the Order of Consecration to be conformed, as nearly as may be, in the judgment of the Bishops, to the one used in this Church. Such Bishops, so consecrated, shall not be eligible to the office of Diocesan, or Assistant Bishop, in any Diocese in the United States, nor be entitled to a seat in the House of Bishops, nor exercise any Episcopal authority in said States." *Restrictions on Jurisdiction, Authority, and Privilege.*

BISHOPS FOR FOREIGN COUNTRIES.

Q. What was the occasion and necessity of the consecration of Foreign Missionary Bishops? *Consecration of Bishops for Foreign Countries.*

A. The General Convention of 1835, announced the truth that "every member of the Church, by virtue of his Baptism, was pledged to be a Missionary of the Gospel in the Church." Missions in China and in Africa were established, soon after, by Presbyters and Deacons, and Lay Assistants of both sexes. A Bishop was applied for from those countries; who, however, could not be Consecrated under the extant Forms. Hence the occasion and necessity of the Constitutional provision in this Article X. which was finally agreed to and ratified in the General Convention of A. D. 1844.

Q. What are the Constitutional restrictions on the Jurisdiction of a Foreign Missionary Bishop? *Restrictions of Episcopal Jurisdiction, Authority, and Privilege.*

A. He " shall not be eligible to the office of Diocesan, or Assistant Bishop, in any Diocese in the United States."

Q. What are the Constitutional restrictions on the Episcopal Privilege and Authority of a Foreign Missionary Bishop?

A. He shall "not be entitled to a seat in the House of Bishops, nor exercise any Episcopal authority in the United States."

Q. What reasons may be assigned for these restrictions on the Foreign Missionary Bishop?

A. No good reasons are obvious. (1) If the Foreign Missionary Bishop be regarded as amenable to the Constitution and Canons of this Church, like any other Bishop, he ought to be on the same footing as the other Bishops of this Church in matters of Episcopal Privilege. Equity and the principle of the Equality of Bishops, demand this identity of responsibility and identity of correlative privilege.

(2) The Clergy and Laity of a Diocese "destitute of a Bishop," are debarred from the right to choose for their Diocesan a *Foreign* Missionary Bishop, because he is prohibited from the exercise of any Episcopal Authority in the United States, while no such restraint exists on their election of any *Domestic* Missionary Bishop. But since the Church is One Church, whether she extend her offices and ministries to Territories and people, living either within or beyond the boundaries of the United States, her Domestic and Foreign Missionary Bishops ought to be considered as on the same footing, and entitled to equal eligibility to Authority; otherwise the principle of the Unity of the Episcopate is violated in unjust discrimination between her Missionary Bishops; besides a violation of the liberties of her Clergy and People.

(3) The privileges of all the Bishops are, likewise, unreasonably restricted by the provision, that the Foreign Missionary Bishop shall "not exercise any Episcopal Authority in the United States;" because the Bishops of the Protestant Episcopal Church in the United States may not invite a Foreign Missionary Bishop, as they do other Bishops, to supply their lack of service in an emergency.

(4) The Foreign Missionary Bishop, during his vacation in this country, and during the Session of the Gen-

eral Convention of the Church, being forbidden "a Seat in the House of Bishops," is a spectacle mortifying to the Bishop, and painful to the Members of the Church: — the spectacle of a vagrant Bishop, in his own country and in his own Church, without official recognition, and, seemingly, without a home or friends, while his Peers are in Council with closed doors. There is, perhaps, reason in denying a vote on Domestic matters to the Foreign Missionary Bishop; but none in shutting the doors against him, by denying him "a *Seat* in the House of Bishops."

Q. Have these Considerations prevailed in the General Convention, in favor of the Equal Episcopal rights of Foreign Missionary Bishops?

A. Imperfectly. The General Convention of A. D. 1865 enacted by Canon, that the Foreign Missionary Bishop "shall be entitled to a seat in the House of Bishops, but shall not become a Diocesan Bishop in any organized Diocese within the United States, unless with the consent of three fourths of all the Bishops entitled to seats in the House of Bishops, and also of three fourths of the Clerical and Lay Deputies present at the Session of the General Convention, or, in the recess of the General Convention, with the consent of the Standing Committees of three fourths of the Dioceses." [2.] § VIII. Canon 13, Title I. Dig.

Q. Is this Canon Constitutional in this respect?

A. No. It is contrary to the positive restrictions of Article X. of the Constitution.

Q. Does this Article X. need amendment?

A. It does need amendment, to restore the Episcopal College to its primitive and continuous Equality of Office. As St. Cyprian testifies, on the Unity of the Church (vol. i. p. 380, Edin. ed.), "Assuredly the rest of the Apostles were also the same as Peter, endowed with a like partnership, both of Honor and Power."

"EPISCOPATUS UNUS EST: CUJUS A SINGULIS IN SOLIDUM PARS TENETUR."

ADDENDUM

TO THE

COMMENTARY ON THE CONSTITUTION.

THE following Official Certificate of the Rev. Dr. Perry, Historiographer of the Church, and Secretary of the House of Clerical and Lay Deputies, concludes the question of the Original text of Article II. of the Constitution.

This certificate should have appeared in connection with that of Judge Bell (p. 99), but was not received until the plates of that portion of the Commentary were ready for the press. It is therefore given in this place : —

EXTRACT FROM THE ORIGINAL CONSTITUTION OF THE PROTESTANT EPISCOPAL CHURCH IN THE UNITED STATES OF AMERICA, ADOPTED THE 2D DAY OF OCTOBER, A. D. 1789:

"ARTICLE 2. The Church in each State shall be entitled to a representation of both the Clergy and the Laity, which representation shall consist of one or more Deputies, not exceeding four of each Order, chosen by the Convention of the State; and in all questions, when required by the Clerical or Lay representation from any State, each Order shall have one vote."

GENEVA, N. Y., *March* 29, 1870.

I hereby certify that the above paragraph copied from Hawks & Perry's reprint of the Journals of the General Convention, vol. i. page 99, and in particular the words " Clerical *or* Lay " in line 5th of Art. 2 of The Constitution, are correctly printed from the reprint of the Journals of the General Convention issued in 1817 by John Bioren of Philadelphia, and edited by Bishop White under the authority of the said General Convention, as appears from a comparison with a copy of the said Edition of 1817 deposited among the files of the General Convention by the said Bishop White, and bearing his name: and that both Reprints, as far as the aforesaid paragraph and words are concerned, are a correct and exact copy of the Original Journal of the said Convention as published in Philadelphia in 1790 (*vide* page

9, line 5th, of 2d paragraph), both having been by me this day compared with a copy of said Original Journal as contained in a volume belonging to the General Convention, and bearing the following autograph certification, namely : —

"This volume is ye only entire collection within my knowledge of
"ye original Journals of the General Convention from the Beginning,
"for the space of thirty years. It may be of use in determining on
"any questions which may arise concerning any particular of the
"Republication of the Journals by John Bioren. Accordingly I de-
"posit it with ye committee appointed by ye last General Convention,
"for ye collection of Journals."

(Signed)   " W^M. WHITE."

And I further certify that the original of the above certification is in the handwriting of Bishop William White.

Witness my hand this Twenty-ninth day of March, in the year of Our Lord one thousand eight hundred and seventy.

WILLIAM STEVENS PERRY,
Secretary H. C. & L. Deputies General Convention.

INDEX OF QUESTIONS

IN THE MANUAL COMMENTARY.

                                                                           PAGE

Question. What are the Grand Divisions of the Law of the Church in the United States 1

PART I. — THE COMMON LAW OF THE PROTESTANT EPISCOPAL CHURCH IN THE UNITED STATES.

Extent of Authority of English Canon Law. — Limitations.

What is the relation of the Church of England and the Protestant Episcopal Church in the United States 2

What is the Extent of Authority of the Ecclesiastical Law of England in the United States 2

What are the Restraints on the Canon Law of England in this country 2

IDENTITY OF THE CHURCH OF ENGLAND IN THE COLONIES.

Acts of Colonial Governments.

What Acts of Legislation demonstrate the Identity of the Church of England and the Protestant Episcopal Church . 2

By whom was the Church of England established in this country 4

Did the Government of England prescribe the Establishment . 4

Did Parliament 4

Did the King 4

What authority had the King in the premises 4

What power in England could establish the Church . . . 4

What was the Supreme Authority in the Saxon Church . . 4

How did the Royal Governors in the Colonies justify their acts — for example, not to prefer any to Ecclesiastical Benefices, except persons lawfully ordained 5

What effect on Colonial Society did the Governors' recognition of the King's sole prerogative produce 5

INDEX OF QUESTIONS.

What apology for the Royal Governors may be offered	5
What was the spirit of the age	5
Mention an Act of Intolerance of the Virginia Legislature in A. D. 1642	5
Mention Contemporaneous Legislation in Massachusetts	5
Did the Church of England in the Colonies owe its existence and support to the Government of England	5
What notable example of earnest and successful rebuke of the indifference of Parliament occurred about this time	5
Was the money paid	6
What else characterized the age	6
To whom, under God, is the Church indebted, in this country, for existence, for support, and for the spread of sound doctrines and the Catholic faith	6
What, briefly, will you say of this venerable Society	6
Who was the "Ordinary" or Bishop of the Church in the Colonies	6
Whence did he derive his authority	6
How did the Bishop of London exercise a personal oversight	6
Name the Commissaries of the Bishop of London in the Colonies	6
Did the Colonial Church apply for Commissaries	7
What attempt by a Colonial Legislature was made against the rights of the Clergy and the prerogative of the Bishop of London	7
Was this Act of the Legislature resisted	7
How was the outrage remedied	7
What other instances of attempts to bring Clergymen of the Church under Lay jurisdiction	7
What course was pursued in conformity with Ecclesiastical Law	7
What Ecclesiastical Law of England ruled the case	7
What Acts further confirmed the exclusive jurisdiction of the Bishop of London	8
What was the effect, finally, of these struggles	8
What do these acts of the Colonies demonstrate in a general way	8
What custom of the Clergy, in Connecticut *specially*, exhibits the Identity of the Church of England and the Church in the Colonies	8
In what particulars do these historical facts indicate the Identity of the Church of England and the Episcopal Church in the Colonies	9
Was the Ecclesiastical Law of England in any way modified	9

INDEX OF QUESTIONS. 195

How did this Common Law of the Protestant Episcopal Church in the United States develop itself 9
Was there any violent disruption at the Revolution, between the Church of England and the Episcopal Church in the United States 9

IDENTITY OF THE CHURCH OF ENGLAND IN THE UNITED STATES.

Summary of Proofs of Identity of Protestant Episcopal Church and the Church of England. — Particulars of Identity of the Church of England with the Protestant Episcopal Church. — Opposing Views. — Refutation of Opposing Views.

What were some of the Acts of the Church in the United States evincing its Identity with the Church of England . . . 9
    1. Acts of the States.
    2. Acts of the Protestant Episcopal Church in General Convention.
    3. Acts of the Protestant Episcopal Church in General Convention, with the acquiescence of the whole Church.
What were the Acts of the States 9
What were the Acts of the Protestant Episcopal Church in General Convention 12
What are the Acts of the Protestant Episcopal Church in General Convention, with the acquiescence of the whole Church . 13
What do these acts prove beyond contradiction 14
What is the summary of the proofs that the Protestant Episcopal Church in the United States is Identical with the Church of England : and as such, is a living and independent branch of the Church Catholic, and subject to the Catholic Law of the Church and to the Ecclesiastical Law of England, so far as those laws are applicable, and not superseded by Special Canon Law of the Protestant Episcopal Church in the United States 14
In what does the Identity of the Church of England with the Protestant Episcopal Church consist 14
What opposing view of the relation of the Church of England with the Protestant Episcopal Church in the United States has been entertained and debated 15
What distinguished body set forth this opponent view . . 15
Where will you find a full account of those discussions . . 15
What does Bishop White say of these opponent opinions expressed in the lower House in A. D. 1789 15
Did the opinion of the House of Clerical and Lay Deputies of A. D. 1789 prevail 16

196   INDEX OF QUESTIONS.

What would such opinions, if prevailing, reduce the Church to . 16
What just dignity do the prevailing sentiments of the Protestant
   Episcopal Church, in regard to her continuous relations with
   the Mother or Sister Church of England, exhibit . . . 16
State some of the Dicta of received and learned commentators
   on the question 16

IDENTITY OF THE PROTESTANT EPISCOPAL CHURCH WITH
THE PRIMITIVE CATHOLIC CHURCH.

Amenability. of the Protestant Episcopal Church to the General Canon Law of the Catholic Code.—Authorities who decide Mooted Questions.— Further Restraints on Private Judgment.— Definition of Discipline.

What is the relation of the Protestant Episcopal Church to the
   General Canon Law 18
What do the Homilies teach on this question 18
Will you mention a recognition of the "Ancient Canons" as
   being cognate with Holy Scripture and as authority in this
   Church 18
Do these Ancient Canons form part of the Catholic Code . . 19
What practice of this Church in the Consecration of Bishops
   follows the injunctions of the Catholic Code 19
Recite the first of the Apostolic Canons 19
What practice of this Church, in other ordinations, is enjoined
   by Canon in conformity with the Catholic Code . . . 19
Where is this practice of Ember Weeks enjoined in the Primitive
   Church 19
Does our Church, in recognizing Ancient Law and the Ecclesiastical Law of England, follow the example of the English
   Church in yielding obedience to the Catholic Code or Body of
   the Canon Law, and also to the Foreign Canon Law . . 19
What is the Analogy precisely 20
Is every member of the Church bound to obey the Canons of the
   Catholic Code, and of the English Church, with the restraints
   abovenamed 20
May any member of the Church, on his own motion, decide what
   is the Common Law or custom of the Church 20
Quote authority for the restraint on private action . . . 20
Who or what are the authorities that may decide on the Law
   of the Church in England, and of the Protestant Episcopal
   Church in the United States 20
What other restraint on individual and private judgment, in
   respect of doctrine or practice in the Church, may you name . 21
Will you illustrate by some examples of the just restraint on

private judgment and action in respect of doctrine and practice 22
What further statement, in the Preface to the Book of Common Prayer, confirms the declaration "that this Church was far from intending to depart from the Church of England in any essential point of doctrine, discipline, or worship, or further than local circumstances require" 22
What is the sense of the term "discipline" in Ecclesiastical writings 23
In which sense is the word "discipline" here used . . . 23
Will you give examples of this use of the word . . . 23
What is the argument, hence derived, that our Church retained the same Ecclesiastical Laws after the Revolution which it possessed before the Revolution, except when local circumstances required a change 23

CANON LAW OF THE CHURCH OF ENGLAND.

Periods of the Canon Law of the Church in England. — British Church Period. — Anglican Church Period. — Norman Period. — Legatine Constitutions. — Provincial Constitutions. — Common Law of the Church, and where it may be best learned. — Foreign and Domestic Laws of the Church of England. — The False Decretals. — Reformation Period of the Church of England.

How many periods are there of the Canon Law of the Church of England 23
What are their respective dates 24
What was the origin of the Laws of the *British* Church . . 24
What are the earliest records of the Church in Great Britain . 24
How were the Ancient Laws of the British Church to be changed 24
What were the sources of Ecclesiastical Law in the *Anglican Period* 24
How were these "Laws" which affected the Laity and Clergy made 25
How were the "Institutions," or Monumenta Ecclesiastica, enacted 25
What do you learn from these Laws and Institutions respecting the British and Anglican Church 25
Give me an example of the force of this Ancient Law in modern times 25
Were these Synods or Gemotes (as they were called) frequently held by the Bishops and Clergy 25
What are the sources of Common Law in England in the third, or *Norman Period*, — middle of the Eleventh Century to Reformation 26

What are the Legatine Constitutions 26
What are the *Provincial* Constitutions 26
What are the Legatine and Provincial Constitutions styled . 26
Where may best be learned this Common Law 26
What higher recognition of these laws and rules now prevails . 27
How is the English Canon Law divided 27
What is the Foreign Canon Law 27
How do you prove that these "Decretals" are false . . . 28
Were these False Decretals received in England . . . 29
How did the Reformers treat this new Law of Rome . . . 29
What are Domestic Canons in the Church of England . . 29
What do you mean by Ecclesiastical Authority 29
What are the sources of English Ecclesiastical Law in the fourth,
  or *Reformation Period* 29
What Canons have been authorized by Convocation . . . 30
What Statute Law is considered as part of the Ecclesiastical
  Law of England 30
Are the Rubrics in the Liturgy a part of the Statute Law . . 30
Are the XXXIX. Articles of Religion a part of the Statute Law 30
What other sources of Ecclesiastical Law are to be regarded . 30
Was this body of English Canon Law the Ecclesiastical Law of
  the Church in the Colonies, at the date of the Royal Charters 31

ERA OF THE FOUNDING OF THE CHURCH OF ENGLAND IN
AMERICA.

*Ecclesiastical Law of England in the Colonies. — Ecclesiastical Law of the Church of
England in the States. — Summary of Extant Ecclesiastical Laws. — Effect of the
American Revolution on the Constitution and Canons of the Protestant Episcopal Church.*

What is the date of the first Church erected on this Continent . 31
Were all the Ecclesiastical Laws, which we have enumerated, in
  full force in England at the time of the settlement of the
  American Colonies 31
What exceptions and modifications in the English Canon Law
  did our Colonial condition superinduce 32
Will you sum up the several ingredients of the English Ecclesi-
  astical Law as it obtained when the Church was planted in this
  country 32
Did this constitute the Body of the Law of the Church in the
  Colonies 33
What change did the American REVOLUTION bring with it . 33
What Law prevails in cases not provided for as above . . 33

APPENDIX I. — SPIRITUAL COURTS AND PROCEEDINGS IN THE CHURCH OF ENGLAND.

What are the Spiritual Courts in the Church of England . . 34
(1) What is the Archdeacon's Court 34
(2) What is the Consistory Court 34
(3) What is the Court of Peculiars 34
(4) What are the Prerogative Courts 35
(5) What is the Court of Arches, Curia de Arcubus . . . 35
(6) What is the Court of the King in Chancery . . . 36
(7) What is the Court of the Judicial Committee of Privy Council 36

APPENDIX II. — THE MANNER OF ELECTING AND CONSECRATING ARCHBISHOPS AND BISHOPS IN THE CHURCH OF ENGLAND.

What is the manner of Electing and Consecrating Archbishops and Bishops in the Church of England 37
    1. Notice of Demise of Bishop.
    2. Writ of Congè d'Elire, or Letter Missive from the Crown.
    3. Election by Chapter.
    4. Confirmation of Election by the Judges.
    5. Translation.
    6. Consecration of the Bishop.
    7. Writ of Commendam.
    8. Bishop's Suit for Temporalities.
    9. Inthronement of Bishop.
What is the origin of the fable of the Nag's Head Consecration 38
What if the Dean and Chapter refuse to elect, or the Archbishop to confirm and consecrate, the nominee of the Crown . 39
    1. Penalty of Præmunire.
    2. Præmunire.
How does the practice of the American Church compare with that of the Church of England 40
    1. Contrast of British Church Liberties.
    2. Royal Supremacy.
    3. Surrender of Liberties of the Church by the Clergy.
    4. Relation of the Church in the United States to Civil Authority.

PART II. — THE CONSTITUTION OF THE PROTESTANT EPISCOPAL CHURCH IN THE UNITED STATES.

I. PRELIMINARY HISTORY.

When did the Church in this country become Independent of the Government of the Church of England 43
Who was the Bishop of the Church in the Colonies . . . 43
What authority declares that the Jurisdiction of the Bishop of London ceased on the Fourth of July, A. D. 1776 . . . 43
What alterations in the Liturgy were made necessary by the Revolution 43
What political condition was assumed by the Colonies after the Declaration of Independence 43
What was the Ecclesiastical condition of the Church in the several States 43
How did the Church "in the first place" proceed to make the "necessary alterations" in the Liturgy 44
Give examples 44
Were these examples followed 44
How was the Independence of the Church in each State illustrated in Connecticut 44
In how many States did the Episcopal Church exist, at the date of the Declaration of Independence 45
What was the relation of the Congregations to each other during the War 45
What was peculiar to Connecticut 45
What was done, after the War, in other States, for the organization of the Church 45
State the *fundamental principles* which the meeting in Philadelphia proposed as the basis of the Union of the Churches . 46
What seems to characterize these "fundamental principles" . 47
Which Articles affirm the Independence of the Church . . 47
Which express the desire and purpose of Union . . . 47
Which evince jealousy of Episcopal and Priestly authority . 47
What sentiment in the Church does the Sixth fundamental Article further evince 47
Repeat the Sixth Article 47
Was there any apprehensiveness that Episcopalians of that era were disaffected towards Episcopacy 47
What confirmation of this suspicion is extant 48
What political circumstances at that time prompted, or at least favored, the proposed introduction of this Sixth "fundamental principle" in the Constitution of the Church 48

Did the Confederation of the States endure 48
What was the complexion of the hindrances to Union, as revealed in the objections of the Northeastern States . . 49
What further objections proceeded from Connecticut . . . 49
What other hindrances from New Jersey 50
Was this Sixth "fundamental principle," in regard to the restricting of the powers of the General Convention to those functions which cannot be exercised by the congregations, favored by the Churches, after a second thought . . . 50
State the character and annals of "*this first general meeting*" of Churchmen 50
What were these "Fundamental Articles". 50
What States were represented by their Clerical Deputies at this meeting in New York, October, A. D. 1784 51
Why was not Virginia duly represented 51
What effect followed the publication of these Fundamental Articles, in respect to the organization of the Church in the States 51
What principles seem to characterize these Fundamental Articles 52
Does not the analysis of these Fundamental Articles of the assembled Clergy in October, A. D. 1784, seem to depress the Episcopacy overmuch, and exalt the power of the Laity . 52
State the grounds of this opinion 53
What justification may be alleged for this departure from the pattern of Primitive and Ancient Ecclesiastical Councils . 56
What does Dr. Hawks say on the subject 56
What evil in *principle* was patent 56
State what followed the adoption of the Fundamental Articles by the Voluntary Meeting in New York in A. D. 1784 . . 57
What Churches were represented 57
What was the character and authority of this proposed Constitution of the Church 57
What followed next 58
Did the Constitution of A. D. 1786 become the fundamental law of the whole Church 58
How was the next General Convention summoned . . . 58
When did the next General Convention convene . . . 58
What was done at this Convention of A. D. 1789 . . . 58
What was done to engage the Churches in the Northeastern States 59
What were the several Dioceses *allowed* to retain under the Constitution of A. D. 1786 59
In what were the several Dioceses *prohibited*; or, as Dr. Hawks states the proposition, "What did they surrender?" . . 60

What further right of the State (or Diocesan) Conventions does Bishop White affirm was "surrendered" and abandoned in A. D. 1789 61

II. THE POWERS AND AUTHORITY OF THE GENERAL CONVENTION.

Argument from Historical Facts. — Adverse Arguments. — Confirmatory Argument. — Recapitulation. — Argument from the Canons.

State the facts to prove the Supremacy of the Convention of the Protestant Episcopal Church in the United States . . . 62
Was there required any *subsequent* ratification of the General Constitution by the State Conventions before it should become "the Fundamental Law of the Protestant Episcopal Church in the United States" 63
Did the State Conventions take action on the subject . . 63
What are the just inferences from these various actions of the State Conventions 64
Was it within the powers of the original State Conventions to claim authority to ratify the Constitution before it should have force, or to refuse their consent to the action of their Deputies in the premises 64
Is this question historically mooted 65
What was the authority of the Constitution (as amended in General Convention, October, A. D. 1789) in those States which had not sent Deputies, or which had not "empowered" them to "confirm and ratify a General Constitution" . . . 65
What further argument may be adduced to prove the Supremacy of the General Convention in respect of Amendments to the Constitution 66
Let us examine this point more particularly. Recite the words of the Eleventh Article of the Constitution as proposed to the State Conventions in A. D. 1785 67
Recite the Eleventh Article of the Constitution, as proposed to the State Conventions in A. D. 1786 67
Where is "the Church" affirmed to be, for the purpose of Ratification 67
Recite the Ninth Article of the Constitution, as passed in General Convention, October, A. D. 1789; being the same as now existing (except the word "States," changed into Dioceses in A. D. 1838) 67
By whom may the Constitution be altered 68
Where must the action of the Church, by such majority, be expressed 68

INDEX OF QUESTIONS.

Where must alterations be proposed	68
Where must *proposed* alterations be finally agreed to, or ratified	68
What must be done with the proposed alterations in the Interim	68
For what purpose	68
State the views and testimony of Bishop White on this point	68
If a majority of the Dioceses, in their respective Conventions, dissent from the proposed alterations, should the General Convention alter the Constitution against such expression of dissent	69
How are the votes of the States (Dioceses) on Amendments to the Constitution, expressed in General Convention	69
What adverse inference has been drawn by Dr. Hawks from the language of Article IX. of the Constitution, as to the relation of the Conventions of the Dioceses to the General Convention	70
What answer to the hypothesis on which this conclusion is postulated, does the History of the Constitution of A. D. 1789 furnish	70
What further argument does Dr. Hawks urge against the Supremacy of the General Convention	71
What answer does Article VIII. of the Constitution, providing for the Amendment of the Book of Common Prayer, furnish to this interpretation and argument of Dr. Hawks	72
What further argument for "diocesan independence" does Dr. Hawks allege	73
What answer is made to this argument	74
What is the upshot and practical conclusion which Dr. Hawks infers from his hypothesis of "diocesan independency"	74
What have you to say to this twofold conclusion of the argument against the Supremacy of the General Convention	74
State what has been the practice, or the precedent, in the mode of altering the Constitution	75
What does this historical enumeration of the amendments exhibit	76
Will you again quote Bishop White on the question of the Supreme Authority of the General Convention under the Constitution of the Church	77
Recapitulate the facts which demonstrate the paramount authority of the General Convention	78
What further confirmation of the Supremacy of the General Convention, may you derive from the enactment of Canons by the General Convention of A. D. 1789	79

III. THE CONSTITUTION OF THE CHURCH.
ARTICLE I.
Origin. — Change of Time and Place of Meeting. — Special Conventions. — Presiding Bishop. — Quorum. — Freedom of Debate.

State, in brief, the origin of this Article	81
Who prescribes the place of meeting of the Triennial Conventions	82
Name the amendments in reference to the time and place of meeting of the General Convention	82
By whom may the place of meeting of the General Convention be changed, when good cause renders it necessary	82
How are Special Meetings of the General Convention regulated	83
Recite the terms of the Canon which regulates the right of calling "*Special* General Conventions"	83
Where shall Special Conventions be held	83
What Deputies shall compose a Special General Convention	83
Who is "the Presiding Bishop" mentioned in this Article I. of the Constitution	84
State what the Rules of the House of Bishops have been, in reference to the Presiding Bishop	84
Has the title of "Presiding Bishop" invested him with *superior rank or authority*	87
Is there any Rule of the House of Bishops fixing and establishing the priority of right to preside	87
What is the Law of the Church in England in respect of dignity and rank	87
What is the Law of the Church in Scotland	87
What constitutes a Quorum	88
What is the language in this Article I. of the Constitution	88
What constitutes a representation of a Diocese in order to proceed to business	88
What constitutes a representation of a *Majority* of the Dioceses, in order to proceed to business	88
Is a Diocese duly represented for the purpose of a Quorum, if only the Clerical Deputies are present; or if only the Lay Deputies are present	89
What then is "a majority of the Dioceses" represented, in order to proceed to business	89
What is meant by Freedom of Debate	89
Specify the authoritative restraints of Rules of Order on the Freedom of Debate	89

Does "Freedom of Debate" include a right to discuss a motion
to enter a Protest in the Journal 90
How long since has it been a settled Rule to deny a claim to
enter a Protest in the Journal 90

ARTICLE II.— HOUSE OF CLERICAL AND LAY DEPUTIES.

Qualifications of Deputies.— Vote by Dioceses and Orders.— Lay Communicants.— Ecclesiastical Residence.— Clerical Residence.— Residence of Laymen.— Manner of choosing Deputies.— Vote by Dioceses and Orders for a Majority.— Dioceses Unrepresented.

How are the Deputies to the General Convention chosen . . 92
May a Diocesan Convention, by Canon or otherwise, delegate the
right and power of choosing Deputies *prospectively*, either to
the Bishop, or a Committee, or any other person or persons . 92
What is the just construction of this provision of the Constitution 92
May a Diocesan Convention delegate to the Bishop, or other
person or persons, the power to fill a vacancy 92
Would a Canon of a Diocese delegating the power and duty of
choice, entirely and prospectively, be valid 93
What is a Vacancy 93
Whom does the House of Clerical and Lay Deputies represent . 93
Does it represent the Diocesan Conventions 93
Who are "the Church in each Diocese" 93
What is the relation between the Diocesan Conventions and the
General Convention 94
Is the Constituency of the General Convention and the Constituency of the Diocesan Conventions, one and the same . . 94
Who are "the Church in each Diocese," represented in General
Convention 94
What are the Qualifications of the Deputies to General Convention 95
What is the origin of the admission of Laymen into the Councils of this Church 95
Is there an earlier origin claimed in this country for the plan of
admitting the Laity into the Councils of the Church . . 95
Does the Coördinate Authority of the Clergy and of the Laity
in General Convention confer on each Order the right to join
in making laws to regulate the other Order 96
Does this provision of Concurrent Majorities of the two Orders
confer unusual Ecclesiastical powers on the Laity . . . 96
Is the voice of the Laity, in making Canons for the Government
of the Clergy, a departure from the primitive Law of the
Church 96

INDEX OF QUESTIONS.

What was the ancient and invariable rule of the British and Anglican Church, as inherited by the Church of England . . 96
In this country, where there is no union of Church and State, how are the respective rights of Clergy and Laity protected under the Constitution of the Protestant Episcopal Church . 97
What error on this point of a call for a Vote by Dioceses and Orders has probably crept into the Constitution . . . 98
When was the qualification of being a Lay "Communicant in this Church" introduced into the Constitution of the General Convention 102
What is meant by "Communicants in this Church," as a qualification of Lay Deputies 102
What Ecclesiastical censure would invalidate the qualification of a Layman 103
If a Layman should incur Ecclesiastical censure during his term of office, would he be qualified to sit as Lay Deputy . . 103
What is meant by the clause "Residents in the Diocese," as a qualification of Clerical and Lay Members 103
What judgment must the Secular Courts give on the question of Residence in a Diocese 103
What is the Canonical Residence of a *Clergyman* . . . 103
State what the Canons on Residence of Clergymen require and enjoin 104
What Canonical Conditions prescribe the *time* when the privilege of Clerical Residence and Removal takes effect under Letters Dimissory 105
Is a Clergyman removing beyond the territorial limits of a Diocese into parts where there is no Bishop, required to maintain his Diocesan Residence 106
To whom is a Clergyman belonging to one Diocese, and charged with an offense committed in another Diocese, amenable . 106
May the Ecclesiastical Authority of a Diocese refuse to accept Letters Dimissory presented by a Clergyman in good standing, who is called into the Diocese to take charge of a Parish . 107
What further interpretation on Clerical Residence do the Canons furnish 107
What conclusion follows as to the meaning of the clause in Art. II. respecting Clerical Deputies, "Residents in the Diocese" which they represent 108
What is the authority of the axiom that "No man may take advantage of his own wrong" 109
What policy of the Church dictates the Constitutional and Canonical Residence of a Clergyman, as independent of Secular Residence or "Domicile" 110

INDEX OF QUESTIONS. 207

Does the removal of a Clergyman into another State or District
or Diocese, *ipso facto*, vacate his Ecclesiastical Domicile . 110
How is the principle that a Clergyman's Residence in a Diocese
is determined exclusively by the fact of Episcopal Jurisdiction
over him, and not by the laws of secular domicile, evinced by
Article V. of the Constitution of the Church 111
What is the doctrine of the Canon of "Episcopal Residence" . 112
Repeat what special immunity is accorded by Canon (in view of
the rights of the Clergy and the *Laity*) to a Clergyman called
to take charge of a Parish or Congregation 113
What is the conclusion of the question as to the meaning of the
phrase "Residents in the Diocese," in respect of Clerical
Deputies to the General Convention 114
When are Laymen "Resident in the Diocese" and qualified to
represent it in the General Convention 117
Suppose he fails to comply with the Canon 117
Does the Canon contemplate a *dispensation* from the consequences of the Lay Communicant's negligence and fault in not
procuring a Letter Dimissory 117
Repeat the provision in the Constitution for choosing Deputies . 118
Does this provision give color to the idea that the Deputies chosen
by the Convention, represent the *Convention* 118
What is a Vote by Dioceses and Orders 118
What number of votes in either order, is a Vote of that order . 119
Suppose the vote of either order be divided, as two against two. 119
What is the specific usage of the General Convention in regard
to divided votes 119
Were divided votes counted 119
State what Bishop White says on this Vote in A. D. 1786 . . 120
What was the Article of the Constitution under which the Vote
by Orders in A. D. 1786 was taken 120
How is this seeming *Plurality* Vote to be construed as that of
the majority of Suffrages of the Church in each State represented 120
Is this example of the General Convention of A. D. 1786 followed
by the Church in subsequent Conventions 121
What is the Parliamentary Rule respecting Blank Votes in a
Balloting 121
Is a Divided Vote equivalent to a Blank Vote 121
Is this Parliamentary Rule applicable to *Divided* votes under the
Constitution of the General Convention 121
What is the proper mode of counting a Vote by Dioceses and
Orders, under Article II. of the Constitution of the General
Convention 121

What principle in respect to the rank of Dioceses, and the Coördinate rights of Clergy and Laity, does the Vote by Dioceses and Orders establish 122
Is it true that "diocesan *independency*, in all matters not surrendered for the great end of union, is asserted" by the fact that "any Diocese may demand a vote by Dioceses" . . 122
If the Convention of any Diocese appoint Lay Deputies, or Clerical Deputies, of whom some do not attend, what constitutes a Representation of the Diocese in General Convention, in a vote by Dioceses and Orders 122
If only a Lay Deputy, or only a Clerical Deputy attend, does he, in a vote by Dioceses and Orders, represent the whole Diocese 122
If a Diocese "has but a single Deputy of either order, upon a call for a vote by Dioceses and Orders, has that Diocese a voice, in that order that may chance to be present, equal to that of the largest Diocese with all its *eight* delegates . . 123
What is a Quorum of the House of Clerical and Lay Deputies, for a vote by Dioceses and Orders 123
If the Convention of any Diocese should neglect or refuse to appoint Clerical and Lay Deputies; or if Deputies, Clerical or Lay, should not attend at any General Convention, would the Church in that Diocese be discharged from amenability to the Canons of that General Convention 123
Does this clause of Article II. contradict the hypothesis of "diocesan independency" 123
What relation does this clause of Article II. establish between the General Convention and the Church in any Diocese . . 124

ARTICLE III.—HOUSE OF BISHOPS.

Quorum of the House of Bishops.

How many Bishops of this Church form a House of Bishops . 124
What are the powers of the House of Bishops 125
Is this negative absolute and unconditional 125
What result follows from the failure of the House of Bishops in complying with these conditions, or either of them . . . 125
Suppose the Act of the House of Deputies be reported to the House of Bishops for their concurrence, within three days of the adjournment of the Convention 125
What constitutes a Quorum of the House of Bishops . . . 125
How is this manifest? State the History of the organization of the House of Bishops 125

Mention the subjects which engaged this House of Bishops . 128
On what principle did the House of Bishops proceed in revising
 the Liturgy and Offices 130
Did the House of Deputies adopt the same *principle* — the revision of the English Book 130
How does Bishop White account for the celerity in the dispatch
 of business in the House of Bishops 131

ARTICLE IV. — DIOCESES.

Jurisdiction of Bishops. — Assistant Bishops. — Suffragan Bishops. — Coadjutor Bishops. — Organization of Dioceses under Catholic Canon Law.

What is a Diocese 131
What is the derivation of the word Diocese 131
What is the historical Origin of Dioceses 131
What are the bounds of a Diocese by Canon Law . . 132
How were the bounds of Dioceses determined in this Church . 132
How are the bounds of Dioceses now fixed 133
How may new Dioceses be formed in outlying Missionary dis-
 tricts 133
By what claim and authority does the Church appoint Domestic
 Missionary Bishops 133
By what authority does the Church appoint Foreign Missionary
 Bishops 133
What is the relation of the Bishops of this Church to the Apos-
 tles, to whom the Lord gave mission 134
What are the bounds and limits of the Jurisdiction of Domestic
 and Foreign Missionary Bishops 134
Is it possible that, in the same place, there can be several differ-
 ent *Churches* 134
Is it possible that, by the law of God, there may be more than
 one *Apostle* or *Bishop* in the same place, without disturbing the
 Unity of Communion in the Church 134
What do you gather from these examples of Holy Scripture re-
 specting the original *Norm* or rule of Apostolic or Episcopal
 jurisdiction 135
Does this Church legislate on the principle, that a Diocese is the
 Bishop's *Jurisdiction*, in its normal character, and is over per-
 sons and not defined by places 136
What is the force of the Limitation on the Bishop's Jurisdiction
 in this Article IV. 136
What is the Canon Law on this point 137
By what authority may a Bishop exercise his Episcopal office

outside of the local limits of his own proper Diocese, according to Article IV. of the Constitution of this Church . . 137
Does this Article prohibit the Bishop of the Diocese from inviting another Bishop to exercise his Episcopal functions in his Diocese 137
How can a Bishop of a Diocese justify his own invitation to another Bishop to exercise the Episcopal office in his Diocese . 137
What further does this Article contemplate 137
May an Assistant Bishop be consecrated without assurance of his continuance in some Episcopal Jurisdiction after the demise of his principal 138
What is a SUFFRAGAN Bishop 138
What were the duties of Suffragan Bishops in England . . 139
What were the privileges of Suffragan Bishops 139
How long have Suffragans been disused in England . . . 139
What was a COADJUTOR Bishop 139
What relation does an Assistant Bishop in this Church bear to the Suffragan and Coadjutor Bishops of the Church of England 139
Give a succinct statement of the organization of the Church under the Catholic Canon Law, which has been established or atified by the Œcumenical Councils and received by the Church Universal 140

ARTICLE V.—ADMISSION OF NEW DIOCESES.

Diocesan Rights of the Bishop and Assistant Bishops.—Constitution and Canons of New Dioceses.

How may a new Diocese be admitted into union with the other Dioceses and with the General Convention 143
Does the act of "acceding" to the Constitution imply the right of any Diocese to *secede* from the union established by the Constitution 143
State the other powers of "independency" which Dr. Hawks says the Dioceses "surrendered" 143
What supreme function of "diocesan independency" does Bishop White say was *abandoned* by the State Conventions, under the Constitution of A. D. 1789 144
What is the process by which a Church in any of the United States is admitted into Union 144
What is the process by which a "New Diocese, formed from one or more existing Dioceses," is admitted into union . . 145
What are the Constitutional Restrictions on the dividing of an existing Diocese 145

Into how many Dioceses does this Article of the Constitution contemplate the Division of a Diocese 145
What was the interpretation of this Article whereby the Diocese of New York, in A. D. 1868, was divided into *three* Dioceses with the consent of the General Convention of that year . 145
What is the further restriction on the erection of New Dioceses 146
What is the principle adopted and published in these "restrictions," respecting the definition of a Diocese 146
When was Article V. put into its present form . . . 147
What was the principle of the old Fifth Article respecting the defining of Dioceses, which is now superseded . . . 147
What is the right of Jurisdiction of the Bishop when his Diocese is divided 147
What is the right of Jurisdiction of the Assistant Bishop . . 147
What is the Fundamental Law of New Dioceses . . . 147
May two or more Dioceses be united into one Diocese . . 147
What is the Fundamental Law of the Consolidated Diocese . 147

ARTICLE VI.—COURT AND TRIAL OF BISHOPS.

Diocesan Courts and Trials.—Imperfection of the Judiciary.—Sentences.

What is the mode of trying Bishops 148
Who may constitute the Court for the trial of Bishops . . 148
What was the corresponding article of the Constitution of A. D. 1785 148
What comment on this Article was made by the English Bishops 149
What comment does Bishop White make on this portion of the communication from the English Bishops 149
What is the further comment of Bishop White on the remonstrance of the English Bishops 149
On what legal and equitable principle did the English Bishops object to the provision for the Trial of the Clergy . . . 150
What modification did the General Convention of A. D. 1786 make in Article VIII. of the Constitution 150
Does this amendment remove the objection of the remonstrance of the English Bishops 150
How did the General Convention of A. D. 1786 treat the remonstrance of the English Bishops 150
How long did Article VIII. remain in the Constitution unchanged 151
What notable advance toward Catholic Canon Law was made by the Amendment of A. D. 1841 151

What further change was made in this Article respecting the
  trial of Presbyters and Deacons 151
What advance towards Catholic Law was made by this Amendment of A. D. 1848 152
Is the equal amenability of the Clergy of this Church established
  by the provision for Diocesan Courts and Canons . . . 152
What remedy does this Article provide 152
Would the Canon of the General Convention supersede an existing Diocesan Canon, on the trial of Presbyters and Deacons . 152
Has the General Convention exercised its Constitutional and inherent Prerogative, in providing a Code of Laws and a system
  of Judicial Proceedings 153
What crying enormity prevails, for lack of just and wise General
  Canons for the trial of Presbyters and Deacons . . . 153
Why is the denial of the power of Appeal so enormous a wrong 153
What Commentary does Dr. Hawks make on this Article . . 154
What is the view of Judge Hoffman 154
What sentences may an Ecclesiastical Court pronounce . . 154
What is Admonition 155
What is Suspension 155
Is there such a Sentence known to Canon Law as "Indefinite
  Suspension" 155
What is Degradation 155
Does the Sentence of Degradation, Deposition, or Displacement
  (equivalent terms in the Canons), take away the *office* of a
  Minister in this Church 155
May a deposed Minister be restored to the Exercise of his Office 155
Must he be ordained again, if restored 155
What notice shall be given to the Church when a Clergyman is
  sentenced to "Degradation" 155
Who alone may pronounce a Sentence 156
Under what Solemnities shall a Bishop pronounce a Sentence . 156

ARTICLE VII.

Origin. — Requisites for Ordination. — Declaration. — Container of the Faith. — Teacher of the Faith. — Extent and Limitation of Private Judgment. — Admission of Foreign Clergy.

What was the origin of this Article 157
What are the foremost requisites for Ordination . . . 157
What Canons provide the regulations for Candidates for the Holy
  Order of Deacons 158
What Canons provide the regulations for Candidates for the Holy
  Order of Priests 158

INDEX OF QUESTIONS. 213

What is the next condition precedent to Ordination into the Ministry of this Church 158
Why is not a subscription to the "Articles of Religion" required, as in the Church of England 158
State the authority for this answer, from the records of the General Convention in A. D. 1804 158
What is the force of the Declaration that the Holy Scriptures "*contain*" all things necessary to Salvation" 159
Do you distinguish between "The Faith" and the Doctrines contained in the Holy Scriptures of the Old and New Testaments 159
Does this Declaration, as interpreted by this Article of Religion, affirm that the Holy Scripture *teaches* what is the Faith . . 159
What would be the effect of the dogma that the Holy Scripture is the only or the foremost *Teacher* of the Faith . . . 159
Whence do we derive the Holy Scriptures of the Old and New Testaments 160
What are the tokens and demonstration of the truth of the testimony and tradition of the Church 160
Where is the TEACHER OF THE FAITH to be found . . . 160
Where is the "Faith" taught 160
Is the particular Church, as of Jerusalem, of Alexandria, of Rome, of England, of the United States of America, liable to err 160
What limitation is there on the authority of a particular or national Church 161
Is this limitation of authority applicable to the Church Universal 161
May not the Church Universal err 161
What is the visible Church 161
What is meant by "faithful men" 161
Are the Creeds to be received as Symbols of the Faith, simply because they are put forth by the witness of Œcumenical Councils of the Church 161
Is there, then, both a Limitation and a Latitude of private judgment 162
What then is the final or ultimate Rule of Faith . . . 162
What if a Searcher of the Scriptures disagree with the testimony of the Church, as to the Faith 162
May a *Minister* of this Church have any Latitude of private judgment, in matters of the Faith, Doctrine, Sacraments, or Discipline of CHRIST 162
What is the authority for this answer 162

214   INDEX OF QUESTIONS.

What if the Priest teaches contrary to the Faith, Doctrine, Sacraments, or Discipline of this Church 163
Repeat the words of the engagement of Conformity, in the Declaration 163
Where are to be found the Doctrines and Worship of the Protestant Episcopal Church, to which the Clergymen of this Church engage to conform 163
Where are the directions for Divine Worship in this Church to be found 163
Does the Clergyman engage to conform to the Rubrics and Canons 163
What is the Canon Law on Conformity to the worship of this Church 163
What duty do these Canons enjoin 164
In the interpretation of these Canons, confining the use of prescribed prayers in *"public worship"* and *"before* all sermons," may a Clergyman *after* the sermon use any other prayers or services than those which are prescribed 164
May a Clergyman use other prayers or services before the public worship shall have commenced 164
Are processional and recessional Hymns allowable, on the literal interpretation of these Canons 164
May Clergymen, during public worship, neglect or omit to use, any part of the prescribed Form of Prayer . . . 164
What is the duty of a Clergyman in officiating in Missionary work, or where the Prayer Book is unknown . . . 164
Would the publication of opinions tending to the derogation or depraving of the Prayer Book, be a violation of the Clergyman's subscription and promise of conformity to the Doctrines and Worship of the Protestant Episcopal Church . . 165
Recite the clause in Article VII. touching the admission of Foreign Clergy into the Protestant Episcopal Church in the United States 166
What are the Canons in that case provided . . . 166

ARTICLE VIII.—HISTORY OF THE BOOK OF COMMON PRAYER.

The Book of Common Prayer. — Articles of Religion. — Use of the Book of Common Prayer. — Alterations and Amendments of the Book of Common Prayer.

What is the History of the Compilation of the Book of Common Prayer of the Protestant Episcopal Church in the United States 167
What was done by the next Convention of A. D. 1785, on this subject 167

INDEX OF QUESTIONS. 215

What notable alterations in the Symbols of the Faith were made
in the "Proposed Book" of A. D. 1785 169
What notice of the alterations in the Faith did the English
Bishops take 169
What heresy do the English Bishops refer to, as contradicted by
the Catholic Church, in the Article in the Apostles' Creed, on
the "Descent into Hell" 169
What else was done in the premises, by the Convention of A. D.
1785 170
What was done in General Convention, in A. D. 1786, in respect
to the restoring of the Creeds in their integrity . . . 170
What was done with the Athanasian Creed 171
What do you observe in this sketch of the History of the Com-
pilation of the "Proposed Book" of Common Prayer . . 171
Were these expectations realized 172
What was done in the next General Convention in A. D. 1786 . 172
How did this motion of Bishop White settle the question of the
Supreme Authority of the General Convention, and prevent
all future interfering instructions from the Dioceses . . 173
Repeat the Article of the Constitution introduced by Bishop
White, and the Article for Amendments, adopted by that Gen-
eral Convention at its first Session in June, A. D. 1786 . . 173
What became of "the Proposed Book" 174
State the proceedings of the General Convention of A. D. 1789,
in regard to the Book of Common Prayer 174
On what principle did the Convention proceed 175
What was the opinion of the Bishops 175
Whose words are you reciting 176
What does Bishop White say of the Rubric allowing the *omission*
of the Article in the Apostles' Creed on the "Descent into
Hell," as printed in the Prayer Book of A. D. 1789 . . 176
Recite the Resolution of the House of Deputies of A. D. 1789,
appointing "the Committee on printing the Prayer Book" . 176
What was done by Bishop White when he discovered the unau-
thorized interpolation of that part of the Rubric allowing the
Omission of the Article in the Apostles' Creed on "the De-
scent into Hell" 177
How was the Prayer Book compiled 177
What is the characteristic of the change, or growth of sentiment,
as evinced in this History of the Compilation of the Prayer
Book 178
What intimation have we that the Church regarded her Polity
as completed and fixed in A. D. 1789 178

216 INDEX OF QUESTIONS.

Were the Articles of Religion adopted at the Convention of A. D. 1789 178
When were the Articles of Religion established by the General Convention 178
Is there any force in the assertion of some persons, that the Articles of Religion were not "adopted" by the General Convention of A. D. 1801, but only "set forth" 179
Are the Articles of the same authority as the Book of Common Prayer 179
Why was the establishment of the Articles postponed . . 179
What account does Bishop White give of the Articles . . 180
When were the other Offices of the Church compiled . . 180
What is the difference between "Induction" and "Institution" 181
Why was the title "Induction" changed by General Convention in A. D. 1808 to "Institution" 181
What ought our emotions to be in view of this History . . 182
How does this Article VIII. distinguish the Book of Common Prayer 182
May the Offices be printed in a separate Book 182
What is the authority for the use of the Book of Common Prayer, the Offices, and the Articles of Religion 182
To what extent is the use of the Book of Common Prayer, and the Offices enjoined 182
What is the obligation due from Clergy and Laity to the Articles of Religion 182
What is the advantage of the Common Prayer Book, Offices, and Articles of Religion 183
How are Alterations and Amendments made 183
Why are proposed alterations "made known" to the Conventions of every Diocese 183
Are the Deputies bound by their Instructions 183
How is the Alteration to be made in the Book of Common Prayer, and the Offices, and the Articles 183
Does this Article of the Constitution specify the necessity of voting by Dioceses and Orders 184
What do approved Commentators say on this point . . 184

ARTICLE IX.—ALTERATIONS OF THE CONSTITUTION.

Where shall the Constitution be altered 184
By whom may the Constitution be altered 185
How must the voice of the Church in the Dioceses be expressed 185
What constitutes a majority of the Dioceses in General Convention 185

INDEX OF QUESTIONS. 217

Where must the Alteration be proposed 185
Where and by whom must the Alteration be "finally agreed to or ratified" 185
What is directed to be done with the proposed Alteration, in the *interim*, between the two Conventions 185
For what purpose is the proposed Amendment "made known". 185
What action in the premises may the Church in a Diocese take . 186
If a majority of Diocesan Conventions should oppose a proposed amendment, what then 186
What is the testimony of Bishop White 186
What does Dr. Wilson, in his "Memoirs of Bishop White," say of the purpose of the clause of this Article, requiring the proposed alteration to be "made known" to the Diocesan Conventions 186

ARTICLE X.—BISHOPS FOR FOREIGN COUNTRIES.

Consecration of Bishops for Foreign Countries. — Restrictions of Episcopal Jurisdiction, Authority, and Privilege.

What was the occasion and necessity of the consecration of Foreign Missionary Bishops 187
What are the Constitutional restrictions on the Jurisdiction of a Foreign Missionary Bishop 187
What are the Constitutional restrictions on the Episcopal Privilege and Authority of a Foreign Missionary Bishop . . 187
What reasons may be assigned for these restrictions on the Foreign Missionary Bishop 188
Have these Considerations prevailed in the General Convention, in favor of the equal Episcopal rights of Foreign Missionary Bishops 189
Is this Canon constitutional in this respect 189
Does this Article X. need amendment 189

INDEX OF AUTHORITIES
ON

1. THE COMMON LAW OF THE CHURCH.
2. THE SPIRITUAL COURTS AND PROCEEDINGS OF THE CHURCH OF ENGLAND.
3. ON THE MANNER OF ELECTING AND CONSECRATING ARCHBISHOPS AND BISHOPS OF THE CHURCH OF ENGLAND.

COMMON LAW OF THE CHURCH.

Acts of Colonial Government.
Acts of States.
Alumni Association, General Theological Seminary.
Apostolical Canons.
Appendix to Dr. Wilson's Memoir of the Life of Bishop White.
Ariminium, Council of.
Arles, Council of.
Articles XXXIX., The.
Augustine, St.

Baronius, Bishop.
Beardsley, his Bill.
Bede, Venerable.
Berkeley, George, then Dean of Derry, Ireland.
Beveridge, his Synodicon, et Cod. Can. Ecc.
Bogardus v. Smith, case of, 4 Paige Rep. 178.
Bramhall, Bishop, Tracts of.
British Bishops, A. D. 314; A. D. 325; A. D. 350; and A. D. 359.
Burnet, History of the Reformation.
Bushrod, Washington, Opinion of.

Canon Law of the Latin Church.
Canon Law, Special.
Canons. (passim).
Canons, Ancient.

Canons of Catholic Church.
Cardwell, his Synodalia — Preface to.
Chalmers, Dr.
Charter of Duke of York, 1664 to 1683.
Church-Register, Bishop White on " Primitive Facts."
Churton's Early British Church.
Code of African Church.
   Latin Church.
   Oriental Church.
   Photius.
   the New Canon Law of the Latin Church.
Colonial Assembly of 1706.
Colonies. See several States.
Commendam, Writ of.
Common Law. See case of Bogardus v. Smith.
Compilation of Constitution, Baltimore, 1849.
Congè d'Elire, Writ of.
Convention, General.
Cotelerius, his Pat. Apostol.
Courts, Ecclesiastical and Temporal.
   Spiritual.
    1. Archdeacons.
    2. Consistory.
    3. Peculiars.
    4. Prerogative.
    5. Arches.
    6. The King in Chancery.
Cranmer, his Reformatio Legum.

Dalcho's History of the Church in South Carolina.
Dawson, his Origo Legum.
Decretals. False Decretals.
Dicta of Received and Learned Commentators.
Diocletian, persecution during reign of.
Dionysius, Exiguus.

Ecclesiastical Law of England.
   Case of Gaskins v. Gaskins.
   Ex. of the Authority of.
Edmund, King of England (A. D. 950), one of his laws referred to.
Eusebius, A. D. 337, 340 : Vit. Constant. II. 28.

Fleury, Cardinal, Hist. Ecc. xliv. liv.
Foreign Canon Law (Body of).

INDEX OF AUTHORITIES.

Gaskins v. Gaskins (case of), 3 Iredell's Law Rep. 155.
Gelasius' Decrees.
Gibson's (Bishop) Codex. Introductory Discourse.
Gibson's Codex.
Grey's Ecc. Law.
Guettée (Abbé), On the Papacy.

Haddan & Stubbs, Records by, from A. D. 200. Ox. 1869.
Hawkins' Annals of the Society for the Propagation of the Gospel in Foreign Parts.
Hawks, Dr., on Constitution and Canons.
        Contributions to Ecclesiastical History.
Hilary, and others, History of Martyrdom of St. Alban.
Historical Record of Maine.
Hoffman, Murray, Judge, his Introduction to the Law of the Church.
        Law of the Church.
Hooker, his Ecc. Pol.

Ignatius, St. (his Maxim).
Iredell, Law Rep.
Isidore (Mercator or Peccator).

Johannes Scholasticus, Patriarch of Constantinople.
Johnson's English Canons.
Journal, General Convention.
        N. Y. Convention.

Kenneth's Ecclesiastical Synods.
Kent's Commentaries.

Legatine Constitutions.
        Constitution of Otho.
                of Othobon.
Legislatures (see Hoffman, L. C.).
Letters, Missive.
Liberties of the Church of England.
Lords (House of).
Lyttleton.

Minute Summary of Ecc. Law, in Odenheimer's Essay, Assoc. Alum., 1847.
" Monumenta Ecclesiastica."

Nice, Council of.
Nicholas (Pope), A. D. 836.

Oath of Supremacy.
Odenheimer (Bishop).
          (Essay), Alum. Assoc., 1847.
" Option," Archbishop's.
" Ordination Office." See Bishop White.
Origen (Homilies), A. D. 239.

Paige. 4 Paige Rep. 178.
Palgrave. History of the Anglo Saxons.
Parker (Archbishop).
Parliamentary (Acts and Rules).
Parliaments, Acts of. (See Statutes.)
Photius (Code of).
Præmunire (Writ of).
Preface to Book of Common Prayer.

Queen *v.* Mills, Decision in the case of.

Randolph, Edmund, his Opinion.
Rubrics of the Church.

Sozomen (A. D. 300), Hist. Ecc.
Statutes, Ann c. 5; 13 Car. II. c. 4; Edw. I.; Edw. III.; 5 Edw. VI.; 13 Eliz. c. 12; Hen. I. A. D. 1108; Hen. III. A. D. 1225; Hen. VII. c. 21; 24 Hen. VIII. c. 12; 25 Hen. VIII. c. 19; 26 Hen. VIII. c. 1.

Tertullian, his Apology against the Jews.
Toleration, English Act of.
Turner's (Sharon) Anglo Saxons.

Usages and Statutes in the Colonies.

Walpole, his Administration from 1723 to 1742.
White, Bishop, on the Ordination Offices.
              his Comparative View of the Calvinistic and Arminian Controversy.
Wilkins' Concilia Magnæ Britanniæ et Hiberniæ.
Wilson's Memoir of the Life of Bishop White.
Witenagemote, Council of the.
Wood's Institutes.

INDEX OF AUTHORITIES.

PARTS I. AND II.—PRELIMINARY HISTORY, POWERS, AND AUTHORITY OF THE GENERAL CONVENTION.

Acts, Apostles, of the.
Articles, Confederation of, 1774.
Boyle, his Lectures.
Constitution, Articles of.
Dawson, Origo Legum.
Digest of Canons.
Eusebius Pamphylias.
    his "Life of Constantine."
Hoffman (Murray, Judge).
    his "Introduction."
    his Law of the Church, *passim*.
Kenneth, Ecclesiastical Synods.
Memoirs, Protestant Episcopal Church of the, by Bishop White.
Merivale, History of the Romans.
Parker, Right Rev. Bishop, of Massachusetts.
Seabury, Right Rev. Bishop, *passim*.
Webster, Noah.
White, Right Rev. Bishop, *passim*.
Wilson, Dr., Memoir of the Life of Bishop White.

PART III.—"CONSTITUTION OF THE PROTESTANT EPISCOPAL CHURCH IN THE UNITED STATES."

Acts of the Apostles, quoted.
Apostolical Canons.
Appendix to the Journal of General Conventions.
Articles of the Constitution.
Bingham, Ecclesiastical Antiquities.
Bouvier, quoted.
Buck's Massachusetts Ecclesiastical Law.
Burns' Ecclesiastical Law.
Canon Law, *passim*.
Canons and Institutions under the Saxon Kings, styled "Monumenta Ecclesiastica."
Canons, Church of England, A. D. 1603.
Comments of English Bishops, referred to.
Common Law of the Church.
Convention, General, Proceedings of.
Council of Antioch.
Council of Constantinople.
8 Cowen's Reports, 1826, Dutch Church *v.* Bradford.

CONSTITUTION OF THE CHURCH. 223

3 Curties' Reports, 565, Sanders v. Head.
Cushing's Rules of Proceedings and Debate in Deliberative Assemblies.
Cyprian, St., on the Unity of the Church.
    Epistles.
Degge's Parson's Counsellor.
Digest of Canons, *passim*.
Discourse of Ignotus, Philadelphia, 1855.
Galatians, quoted.
Gibson's Codex.
Grey's Ecclesiastical Law.
Hatsel, Rules of Parliamentary Debate.
Hawks, Dr., Constitutions and Canons, *passim*.
Henry VIII. ch. xxv. xxvi. etc.
Historical Notes and Commens to Journal of General Convention.
Hoffman, Judge, Law of the Church.
    Ecclesiastical Law of New York.
Jefferson's Manual.
Journal, General Convention, Hawks & Perry's Edit. and Notes.
    House of Bishops.
    New York Convention.
    Preface to.
Kenneth, Ecclesiastical Synods.
Law of Suspension in the Primitive Church.
Letter to Bishop Seabury by Bishop White.
Lyndwood's Provincial Constitutions.
Mark, St., quoted.
Matthew, St., quoted.
Memoirs of the Protestant Episcopal Church, by Bishop White.
Ortolan, Histoire de la Legislation Romaine.
Palmer on the Church.
Preliminary History of this work referred to.
Report of a Sub-Committee, Journal New York Convention, 1867.
Seabury, Bishop, Letter to Dr. Smith.
1 Spear's Equity Reports, Court of Appeals of South Carolina (1843),
  Harmon v. Desher.
St. Cyprian, Epistle to Pope Stephen.
    de Unitate Ecclesiæ.
Suspension. See Law of.
Van Espen, his Supplement.
Webster, Noah.
Wilson, Dr., Memoirs of the Life of Bishop White.

www.ingramcontent.com/pod-product-compliance
Lightning Source LLC
Chambersburg PA
CBHW060508090426
42735CB00011B/2146